TriQuarterly

T0164111

TriQuarterly is

an international

journal of

writing, art and

cultural inquiry

published at

Northwestern

University

TriQuarterly

issue 132

Editors of this issue: Susan Firestone Hahn and Ian Morris

TriQuarterly is pleased to announce:

Mark Slouka's story "Dominion" (*TriQuarterly* 121) was selected by editor Ann Patchett to appear in *Best American Short Stories 2006*.

Michael Collier's poem "Common Flicker" and David Rivard's poem "The Rev. Larry Love Is Dead" (*TriQuarterly* 120) were selected by editor Heather McHugh to appear in *Best American Poetry 2007*.

Richard Burgin's story "Identity Club" (*TriQuarterly* 118) was selected by editor Joyce Carol Oates to appear in the *Ecco Anthology of Contemporary American Short Fiction* (Ecco/Harper Perennial, 2008).

Kathleen De Azevado's story "Together We Are Lost" (*TriQuarterly* 125) was selected by editor D. Seth Horton to appear in *New Stories of the Southwest* (Ohio University Press, 2008).

The following *TriQuarterly* authors received special mentions in the Pushcart Prize XXXII (2008) anthology: from *TriQuarterly* 122, the poem "Snake Key" by Carol Frost; from *TriQuarterly* 123, the story "Steps through Sand, through Fire" by David H. Lynn and the story "Jonathan and Lillian" by Richard Burgin; from *TriQuarterly* 124, the essay "The Ghost Light" by ArLynn Leiber Presser; from *TriQuarterly* 125, the story "Mijo" by Carolyn Alessio, the story "Life During Peacetime" by Jason Brown, and the poem "The Great Fugue" by John Balaban.

The following *TriQuarterly* authors received special mentions from Pushcart Prize XXXIII (2009) anthology: from *TriQuarterly* 126, the story "Indie," by Steven Schwartz and the story "Frances the Ghost" by Joe Meno; from *TriQuarterly* 129, the story "A Letter in Las Vegas" by Richard Burgin, the story "The Daughter of the Bearded Lady" by Vincent Precht, the poem "Don't Come Home" by Todd Boss, and the poem "Ode on the Letter M" by Barbara Hamby.

Contents

Cover photo: Doug Macomber

Donna Seaman

The Empress of In-Between:
A Portrait of Louise Nevelson

She was a bird of rare plumage.

Edward Albee

My total conscious search in life has been for a new seeing,
a new image, a new insight. This search not only includes
the object, but the in-between places, the dawns and dusks,
the objective world, the heavenly spheres, the places
between the land and the sea.

Louise Nevelson

Louise Nevelson was a late bloomer, a mythmaker, and an art world
icon. Tall and fierce, she favored floor-length embroidered robes and
furs, headscarves and hats, warrior-trophy necklaces, and dagger-like
false eyelashes. With smoke rising from her ever-present cigar, she
looked like an empress from a cold and distant land. A priestess of the
steppes. A Siberian shaman. Indomitable, irascible, and fluently creative, Nevelson built large, complex abstract black wood sculptures that
look like the abandoned temples and shrines of a lost tradition. The
artist was in her sixties when the mainstream media finally took notice

of her striking assemblages and dramatic presence, and she held the spotlight until her death at age eighty-eight.

Nevelson could be *Vogue*-elegant, thanks to photographer Richard Avedon. She could also be campy, even grotesque as one of the more grandiose of the self-appointed deities of the era of disco kitsch and cocaine decadence. Nevelson was photographed with Andy Warhol (but then, who wasn't?), New York's Mayor John Lindsay, and Merce Cunningham and John Cage, who in one shot are laughing so hard their eyes slit shut. She looks demur as she shakes hands with President Jimmy Carter after receiving the Women's Caucus for Art Award, and radiant as President Ronald Reagan and First Lady Nancy Reagan present her with the National Medal of Arts award. Recognition was long in arriving, and Nevelson eagerly wrapped herself in the shimmering cloak of fame like a shipwreck survivor pulls a blanket tight around her shoulders.

Nevelson courted the camera and the press, and was more than willing to ham it up. Photographer Hans Namuth cleverly combined two images to give the artist four arms, so that she looks like a magician, a card shark, an undercover incarnation of the fearsome goddess Kali, the dark mother. In other, far less flattering portraits, Nevelson looks like a sinister character out of such old films as *The Cabinet of Dr. Caligari* or *Metropolis*, a creepy look immortalized by Robert Mapplethorpe in 1986, two years before Nevelson's death. Cecil Beaton caught Nevelson in a vulnerable moment: her gray hair disarrayed, as though she has just stopped raking her hands through it in despair; her expression weary, sorrowful; the black sculpture behind her a post-apocalyptic ruin.

The most dismaying image appeared in *Life* magazine in the May 24, 1958, issue with the trivializing headline: "Weird Woodwork of Lunar World." The usually regal and impervious Nevelson crouches awkwardly behind her sculpture, "Moon Garden," as a cheesy green light illuminates the ludicrous scene. The artist wears a peaked black hat that could be witchy but instead resembles a stubby dunce's cap, and she looks for all the world like a colonist in the stocks, humiliated and punished for some petty crime against propriety.

Photographer Pedro E. Guerrero observed that "Louise loved being provocative."[2] He took pictures of Nevelson in her ferocious prime, her late seventies, and created one of the most beautiful and revealing published portraits of the artist: a stunning work of chiaroscuro in which Nevelson, her skin golden, wears a pale blue paisley headscarf and silvery blue fur and leans her head on her hand on a black glass table in front of a black wall. She is a study in sun and moonlight, a graceful predator in repose.

Classical Western sculpture involves the liberation of the human form from great blocks of marble. Surely such master sculptors as Praxiteles and Michelangelo possessed superhero X-ray vision that enabled them to peer into pearlescent stone wombs and discern figures of astonishing beauty awaiting birth via chisel and mallet. Mighty limbs, divine torsos, heads noble or monstrous, Olympian muscles, massive shoulders, lavish locks of hair, extravagant drapery, engraved armor—all enclosed in a fortress of white, a mineral holdfast pried from the earth's clasp and turned malleable beneath the artist's sure hands. This miraculous metamorphosis from rough-hewn stone to finely carved and polished sculptures of gods and goddesses, men, women, and animals took place in a world that was all of a piece. In the atomic age, we see the world in pieces.

How disconcerting it is when the myth of solidity is exploded by the utterance of the words "molecule" and "atom." Suddenly your child's-eye-view is recalibrated and the very desk you lean on becomes a whir of tiny spheres, each containing its own spinning galaxies. Zoom in, zoom out, the cosmos is comprised of galaxies within galaxies, a continuum without end from the tiniest itty-bittiest specks to the grand circle dance of planets and stars. The cosmos is a sea of choreographed particles and waves. All is in flux, even an imposing hunk of marble.

Subatomic awareness aside, marble is heavy, obdurate, and expensive. Far out-of-reach for a penniless middle-aged woman artist working out of a shabby apartment in mid-twentieth-century New York City. And besides, stone did not speak to Louise Nevelson. It was wood that called out to her. In her extemporaneous self-portrait-in-words, a torrent of observations, anecdotes, and pronouncements diligently recorded and transcribed by her assistant, Diana MacKown, and turned into a book titled *Dawns & Dusks*, Nevelson explains:

> I wanted a medium that was immediate. Wood was the thing I could communicate with almost spontaneously and get what I was looking for . . . the textures and the livingness . . . when I'm working with wood, it's very alive. It has a life of its own."[3]

But the sculptor began her long practice of visual expression as most artists do, by drawing and painting. As a girl, she composed remarkably vital interiors in which the furniture is about to shimmy and lift off the floor, thick black lines revel in the illusion of perspective, bookshelves look ready to burst, and the curlicues of fabric and carpet designs refused to be confined. An upholstered chair in the lower left-hand corner of a 1918 watercolor even displays what looks like a molecular pattern. As an adult, Nevelson created free-flowing drawings, paintings, and prints, many depicting substantial female figures, and one in particular, "The Lady Who Sank a Thousand Ships (Helen of Troy)," offers intriguing clues to her feelings about womanpower.

But two dimensions were not enough for Nevelson. Captain of her high school's girls' basketball team, she was vibrant, high-strung, and restless. She later channeled her physicality into dance and eurythmics, the art of expressive, improvised movements in response to music. These disciplines put her in closer touch with the creative force and helped her focus her energies. Nevelson used her entire body when she made art. Working quickly and intuitively, she was inspired and guided by the heft, texture, and shape of her materials. She needed to work with and against gravity.

When Nevelson speaks of wood, she isn't referring to freshly milled lumber like that produced in Rockland, Maine, where Louise, a young Russian Jewish immigrant, came-of-age. No, she is praising used and discarded wood. Cast-off wooden objects, fragments, remnants, rejects. Street debris. Scraps. All treasures for hand-to-mouth-poor Nevelson.

In the late 1930s, the artist and her son, Mike, trawled through the streets of their Lower Manhattan neighborhood, collecting wood to burn in the fireplace to keep warm. But even as Nevelson struggled to keep body and soul together, she was stubbornly resourceful in her determination to make art. "I had all this wood lying around and I began to move it around, I began to compose. Anywhere I found wood, I took it home and started working with it. It might be on the streets, it might be from furniture factories. Friends might bring me wood."[4] Nevelson later called herself "the original recycler."[5]

Going out with a wheelbarrow in the dead of night, and later, in better times, riding around in a black Ford station wagon she dubbed Black Beauty, she collected battered and busted and thrown-away pieces of wood in great quantities. From this harvest of damaged goods and banished materials, Nevelson began to construct "wonder boxes" and "dream houses." Altars and wailing walls. Palaces and monuments. And as she constructed these mysterious works, she transformed junk into a precious substance through a simple alchemy: she painted everything black. Profound, complete, irrevocable, mystical, holy black. The black of night, the underworld, silence, and blindfolds. Of despair and death. But also the black of life's hidden ignition in a seed, an egg, pod, womb, the ocean depths, the nourishing earth. And the black of coal, obsidian, sable, velvet, tuxedoes, grand pianos, chess pieces, record albums, patent leather, caviar, the eye's pupil, ink, a crow, a panther. The beginning and the end.

For Nevelson, black was "the total color." She explained, "It means totality. It means: contains all. . . . it contained all color. It wasn't a negation of color. It was an acceptance. Because black encompasses all colors. Black is the most aristocratic color of all. The only aristocratic color . . . I have *seen things* that were transformed into black, that took on greatness. I don't want to use a lesser word."[6]

As for form, Nevelson credited Picasso with laying the groundwork for her sculpture. "Without Picasso giving us the cube, I would not have freed myself for my own work."[7] And like her contemporary and fellow assemblage pioneer, Joseph Cornell, Nevelson loved boxes. Boxes bring order to chaos. Boxes contain fear and conceal valuables. Open-faced boxes serve as little stages and dioramas, the precincts for fantasy. But while Cornell used boxes to preserve and showcase objects he collected and cherished in all their resonant detail and romantic allusion, Nevelson sought to obliterate all surface distinctions and cultural associations. As she filled her black boxes with strata of black forms, she emphasized their essence and sought to erase their former lives as banisters, bentwood chairs, pallets and crates, bowling pins, wooden spools, guitars, even toilet seats. Each piece has been purified and born again, each curve and angle is sharply defined, caressed, revitalized. Nevelson then used these packed, open-faced boxes to build walls and towers, mysterious and sublime structures of many shades of black. Of shadows and secrets.

Nevelson's wood sculptures are at once archaic and innovative. Imposing and elegant. Brooding and witty. Intuitive and free-spirited, she was inspired by the art of Native North Americans and the Maya, and attuned to the realm of archetypes and dreams, and the very energy of the cosmos itself. Nevelson's titles convey her mysticism. A 1955 exhibition, "Ancient Games and Ancient Places," included *Bride of the Black Moon*, *Black Majesty*, *Forgotten City*, *Night Scapes* and *Cloud City*. Her next exhibition, "The Royal Voyage," featured *The King and Queen of the Sea* and *Undermarine Scape*. Later came *Moon Garden + One*. *Sky Cathedral*. *Sky Garden*.

How many clever quips, bad jokes, and tiresome remarks have

been made mocking abstract art? Skeptics claim a child could do better, even a monkey. Abstract expressionism has been dismissed as the visual ravings of a crazy person, or an outright hoax, the artistic equivalent of the emperor's new clothes. Yet beginning with Wassily Kandinsky—whose concept of "inner necessity"[8] and belief in the spiritual power of art inspired him to forego representation and explore the deep resonance of abstraction—abstract artists, who only trust spontaneity after achieving technical mastery through traditional training, have been anything but glib. Carrying forward what art historian Frederick Hartt describes as "Kandinsky's imaginative legacy of form inflamed by emotion,"[9] the first abstract artists grappled with the boundary-dispelling perceptions of Impressionism, Freud and Jung's theories of the unconscious, the free-associations of surrealism, Einstein's disconcerting revelations, and the shocking devastations of mechanized world war.

The initial Abstract Expressionist movement was dominated by male painters, yet women artists, including sculptors, kept abstract art alive and thriving in the ensuing decades. In the third and final edition of his influential magnum opus, *Art: A History of Painting, Sculpture, Architecture,* Hartt observes that abstract sculpture was "more exciting than recent painting in the richness of its development and the multifarious shapes of its creations," and credits the ascendancy of abstract sculpture in great part to Nevelson, "who ranks as one of the finest artists of the twentieth century."[10]

Abstract art is an invitation to imagine, to interpret, to reflect. Abstract art induces reverie. It liberates us from the literal and the everyday, and provides a bridge to the realm of the collective unconscious. Like jazz musicians—who begin with a deep knowledge of song and traditional composition, then venture out into new territory, making fresh connections and creating unforeseen variations on a theme—abstract artists improvise on line and form, light and dark, emptiness and presence. Abstract art is about mass and energy, being and nothingness, moods and correspondences. We absorb its emotional valence, its action or stillness, cacophony or silence. Our busy minds instinctively seek patterns and images in abstract art just as we do when we gaze at clouds, fire, rain, and falling, whirling snow. The rigorous theorists and critics of the day who provided the intellectual framework for abstract expressionism—Hilton Kramer, Clement Greenberg, and Harold Rosenberg—would strenuously object, but why not admit that much of the power of Nevelson's work resides in the way it evokes:

Oceans and oceanic forms, from waves to currents,
seaweed, fish, coral reefs, shells.

Landscapes, from hills and valleys to ravines,
rivers, oxbows, canyons, cliffs, deserts, forests.

Books open and closed. A rebus. Type cases. Musical scores.
Libraries, archives, punch cards, puzzles, mailboxes.

Cells. Hives and honeycombs. Pueblos.
Apartment buildings. Dovecotes.

Geodes. Fossils. Catacombs. Morgues.
Mausoleums, coffins, tombs.

Machines, motors, circuits, the insides of old televisions,
furnaces, factories, mainframe computers.

Shadow boxes and tabernacles.
Stage settings and puppet theaters.
Secret nooks and crannies.
Cabinets of wonder.
Cluttered attics and basements.
Old dark rooms.

Laboratory slides. The periodic table.
Apothecary bottles and cases. Medicine cabinets.

Jewelry boxes. Safe depository boxes.
Wardrobes. Doll houses.
Tool boxes, sewing baskets.

Offerings. Reliquaries.
Arks. Scrolls.
Lost cities. Sacred ruins.
Temples, chapels, churches, mosques.
Treasure chests.
Prayers. Sanctuary.
Mindscapes and memory.
The genome.

Born in 1899, Nevelson was "a modernist down to the very core of
her being,"[11] according to professor of Jewish history Michael Stanis-
lawski. She came to art as a teenager just as America entered World War
I and fully embraced mass industrialization. Nevelson tried to take

advantage of the bounty of the robber baron era and got slammed by the Great Depression. She took shelter in art during the life-altering horrors of World War II, and gradually benefited from the mad abundance of the postwar consumer frenzy. Nevelson knew displacement, exodus, exile, prejudice, and eviction. Middle-class comfort and abject poverty. Her work was rooted in her faith in action, improvisation, and thrift. Nevelson said, "I trained myself not to waste. I feel that if you know you're going to live your life as an artist, you steel yourself daily. You don't develop fancy tastes, fancy appetites." As for her choice of materials, she explained, "During the war there was a shortage of media, and I decided that creativity was the important thing and I would see things that I could use, everywhere."[12]

Nevelson continues,

> I feel that what people call by the word *scavenger* is really a resurrection. You're taking a discarded, beat-up piece that was of no use to anyone and you place it in a position where it goes to beautiful places: museums, libraries, universities, big private houses ... These pieces of old wood have a history and a drama that to me is—well, it's like taking someone who has been in the gutter on the Bowery for years, neglected and overlooked. And someone comes along who sees how to take these beings and transform them into total being.
>
> I always wanted to show the world that art is everywhere, except that it has to pass through a creative mind ... In my environment as a child I was very aware of relationships. The injustices of relationships. And I suppose I transferred that awareness to material, what we call "inanimate." I began to see things, almost anything along the street, as art. I don't think you can touch a thing that cannot be rehabilitated into another life." And once I gave the whole world life in that sense, I could use anything.[13]

Nevelson goes on to talk about what happens when she works with pieces of found wood:

> ... when you do things this way, you are really bringing them to life. You know that you nursed them and you enhance them, you tap them and you hammer them, and you know you have given them an ultimate life, a spiritual life that surpasses the life they were created for. That lonely, lowly object is not used any more for what it was—a useful object. It becomes a work of art. It transcends

the third dimension and it too arrives beyond. It takes part in a great creative act *after* practically becoming ashes.[14]

Her empathy for old, battered, broken wood, her sense not only of bringing wood scraps back to life, but also of elevating them to a better life, is at once childish, poignant, grandiloquent, and mystical. And the psychological implications are compelling. Did Nevelson identify with used and abused wood? She, too, had been maligned, mistreated, rejected, dismissed, injured, and cast-off. She came damn close to landing in the gutter herself, and she rose from the ashes of her severe depressions and setbacks resurgent and resplendent, a phoenix in brocade and fur.

How low did Nevelson go? She began life outside Kiev, Ukraine, as Leah Berliawsky. The Berliawskys lived next door to the Yiddish writer Sholom Aleichem's sister, and legend has it that when he visited and saw baby Leah he declared she was " 'built for greatness,' potent words Leah's mother, Minna, never let her daughter forget."[15] But benediction aside, Leah's early years were difficult. Her father, Isaac, the son of a lumberman, immigrated to America a few years after her birth, seeking a freer life than the one they had in Pereyaslav, a small town fifty miles southeast of Kiev, in a region where pogroms, anti-Semitic restrictions, and epidemics ravaged Jewish communities. His wife and two children joined him in Rockland, Maine, of all places, in 1905, and promptly changed their names to sound more American. Leah became Louise.

Curiously, Rockland, Maine, was also home to the poet Edna St. Vincent Millay (1892-1950), who fled as soon as she could, and, who, like Nevelson, found paradise in New York City. Few Jewish families lived in Rockland when the Berliawskys were reunited there, and Louise later described it as a "WASP Yankee town,"[16] and bluntly said, "Look, an immigrant family pays a price."[17] As outsiders they were not welcome and were viewed forevermore as alien, or exotic. So wrenching was her father's fall from being somebody in the old country to being nobody in the new world, he suffered a breakdown, which frightened his family. He did recover, and promptly put himself to work as a peddler, "scavenging bottles, paper, scrap metal, wheels, rags, old clothes, used furniture and other discarded items to sell from a junkyard near his home."[18] As he regained his strength, optimism, and determination, he became successful enough to hold a stake in a lumberyard and work in construction and real estate. The parallels in Louise's up-and-down, junk- and wood-centered life are intriguing to say the least.

But Louise was devoted to her lovely mother, who was terribly lonely, and often bedridden with elusive ailments and untreated depression. Minna suffered the hidden trauma of immigration, the shock of losing one's homeland and sense of belonging. Her very identity was erased, her standing in the world much reduced. To her new American neighbors, Minna, called Annie, would never be anything but an intruder. Immigrants have to recreate themselves to become part of their new community, and Minna wasn't able to affect this change. It was left to her eldest daughter to make the leap, and willful Louise had no trouble inventing an American persona, a personal mythology, and a world of her own.

In an effort to make a good impression, Minna dressed herself and her children in the finest clothes she could buy. But in this chilly Yankee town, frugality and plainness were virtues. Consequently, sensitive Louise was embarrassed by her mother's elaborate attire and make-up, and often felt conspicuously overdressed herself. Yet she loved her mother and understood that dressing well "was her art, her pride, and her job."[19] She also described her mother as "a woman who should have been in a palace."[20] In *Louise Nevelson: A Passionate Life*, the first and only full Nevelson biography, published in 1990, Laurie Lisle quotes Nevelson saying, "My mother wanted us to dress like queens."[21] Lisle believes that Nevelson sought to redeem her mother's life by transforming herself into a regal figure who ruled over her sculpture palaces and virtual empire with head held high.

But first Louise had to overcome her discomfort with English (the family spoke Yiddish at home, and Nevelson's English remained gnarly), the town's low-key but palpable anti-Semitism, and her dislike of everything at school except Shakespeare and art classes, in which she excelled. Energetic, olive-skinned, and curvy, she possessed, Lisle writes, "an extravagant dark beauty."[22] Louise enjoyed her good looks and used them to her advantage. As she developed her considerable drawing and painting skills, which guided her all her life (in talking about sculpting she later said, "Without drawing, you wouldn't *do* anything."[23]), she also began to make her own eye-catching clothes, cleverly using aprons, cloth napkins, and draped fabrics. Her penchant for unusual get-ups became intrinsic to her identity.

At eighteen, Louise was working as a legal stenographer in a Rockland law office when she met and impressed Bernard Nevelson, one of four sons in a wealthy New York shipping family. He basically arranged her marriage to his younger brother, Charles. Their 1920 wedding pleased Louise's parents, and granted her a ticket out of the forested wilderness of Maine and into the promised land of New York City. But Louise was soon bored by the plush and conventional life she bartered her independence for. More alarming was her reaction when she became pregnant. She was absolutely traumatized. Terrified and appalled by the very idea of giving birth, she insisted on having a cesarean section. Myron, called Mike, was born in 1922, and Louise proved to be a rotten wife and a wretched mother. She spent so little time with her son, he had trouble learning to speak.

When the Nevelson fortune was vaporized in the crash of 1929, Louise refused to curb her rebelliously lavish spending and impractical ways, and she continued to embarrass her husband and son with her flamboyant attire. Years later she told MacKown, "I was never married in the true soul sense."[24] She remembers reading a newspaper article about a woman who pushed her husband out of a window during an argument and thinking, "there but for the grace of God go I."[25] Equally disturbing was her response to motherhood. "Here I had a son, and I didn't feel like living. I just felt like I was lost."[26] Her depression was severe. She described what went through her mind: "I can't stay here because I'll do something desperate. I must get out of this. So I began working toward that end. The only thing that I felt saved my life was work because there was always a straight line there. I found that this was my stability."[27]

After Nevelson began taking art classes, an epiphany at the Metropolitan Museum of Art affirmed her calling. And how fitting it is that her revelation was sparked by an exhibition of golden Noh kimonos. These exquisite ceremonial robes designed for classical Japanese theater moved her to tears. "I said, oh my God, life is worth living if a civilization can give us this great weave of gold and pattern."[28] This was an abiding vision, made manifest in the elaborate robes she favored and the stage-set qualities of her sculptural installations, especially her late, still controversial gold-painted assemblages.

Finally admitting that she cared not a whit for family life or material comfort or conformity, Nevelson enlisted her family's help (her brother Nate was a loyal and essential ally), and took off for Europe to further her art studies. Guilt over abandoning her son soon brought her back home, but she fled again a few months later in 1931, financing this trip by pawning the diamond bracelet Charles gave her in celebration of Mike's birth. When she returned for good a year later, she rented a place of her own in Lower Manhattan, and dedicated herself wholly to her art.

Nevelson declared, "I am closer to the work than to anything on earth. That's the marriage."[29] She was so absorbed in her struggle to survive and make art, she missed her son's bar mitzvah. When Mike tried to live with her, the steady stream of his mother's casual lovers soon sent him packing. Without a gallery, Nevelson could not sell her work, and so she scrounged, drank too much, plunged into depression, and made art out of scraps.

Indomitable and gifted, Nevelson did succeed in exhibiting her work in group shows, but her relationships with other artists were thorny. Inspired by Diego Rivera's murals and seduced by his infamous charm, she had an affair with him that she quickly regretted because it created a rift between her and Frida Kahlo, Rivera's wife, whom she admired. As much as she wanted admission into New York's now fabled abstract art circles, Nevelson didn't talk the talk or adopt the look. She simply refused to walk around looking like the starving artist she truly was. While other women artists dressed plainly and offhandedly, implicitly stating that they had more important things on their minds then fashion, Louise was provokingly glamorous. When Alice Neel asked her how she managed to dress so beautifully, Nevelson replied, "Fucking, dear, fucking."[30] Another woman friend (with friends like this, as they say, who needs enemies) described Nevelson as "slightly whorish."[31] Brazen to the end, Nevelson told Lisle that "if she revealed all the ways she had survived during those financially difficult years, she would be arrested and put in jail."[32]

Nevelson's confident, even aggressive appearance, coupled with her reluctance to theorize about her work, fueled the misogyny that ran rampant in the art world at the height of the abstract expressionist movement. Male artists and critics did not take her seriously, thus underestimating her grievously. But she stood her ground. When an obnoxious male artist tells her, "You know, Louise, you have to have *balls* to be a sculptor," she replies, "I *do* have balls."[33] She kept her troubles to herself, and wore her regalia as armor.

After being forced to destroy many sculptures because she had no place to store them, after enduring poverty and despondency and rage, Nevelson, a hunter-gatherer in the urban jungle who refused to compromise or beg, finally insisted that gallery owner Karl Nierendorf come look at her work and give her a show. He looked, he liked, and Nevelson had her first solo exhibition in 1941, the same year she became legally divorced. Nierendorf represented her for seven years, in spite of a rocky start with an egregiously sexist review, which includes these immoral lines: "We learned the artist is a woman, in time to check our enthusiasm. Had it been otherwise, we might have hailed these sculptural expressions as by surely a great figure among moderns."[34] It's enough to drive anyone to drink and fury.

Nevelson could be unnervingly confrontational. Even atavistic and out of control. One of the more sad and shocking stories Lisle tells places a wrathful Nevelson at the ritzy opening for a 1959 group sculpture show at the Museum of Modern Art. Enraged not to have been included, Nevelson slips behind a curtain concealing a stash of liquor and tubs of ice, lifts her long skirt, and pisses on the cubes.

Both Nevelson and the twentieth century were in their fifties when her work finally began to receive respectful critical attention. And she was well into her seventies and eighties when she began to create large outdoor sculptures. As much as she fought to be treated as equal to men artists, Nevelson believed that women did make art differently than men, and that this was a fine and wonderful thing. Furthermore, she said, "I think that if a woman is gifted and she's attractive she's going to have a great time on earth. Why would she want to be anything else? I don't think of myself as a strong woman. I never even heard that word about me until recently. I always thought bluntly that I was a glamorous goddam exciting woman."[35]

When Nevelson wasn't hustling rich men, she liked to pick up stevedores who worked on the docks nearby. She got lucky in her relationship with one longshoreman named Johnny (last name lost), who for several years squired her around town and helped her with the heavy lifting in the studio. Too bad the injuries he sustained after being shot in a brawl with police ended up causing him "chronic stomach trouble."[36] As Lisle so succinctly puts it, "Louise did not want to be bothered with the needs of a sick person."[37] Heck, she had little patience with her own physical needs, although at seventy-six she chose to undergo breast-reduction surgery. She claimed her breasts got in her way when she worked. Maybe, but she also didn't want to look matronly or old. She wanted to be svelte and unencumbered and desirable.

As her fame increased, so did the quality of her clothing. The fashion designer Arnold Scaasi was quite taken with her unique chieftain/sorcerer style, her bold mixing of different prints and unexpected combinations of the opulent with the utilitarian, a flannel work shirt, for instance, with a sable coat. Scaasi designed extravagant clothes fit for the "empress of art"[38] that Nevelson adored, even as she refused to wear high heels because she like to take long, free, and easy strides. She not only craved the attention her colorful, flowing garb attracted, she also, the truth be told, felt shy and defenseless without her robes, hats, and amulets. And besides, her outfits were works of art. Nevelson told MacKown,

> I love to put things together. My whole life is one big collage. Every time I put on clothes, I am creating a picture, a living picture, for myself . . . I like clothes that are upholstered. I like that you build up your clothes, and build up, and even the hat . . . I feel the clothes that I have worn all my life have been freedom, a stamp of freedom—because I have never conformed to what is being worn.[39]

Nevelson was no hypocrite. She had "such esteem for the creative mind,"[40] she refused to stifle her artistic impulse and dress down in order to look like everyone else. And why not flaunt her success? Hers is a tale of rags-to-riches, shmattes-to-fame.

Nevelson started making abstract free-standing sculptures in the heyday of abstract expressionism, and she began filling boxes with found objects in the pop art days, when a can of Campbell's soup was elevated to fine-art status. But Nevelson couldn't have cared less about consumerism and mass culture, ensconced in her empire of scraps. She was seeking a deeper level as she put together her intricate puzzles. By the late 1960s and early 1970s, Nevelson's attunement to the "livingness" of wood, passion for ancient cultures, and mysticism were in sync with hippie culture, as were her flowing, paisley thrift-shop clothes, her beads and bandanas, her love of Native American art, and her penchant for crazy-quilt juxtaposition and do-it-yourself handicraft.

The 1970s were also a time of renewed feminism and the women's history movement. Women critics were intent on reclaiming the work and life stories of forgotten women artists of the past, and on fighting for space in galleries and museums for women artists of the present. Women artists were also transforming art itself. Miriam Shapiro and Judy Chicago brought traditional women's crafts—sewing, embroidery, china-painting—into the fine-art arena, most radically in Judy Chicago's ambitious group effort, *The Dinner Party*, which debuted in San Francisco in 1979 and which remains scandalous thirty years later.

Like her sister artists, Nevelson knew that the ordinary contains the extraordinary. In a 1976 interview with Arnold Glimcher, her most devoted and simpatico art dealer, she said,

> Well, don't forget that the lace curtain is not only a lace curtain. I am saying that it isn't just something to put on a window. . . . It has

a whole architectural structure of its own. It has its own life. It is constantly in movement. A breeze gives you new forms; and the glitter is like a river, or an ocean really. So we have to realize that when a mind is working in a medium, it means that you're using this kind of a medium to encompass into your consciousness all the creation that was put on this earth and also beyond.[41]

Life on earth was at once too much and too little for Nevelson, who beneath her queenly robes was porous to the suffering of others, even as she was impatient with the needs of family and friends. She relied on the discipline of art to channel her unruly emotions and tame her demons. She built an empire for herself out of "a thousand destructions of the real world"[42] as a retreat, a hermitage, a sanctuary. And yet she did not work in isolation. She cultivated studio assistants and flourished in collaborations that allowed her to give full rein to her imagination while others took care of the technical challenges. Even her vivid autobiography was not written in solitude, but rather spoken aloud to a trusted friend and disciple, who then turned ensorcelled talk into shaped prose. And in spite of her inability to maintain intimate relationships or to be social in the usual ways, Nevelson supported the efforts of other artists, especially women, and she never ceased to learn and grow. She never got stuck in ruts; she never closed doors to new adventures, she never permitted herself to be pigeonholed.

Once she was known the world over as the artist who painted everything black, Nevelson started painting her work white and gold. Revered for her adeptness with wood, she began to make sculptures out of glass and Plexiglass. When commissions for large outdoor sculptures began to pour in from across the country, she decided to explore the possibilities of aluminum and steel. As with wood, she composed with metal scraps and remnants to create "sculpture-collages," remarkably buoyant landscape-scale studies in balance, shadow, and reflection. Penetrating and imaginative, Nevelson became fascinated with all the effort that went into manufacturing these tough, manmade materials, conceiving of each substance as an "accumulation of thought."[43] As with wood, she detected the life force in plastic and steel, and recognized that these new materials profoundly altered our perception of the world.

Nevelson brought this same insightful understanding of how the things we invent and construct change not only the tangible and visual world, but also our mindscape to her impressions of the then three-year-old World Trade Center:

The World Trade Center is two giant cubes and the tallest cubes in the city. They stand there among the rest of the sculpture-city and they are fine. They're magnificent. When the lights go on at night they're touching beyond the heavens. But when you think of the concept of building involved in the World Trade Center, it has set a precedent and challenge to the world that the human mind has encompassed the engineering of that space. From that point of view the World Trade Center is a landmark. And you can understand, if you want to tie it up with the evolution of humanity, how the human mind is going to have to move and expand to accept it.[44]

Or not. Leave it to sibyl Nevelson to recognize the immense and problematic symbolic import of the World Trade Center, which, of course, led to its destruction. Naturally, she was thrilled to be commissioned to create an immense black wood wall relief for the towers, *Sky Gate-New York*. It was prominently displayed until all was destroyed on 9/11, in a tragedy we've yet to wrap our minds around, let alone all the horrors, misery, and crimes that have followed.

The endlessly self-aggrandizing sculptor boasts about her handling of Cor-ten steel: "I found that in my hands and in my way of thinking at this point, it was almost like butter—like working with whipped cream on a cake. I was using steel as if it was ribbon made out of satin. And somehow it gave me another dimension."[45] Of course, Nevelson had the skilled assistance of metal fabricators. The tough gal who relished the company of longshoremen had a ball with the steel men, and there are photographs to prove it. Both MacKown and Guerrero documented Nevelson working at the Lippincott Foundry in North Haven, Connecticut, and these are the most vital and relaxed pictures of the artist available. Nevelson is in her element. You can just imagine her calling these guys "sweetheart" and "darling" and "dear" in her husky smoker's voice as she bosses them around, a slim cigar burning between her nimble fingers. Eyelashes jutting, headscarf snug, plaid and flower patterns in competition on her layered attire, Nevelson directs the men to do strange and marvelous gravity-defying things with curvilinear pieces of steel, resulting in the construction of tremendous sculptures of amazing lightness and beauty.

But creativity is no party. Nevelson said, "The very nature of creation is not of a performing glory on the outside. It's a painful, difficult search inside."[46] In spite of the fact that she worked with pieces, with scraps and fragments, her search was for "the achievement of unity."[47]

Nevelson questioned all assumptions about reality, and thought a lot about how appearances deceive. She pondered the significance of the fact that everything that seems to be solid is actually a tenuous gathering of atoms, that everything is forever in the process of becoming something else. She also considered the conundrum that there is no such thing as nothing. She said, "I think often people don't realize the meaning of space. Space, they think, is something empty. Actually, in the mind and the projection into this three-dimensional world, space plays the most vital part in our lives. Your concept of what you put into a space will create another space. . . . Space has an atmosphere. . . . The whole body is in space. We are space."[48] Lisle writes, "Near the end of her life, Nevelson's metaphysical sense of the insubstantiality of objective reality deepened."[49]

Nevelson was even prescient in her anticipation of the lure of the virtual world. She riffs in her knotty, oracular way on the laws of nature. They are still necessary, she muses,

> But the thing is, the time may come, with computers, with technology, when humans will not need this manifestation, this projection into three dimensions. Even in sacred books, like the Indian philosophies, they don't feel—as long as you are laboring and working—that's the height. It's the place of contemplation, you see, that is where you don't have to make anything or do anything. But I, for my own needs, prefer to play the game with awareness, on earth, three-dimensionally. It's a choice I've made. I could easily have moved into an area of meditation and contemplation, and it is higher according to all philosophers. But I claim physical activity teaches me so much. My feeling is that there is great intelligence in labor . . . That living awareness moves me as I move it to an activity that encompasses the mind, the body, and the total consciousness. So I feel that I could not have projected my world only through contemplation. Since I *did* want to project a three-dimensional world for myself, it could not have been done without physical activity.[50]

How could we wish it to be otherwise? We are creatures of the earth, members of one of the animal tribes. Our minds are fed by our senses. Our bodies evolved, brain and all, to move through space defined by the planet's precious atmosphere and sculpted terrain with its lush and sustaining mantle of trees, shrubs, and grasses. We are wholly dependent on the many-stranded web of life, in which everything serves a purpose at each stage of its existence, cessation, and decay. Nevelson was no nature girl, yet she perceived the interconnectivity and cycles of life as she prowled the wild, secretive streets before dawn, her predator's eyes picking out hidden treasures. And she summoned the moon and the sun, oceans and trees, collective memories and shared dreams as she worked the brilliant black, white, and gold magic of her art.

Yet during the years in which Nevelson built her imaginary empire, the gorgeous complexity and perfection of creation was being diminished by humankind's industriousness. Here and now in the twenty-first century, the entire living world is imperiled. Humankind has inadvertently put the glimmering, miraculous balancing act that is life at grave risk. We've assumed that nature can take care of itself while we, the planet's storytellers and inventors, tinkerers and garbage-makers, are held spellbound by the objects and machines of our own devising, oblivious to the cost of their manufacture, which is paid for with the irreplaceable currency of clean air and water, fertile earth, and all that keeps the fire of life ablaze. For future generations, the astonishment and bounty of a resplendent world teeming with countless, diverse, symbiotic species may become only a memory, the ultimate story of paradise lost.

Reading *Dawns & Dusks* twenty years after Nevelson's death, one is struck by her spirituality. The creator of *Dawn's Wedding Feast*, *Ocean Gate*, *Cascade*, *The Wave*, *The Forest*, *Tropical Garden*, *Sun Disk*, *Half Moon*, and *Royal Tide* was, in her way, a pantheist. In *Standing in the Light: My Life as a Pantheist*, nature writer and writer of conscience Sharman Apt Russell defines pantheism as "the belief that the universe, and all its existing laws and properties, is an interconnected whole that we can rightly consider sacred."[51] She quotes Marcus Aurelius: "Everything is connected, and the web is holy."[52] Surely, Nevelson would have agreed.

A pantheist by nature, Nevelson was Jewish by heritage. She didn't talk much about being Jewish, but Judaism and the Diaspora are the foundation on which her life and her work were constructed. Her habit of covering her hair is in keeping with the practice of Orthodox Jewish women. Like all the pioneering abstract expressionists, of which a remarkable number were Jewish, Nevelson did not create "graven images," which the second commandment forbids. Her work bears a striking resemblance to historic Jewish art and artifacts: elaborately filigreed Torah cases, carved arks that hold the sacred scrolls, and exquisitely patterned kaddish cups, oil lamps, and candlesticks. Even more resonant in this context is her response to brokenness; her impulse to gather dispersed pieces and reassemble them to create a new unity. However subconsciously, Nevelson was enacting a ritualized form of *tikkun olam*, the Jewish call to repair the world.

Not only was space sacred to Nevelson, she also created works for sacred spaces, including the magnificent installation, *The White Flame of the Six Million*, in the Temple Beth-El in Great Neck, New York, and the Chapel of the Good Shepherd at Saint Peter's Church in New York City. She also created *Homage to Six Million I*, which Lisle describes as "a massive black curved wall of immense dignity and grief, a sculptural kaddish."[53]

Louise Nevelson was everywhere, and then she was nowhere. Would Nevelson have been able to draw on her sense of the mutable nature of reality and taken a philosophical view if she could have known how quickly and completely she was forgotten after her death? After Laurie Lisle's biography came out, there was silence. No one else in the public square was critiquing Nevelson and assessing her contribution to modern art and enormous influence on contemporary artists. There were no major retrospective exhibitions. No one found her life alluring enough for fiction or film. Her work was rarely reproduced. Museums put her large installations in storage. Perhaps they are too difficult to maintain; imagine the tedium of dusting every nook and cranny. New books about American art, modern art, abstract sculpture, assemblage, installation art—all spheres in which Nevelson was a pioneer and driving force—omit her entirely, or relegate her to one inadequate, often condescending mention.

As Nevelson was eclipsed, Georgia O'Keeffe ascended. Book after book documented and analyzed her life and work, from the stunning nude photographs taken by her husband, Alfred Stieglitz, to lush reproductions of her paintings to photographs of her desert refuge. Hunger for all things O'Keeffe sustains a veritable industry, and an entire museum devoted to the sainted artist of the southwest was erected in Santa Fe, New Mexico. Sunny O'Keeffe waxed; lunar Nevelson waned. And Frida Kahlo had her revenge. Like O'Keeffe, she became a mainstream emblem of female creativity, albeit as a martyr to pain and betrayal. Her life of physical agony and psychological anguish, of great courage and trailblazing artistry, of audacious and indelible self-portraits was celebrated in a torrent of beautiful and affecting books and in an acclaimed film. Like the forgotten Nevelson, Kahlo was a living work of art with her crown of braids, elaborate earrings, embroidered blouses, and great ruffled skirts. But Kahlo is enshrined; Nevelson obliterated.

Master playwright Edward Albee and master sculptor Louise Nevelson were close friends for more than twenty years. What did he think of Nevelson's erasure? In 2001, Albee wrote a play in homage to the sculptor titled *Occupant*, a work of exquisite empathy and dark, knowing humor. It's a duet for two characters: The Man, "40's, pleasant" and Nevelson, who is "much like the later photographs," and, as the stage directions explain, "encased in a costume 'cage,'" As the play begins, The Man starts to introduce her and Nevelson interrupts, "Look, dear, everybody knows who I am." He demurs, "Time passes. You're not as . . . recognizable now as you were." Nevelson says, "You're kidding!" The Man then has the unenviable task of explaining that today few people know who she is. She bristles; she laughs; she exclaims "All right! So I'm invisible! Or I don't exist! Which do you want?" He tells her that more people know what she looks like than what she did: "You're a very famous image, Louise . . . you were."

Is Albee's Nevelson character devastated by the fact that her work has been forgotten? No, she's too tough, smart, and cynical. She's been around; she knows how the world works. Sharp-tongued and at once combative and evasive, she banters and argues with The Man as he attempts to chronicle each phase of her life. The Man struggles to keep Nevelson honest. She balks and protests, at one point telling the audience, "Pay no attention to him." But as the duel continues, she recognizes that he is well-informed and well-intentioned, and she becomes almost grateful for a chance to reflect on her life. It's an interrogation, a reckoning, a therapy session. Finally, The Man asks her about her last days in the hospital. Her name was on the door to her room, he reminds her, in capital letters no less. "As big as *death* maybe," she says. "Yes, there's no privacy anywhere." So she had them replace her name with "Occupant." The brash and ironic final gesture of a self-made queen.

In keeping with the odd and inexplicable Nevelson blackout, *Occupant* began previews in New York City in 2002 with Anne Bancroft cast as the artist. But as Albee notes in the published version of the play: "Due to illness, Anne Bancroft was not able to continue in her role as Louise Nevelson, so the production never officially opened." Bancroft died in 2005.

Why was Nevelson forgotten? Was she too flamboyant? Too strange? Did she become a caricature rather than an icon? Was she too intense, arrogant, cryptic, ornery, primitive? Too dramatic? Too contradictory? Too successful? Too on-in-years when she created her best work? Was she too flinty and rough with her cigars, her stabbing eyelashes, her gravely voice, her mask and armor? Why was her work so quickly dismissed? Was it too decorative, too creepy, too female, too somber, too mystical? Even when she was alive, nearly everyone despised her gold sculptures. They were considered gaudy and crass. But their bold inquiry into our worship of wealth and status comes through loud and clear, as does the artist's delight in opulence as power. Nevelson's romanticism is as misunderstood as her irony. Her gold sculptures reach back to her epiphany in the presence of the golden kimonos and embody her belief that beauty is a precious and healing element of life.

Nevelson's entire oeuvre will be forever open to interpretation. Her sculptures ask to be read, and reread. Her great walls and towers are wooden poems, each box a stanza, each piece a word, yet they are not tethered to any one language. They speak to everyone. Her works alter the spaces they occupy, and change those who stand before them. Nevelson's sculptures emit a mysterious force; they embody memory, dream, trance, and prayer. Nevelson's accumulations and compositions encompass loss, metamorphosis, and reclamation. Her sculptures make what was broken whole, and reveal that what we see as whole is the sum of infinite parts.

Nevelson's work makes us acutely aware of how blithely we throw things away. We churn out more products than we can possibly use, and we are profligate with our trash. Our garbage is amassed in gargantuan landfills, which stand as our pyramids, our Great Wall. We can't seem to grasp that when we throw things "away," there is no away. There is only here, here on the glorious, spinning, orbiting earth. Our waste becomes more toxic and deadly with each generation of digital and nuclear devices. Nevelson discerned and respected the life force intrinsic to each and every made thing. We toss things when they're worn or broken or no longer stylish. We're losing the art of repair, and we're clotting the web of life with plastic bags and bottles and cigarette butts. A society that habitually discards so many objects so obliviously is at some deep level indifferent to life. How great a divide is there between trashing our belongings and seeing animals and other human beings as disposable? How different is the habit of wastefulness from a lack of compassion? A reconsideration of Nevelson's art inspires us to reflect on what we value and cherish, how we live and die. What we hope for, and what we will leave behind.

It seems that when we need the vision and light of a lost artist, when we're ready to appreciate her perspective and discoveries, the veil is lifted, and the artist returns. How fitting it is that in this time of accelerating climate change, environmental crises, and unmanageable waste, an artist who perceived trash as treasure and found illumination in life's cycles has herself been reclaimed and resurrected. In 2000, the U.S.

Postal Service issued commemorative stamps in Nevelson's honor. In 2007 a retrospective exhibition, *The Sculpture of Louise Nevelson: Constructing a Legend*, was organized and displayed by the Jewish Museum in New York, reassembled in San Francisco, and accompanied by an elegant catalog. Nevelson's archives are now available online as part of the Smithsonian Institute's vast and invaluable Archives of American Art. A new documentary film has been released; a Louise Nevelson Foundation has been founded, and Edward Albee's play has finally been produced. Long live the Empress of Art.

Intimate with paradox and contradiction, despair and triumph, Nevelson called herself Louise Neverlands in wry acknowledgment of her attempt to remain forever young, her preference for make-believe, and her longing for magic. For all her mastery of black and white, Nevelson knew that humankind lives in the gray zone. She understood that we are Earth's most conflicted beings. We dwell uneasily in dawns and dusks, the sea of ambiguity, the lost-and-found, the zone between emotion and intellect, the void between dream and reality. We all abide for better and for worse in the in-between.

Endnotes

1. Epigraph: Interview with Louise Nevelson in Glimcher, Arnold B. *Louise Nevelson*. 1976. New York: Dutton, p. 79. (Number not shown)

2. Guerrero, Pedro E. *Pedro E. Guerrero: A Photographer's Journey*. 2007. New York: Princeton Architechural Press, p. 196.

3. Nevelson, Louise. *Dawns & Dusks: Louise Nevelson, taped conversations with Diana MacKown*. 1976. New York: Charles Scribner's Sons, p. 78.

4. *Dawns & Dusks*, p. 76.

5. Guerro, p. 195.

6. *Dawns & Dusks*, pp. 125-26.

7. *Dawns & Dusks*, p. 38.

8. Hartt, Frederick. *Art: A History of Painting, Sculpture, Architecture*. Third edition, 1989. New York: Harry N. Abrams, p. 890.

9. Hartt, p. 890.

10. Hartt, p. 946.

11. *The Sculpture of Louise Nevelson: Constructing a Legend*. Edited by Brooke Kamin Rapaport. 2007. The Jewish Museum of New York/Yale University Press (New Haven and London). P. 36.

12. *Dawns & Dusks*, p. 73.

13. *Dawns & Dusks*, p. 81.

14. *Dawns & Dusks*, p. 83.

15. Lisle, Laurie. *Louise Nevelson: A Passionate Life*. 1990. New York: Summit Books, p. 18.
16. *Dawns & Dusks*, p. 7.
17. *Dawns & Dusks*, p. 7.
18. Lisle, p. 26.
19. Lisle, p. 30.
20. *Dawns & Dusks*, p. 6.
21. Lisle, p. 30.
22. Lisle, p. 40.
23. *Dawns & Dusks*, p. 64.
24. *Dawns & Dusks*, p. 37.
25. *Dawns & Dusks*, p. 37.
26. *Dawns & Dusks*, pp. 35-36.
27. *Dawns & Dusks*, p. 38.
28. *Dawns & Dusks*, p. 37.
29. *Dawns & Dusks*, p. 43.
30. Lisle, p. 126.
31. Lisle, p. 125.
32. Lisel, p. 126.
33. *Dawns & Dusks*, p, 69.
34. Lisle, p. 143.
35. *Dawns & Dusks*, pp. 69 - 70.
36. Lisle, p. 166.
37. Lisle, p. 166.
38. Lisle, p. 263.
39. *Dawns & Dusks*, pp. 184-85.
40. *Dawns & Dusks*, p. 185.
41. Glimcher, pp. 190-93.
42. Lisle, p. 222.
43. *Dawns & Dusks*, p. 171.
44. *Dawns & Dusks*, p. 112.
45. *Dawns & Dusks*, p. 171.
46. Lisle, p. 191.
47. Lisle, p. 191.
48. *Dawns & Dusks*, p. 167-68.
49. Lisle, p. 283.
50. *Dawns & Dusks*, 177.
51. Russell, Sharman Apt. *Standing in the Light: My Life as a Pantheist*. 2008. New York: Basic Books, p. 2.
52. Russell, p. xi.
53. Lisle, p. 20.

All quotes from Edward Albee's *Occupant* are from *The Collected Plays of Edward Albee, Volume 3, 1978-2003*. 2005. New York: Overlook Duckworth.

Robert von Hallberg

Sob-Ballads

The grip of modernism relaxed in the late-1950s, when the Beats and then the Confessional poets recovered the pleasures of directly expressed feeling in poetry—warm feeling that a quarter-century earlier might have embarrassed Pound, Eliot, or Auden, say. But if one thinks broadly of poetry, including the popular song, one realizes that sentiment was enormously popular in the early-1940s and remained so through the next decade. Frank Sinatra was neither poet nor lyricist; he wrote lyrics to only two songs in his entire life. But from 1939 until 1994 he presented popular poetry to large numbers of listeners and television viewers. Like a rhapsode in ancient Greece, he became identified with a distinctive repertoire of songs. He was not a musical technician (he could not sight-read a score); he chose his songs on the basis of the words, not the tune. "I'll leave the music to somebody else," he said, "I pick the lyrics."[1] At the start of his career, his model was Bing Crosby, who was wrongly known as a crooner; Sinatra said that Crosby was instead a "troubadour. He tells a story in every song. . . . He makes you feel like he's singing just for you. I bet I could do that."[2] It was Sinatra whose success effectively introduced, as Mel Tormé said, "a new era in popular music, a vocalist's era."[3] Before him, audiences came to hear the bands; after him, they came to hear the singers. And the bands died.

His stardom began with a single performance, on December 31, 1942, at the Paramount theater in New York. He was added to a bill featuring the Benny Goodman band. When he came out on stage, the crowd let out a roar that stunned everyone, especially Benny Goodman, who said, "What the fuck was that?" With that performance, Sinatra became the biggest entertainer in the U.S.[4] He had already left the Harry James band to join Tommy Dorsey in January 1940. James was a warm trumpeter who, according to Will Friedwald, taught Sinatra "not to be afraid of schmaltz."[5] Dorsey identified himself then as the "Sentimental Gentleman of Swing."[6] And, with The Voice, he recorded plainly sentimental tunes right from the start. "Polka Dots and Moonbeams," recorded in March 1940, is one the best of these early tunes. Dorsey and Sinatra had their first big hit with "I'll Never Smile Again," recorded by a small group from the band billed as "The Sentimentalists."[7] A label of sentimentality helped to sell songs in the late 1930s and the 1940s.

But the literary culture was another matter. I. A. Richards said in 1929 that "among the politer terms of abuse there are few so effective as 'sentimental.'"[8] Intellectuals wanted no part of sentimental art. Following Eliot's effort in his essays of 1919 to urge English taste back to a standard established prior to the "sentimental age [that] began early in the eighteenth century," Richards, John Crowe Ransom, and Cleanth Brooks elaborated cognate critiques of sentimentality.[9] They argued that sentimentality simplifies the representation and interpretation of experience by stressing a single angle of vision—to the exclusion of others. As Brooks said, "The sentimentalist takes a short cut to intensity by removing all the elements of the experience which might conceivably militate against the intensity."[10] The sentimentalist constructs a thin representation of thought and experience. He had Popular Front poets in mind, and named Langston Hughes, Genevieve Taggard, and Don West in particular.[11]

The anti-sentimental critique was pitched against poets who tried to enlist their art in a struggle for social progress, and worse, against women poets in particular, as Ransom's blunt blast of Edna St. Vincent Millay reveals. But the anti-sentimental critique drew justification from two vigorous and still-influential poetic principles expounded by Eliot. First is the anti-discursive idea that "permanent literature is always a presentation: either a presentation of thought, or a presentation of feeling by a statement of events in human action or objects in the external world. . . . The labour of the intellect consisted largely . . . in refraining from reflection, in putting into the statement enough to make reflection unnecessary."[12] An anti-sentimental or ironic poet is doubtful about the adequacy of reflective discourse. Second is the idea that great art encompasses deep heterogeneity. A poet's mind, according to Eliot, "is constantly amalgamating disparate experience; the ordinary man's experience is chaotic, irregular, fragmentary. The latter falls in love, or reads Spinoza, and the two experiences have nothing to do with each other, or with the noise of the typewriter or the smell of cooking; in the mind of the poet these experiences are always forming new wholes."[13] An ironic poet's subject includes disparities, and no single judgment consistently determines the poem's perspective. Ironic poets are heterodox in that they disagree even with themselves. Insofar as poets after Eliot represent experience in such detail that explicit interpretive reflection seems unnecessary to their purposes, encompass heterogeneous subject matter in their poems, and refrain as well from constructing a single angle of vision on their subjects, they have made their own the very objectives served by the anti-sentimental critique. Assessed by this measure, Eliot's influence has been far more extensive than poets realize.

When Sinatra began his career, the bandleader Harry James, who first hired him, urged him to change his name, derived no doubt from sinestro, on the dark side, to Johnny Satin: he was so smooth. The direct, fluent expression of sensitivity: that was his art; struggle was never part of it. He started out with female fans and ended with males, as Pete Hamill observes.[14] How did that happen, and why? From the outset, young women went wild for him. Soon after he got started, young American men began to enlist and were inducted into the armed services. Other stars, like Clark Gable and James Stewart, went willingly to war, but not Sinatra; he had a punctured eardrum. (After the war he played a soldier in eleven films.)

> The male anger against Sinatra came to a head in October 1944, when he played the Paramount again and 30,000 mostly female fans erupted into a small riot outside the theater. When a male dissenter in the Paramount balcony fired a tomato at the stage, he had to be rescued from women who were trying to beat him to death.[15]

William Manchester said that by the end of the war Sinatra had become "the most hated man in the armed services."[16] And consider the competition! Sinatra recovered public authority after the war by performing the role of a soldier, in *From Here to Eternity* (1953), who is sacrificed. Sinatra had to die in the war, as Maggio, to make everything right again; he won an Academy Award for the part.

John Stuart Mill's paradox about lyric poetry has special bearing on the genre of sob-ballads: one *overhears* lyric, he said. But these songs were not only published, as poems routinely are, they were publicly and repeatedly performed before large audiences. Sinatra's sentimentality required a particular public display. He legitimated the expression of male tenderness, and a view of human nature, based on sentiment, that encouraged even hard-boiled types to display themselves as teary.[17] His social activities, widely reported in the press, were notorious: he kept the company of gangsters, and now and then engaged in fisticuffs in public, or had his bodyguards do so for him. He associated himself publicly with hypermasculinity, but on stage he was a strikingly tender, even slightly androgynous, lover, repeatedly forsaken by the ladies. His friend Noël Coward observed that he was "a remarkable personality—tough, vulnerable and somehow touching."[18] Another friend, Pete Hamill, developed the point:

> He could be tender and still be a tough guy. . . . For men, whining or self-pity was not allowed; they were forbidden by the male codes of the city. Sinatra slowly found a way to allow tenderness into the performance while remaining manly. When he finally took command of his own career, he perfected the role of the Tender Tough Guy and passed it on to several generations of Americans. Before him, that archetype did not exist in American popular culture. That is one reason why he continues to matter; Frank Sinatra created a new model for American masculinity.[19]

It is remarkable that he has performed a vaguely feminine sort of persona on stage, and in lyrics, but achieved success as an icon of hypermasculinity. His grander aspiration was the proposal of a model of human sensibility that disregards gender and social distinction altogether. He challenged audiences to overlook the psychic boundaries between men and women, the social ones between black and white men, and the ethical ones between law-abiding and law-evading entrepreneurs. Some features of this challenge were made in the lyrics themselves, others in his stage and television presentation with friends, still others in his own social activities. It is conventional for singers to perform the significance of the words they sing, to appear to live the words of a song for the duration of a song. Sinatra went further than most other singers in presenting for consumption a comprehensive image of his music. The covers of his albums often represented him in the mood of the songs recorded. In 1942 he recorded the Oscar Hammerstein/ Jerome Kern love song "The Song Is You." The title seemed in retrospect to fit his career. More than a half-century later the five-CD boxed set of his recordings with the Tommy Dorsey band was released with the same title. The following year, 1995, his best critic published the most extensive analysis of the music under the title *Sinatra! The Song Is You.* He did more than sing particular songs. He publicly represented the sentimental thematics of his music as a way of living. His aspiration to legitimate the social changes I have mentioned extended from vinyl recordings, to televisions shows, and concert stages, but it included too all his activities reported in the press, even his contact with politicians and mafiosi.

Of course, Sinatra was not the first to legitimate male weeping. Glenn Hendler tells of nineteenth century temperance rallies at which great crowds of men gathered to weep. Sinatra's point is that human nature is universal, that no one is too tough for tears. The scandals about his infidelities, his friendship with Sam Giancana, and even the scuffles in restaurants—they all served to validate his sentimental art. His large point was that people are just people, that gender, class, and social distinctions (as between the legal and illegal economies) obscure our deep, reassuring sameness. This dream of universal manhood came apart spectacularly at the end of 1960, not because of the intransigence of racism or sexism, but because of the stigma of criminality. Anthony Summers explains that Sinatra served as a go-between from Giancana and associates to the presidential campaign of then-Senator John Kennedy. Giancana helped the Kennedy campaign win the elections in West Virginia and Illinois. When Robert Kennedy was appointed Attorney General, it was clear that the social distinction between licit and illicit businessmen was going to be strenuously enforced, not transcended, by the Kennedy administration. Sinatra was thought to have betrayed Giancana, and for a while he even feared for his life. The universal appeal of sentimental art goes only so far.

American songwriters were evidently not indifferent to the corruptions of sentimental writing, though they probably knew little of Ransom and Eliot. When Ransom accused sentimentalists of anti-intellectuality, he saw what some songwriters saw too. The more compelling sob-ballads are often explicitly framed as instructive utterances.[20] Think of the tunes that propose something to be learned from the story of the gal that got away. Johnny Mercer's "One for My Baby" (1943), for instance, is set in a pub. "So, set 'em up, Joe, / I've got a little story you ought to know." Why should Joe even hear, let alone know, one more story of forsaken love? Mercer frames the song as a lesson, not just an expression; someone has to hear it, and benefit from the hearing. Philip Fisher says that compassion is the object of sentimental narrative.[21] But these sob-ballads suggest that compassion is not in fact the end; enlightenment is the real objective. Just what can one learn from pain? From a sentimental point of view: that human life follows set patterns; that my romance isn't different from yours. As Fred Kaplan observes, "Dickens believed that there was an instinctive, irrepressible need for human beings to affirm both in private and in public that they possessed moral sentiments, that these sentiments were innate, that they best expressed themselves through spontaneous feelings, and that sentimentality in life and in art had a moral basis."[22] Mercer's song is ultimately ambiguous concerning the value of the lover's story. The "ought" in the lines I cited suggests that sentimental narrative has the didactic value that Kaplan describes, but Mercer presents this story oddly. He notes that a bartender is professionally obligated to listen and to maintain confidentiality ("to be true to your code"): Joe is a paid listener. What Mercer does not suggest is that the lover enlightened the bartender. "I hope you didn't mind my bending your ear," the lover says, as though the story may have had no value for the listener. More important, though, the story is not told in the song. "Well, that's how it goes," the lover enigmatically says, as though he has at this point completed his story; whereas in fact he has said nothing at all about his romance. A poet truly confident of the universal value of sentiment would provide the gist of the lover's experience, especially after such a build-up; Dickens or Hardy would have delivered what had been promised. Mercer prefers to pretend that he has told the tale. His subject is neither the lover's experience nor the enlightenment of others, but just the desire to speak to others. This lover needs to share words, though his only listener is a mute pro. Mercer presents a late moment in the decline of confidence in universal sentiments; his song is a shell where conviction once lived.

Sob-ballads begin in adversity; their first appeal is the performance of active, articulate melancholy, something more common in art than in life. It is certainly true that many great poems, whatever their actual sources, seem to derive from romantic melancholy. Heartbreak is a subject for all time, and the effort to recover sentiment is a recurrent impulse of literary culture.[23] "The Lord is with the broken-hearted," according to Psalm 34, and the poets are too. My subject is the recovery of sentiment in the popular song after Cole Porter, but also the apprehension concerning the limits of sentimentality, even among popular songwriters. Matthew Arnold warned that no poetical enjoyment can be derived from the representation of prolonged mental distress, a state in which "everything is to be endured, nothing to be done"; Yeats agreed with him.[24] The

Tin Pan Alley poets seem to have agreed too. The great sob-ballads actually propose that one learn from loss, however hard that is to do. Ransom argued notoriously that sentimental poetry is relatively indifferent to intellectual matters.[25] The sob-ballads that interest me demonstrate, to the contrary, efforts to *think* one's way out of melancholy. Consider Ira Gershwin's lyric, "Someone to Watch over Me" (1926).

> There's a somebody I'm longing to see.
> I hope that she turns out to be
> Someone who'll watch over me.
>
> I'm a little lamb who's lost in a wood.
> I know I could always be good   5
> To one who'll watch over me.
>
> Although I may not be the man some
> Girls think of as handsome,
> To her heart I'll carry the key.
>
> Won't you tell her, please,   10
> To put on some speed,
> Follow my lead.
> Oh, how I need
> Someone to watch over me.

Like many, many others, this song has Sinatra boldly expressing male tenderness: "Oh, how I need." The arrangement is especially saccharine from the opening notes on the celestina through the Viennese-style violin serenade before the last verses. Need and longing are repeatedly asserted, without embarrassment, in any number of his songs. What he longs for is subtle, though. He wants a parental Beloved to supervise him, but why? The second stanza is especially revealing. How does a man, in public, sing the effete line, "I'm a little lamb who's lost in a wood"? (Gershwin wrote the line for Gertrude Lawrence to perform in the musical *Oh, Kay!* [1926]; Sinatra might have revised this line, as someone did lines seven through ten, for gender conformity, but he preferred not to do so. He *wanted* the strangeness of a man likening himself to a little lamb.) Back to my question: how to perform these lines? There's always just naïveté, but there is the more productive possibility of ironic, sophisticated role-playing: despite appearances, I'm a little lamb, and so on. Or more explicitly, I am not, as it appears, a wolf; instead I am a little lamb. Hastily one attributes the song to a neglected, forsaken lover who now yearns for attention. But instead, with a male voice, it expresses the situation of a chastised lover, one who has been caught not being good—the Wolf Exposed.[26] (Of a man singing as a lamb, one asks: if you are the lamb, who is the wolf?) A lamb might say that he is good to everyone. Instead Sinatra claims only that, given the right sort of partner, he "could always be good" *to her*, exactly because his goodness has come into question. The word "always" entails its contrary: the category of an exception, which may be how a chastised lover would designate an exposed violation of trust. That is, behind what the lyric says is an implicit narrative of betrayal and exposure. Overcome him with . . . not love, but supervision, and he will be a little lamb; he only appeared to be a wolf because his last lover neglected him. He has learned from loss that he needs a mother-lover. Or at least it's advisable to say so to the next woman. Sinatra's persona is obviously tender, apparently sweet, but also calculating, and resistant to the more difficult changes that self-knowledge might propose. The singer of this tune is less forlorn than self-reckoning, -justifying. He is a proud lover, accustomed to such attention. Pride stabilizes.

The theme of Ira Gershwin and Harold Arlen's "The Gal That Got Away" (1953) is the education of the proud, and not, as it appears, mere forlornness. Nelson Riddle's arrangement is forceful, driving, even melodramatic: it sets off with a blast of horns. The same punctuating phrase—an aggressive, stagey throb—returns after lines eight, twenty-eight, and at the end. It's a relentless effect: the road is set, and the lover is pulled along without ambiguity. Yet there is an oscillation between two ostensible thematic poles, figured first in the emblematic frieze of the first three lines and the distinctive narrative that enters with a reference to the lover's age (as, later, between the first- and second-person address). The lover is too old for romantic failure. The emblematic landscape returns as the "road" gets rougher, with each romantic failure (l. 20). The Beloved pursued and won the lover; she used to call him eagerly. Now, so far as the singer understands, she has simply, enigmatically run off. Or is that how the lover understands her? The singer dismisses any significance to the lover's experience of this "crazy game." No sense is to be had. The lover is just brought low, and then lower, a proud man reduced to calling emptily in the dark. This is "The Gal That Got Away" (possibly in the sense of "escaped"), but it could be "The Guy Who Doesn't Get It." Neither singer nor lover has a glimmer how to sustain a relationship.

The night is bitter.
The stars have lost their glitter.
The winds grow colder
And suddenly you're older,
And all because of the gal that got away.   5

No more her eager call,
The writing's on the wall.
The dreams you dreamed have all gone astray.

The gal that won you
Has run off and undone you.   10
That great beginning has seen the final inning.
Don't know what happened; it's all a crazy game.

No more that all-time thrill,
For you've been through the mill.
And never a new love will be the same.   15

Good riddance, good-bye.
Every trick of hers you're on to.
But fools will be fools,
And where's she gone to?

The road gets rougher;   20
It's lonelier and tougher.
With hope you burn up
That tomorrow she may turn up.
There's just no let-up
The livelong night and day.   25

Ever since this world began
There is nothing sadder than
A lost, lost loser looking for the gal that got away.

Please come back.
Won't you come back?   30

The gal that got away.

The singer's point of view is ostensibly transcendent. One understands his second-person address as a lover's effort to rise above personal
suffering to the viewpoint of one who might use, say, the French third-
person *on* to express generality. He characterizes the forsaken lover so

knowingly that he can foresee the future: "never a new love will be the same" (l. 15). This is a special moment in Riddle's arrangement and in Gershwin's lyric. Riddle establishes a conclusion here, mid-song, by shifting to a slower tempo for lines sixteen through nineteen. Line fifteen is also the most confident utterance of the poem. The syntax is oddly inverted and remote from speech, but it is a variation on the structure of lines six and thirteen: line fifteen concludes a grammatical set of three with a prediction of what can never recur: romantic enthusiasm. In this one dramatic line, the singer has his maximal authority, and the poem pauses.

The singer means to be a knower, like the singer of "In the Wee Small Hours," not a forsaken lover, but he wobbles repeatedly; these are the major terms of the oscillation I mentioned. A transcendent point of view cannot be hampered by a forsaken lover's ignorance, but it is: "Don't know what happened; it's all a crazy game" (l. 12). This sounds like a line not for a knowing singer but for a benighted, forsaken lover, though there is no marker of such a shift. Two lines later the singer must be the source of the line "For you've been through the mill."[27] The conventionality of the figure itself transcends any one lover's experience; this voice rises to impersonal, proverbial understanding, but that level cannot be held. The singer, in his impersonal mode, actually knows no more than the lover; there is nothing to be had beyond plaintive, passive suffering. The singer narrates a familiar story, but without distinctive comprehension, and this, for him, is an intellectual failure. The oscillation between first- and second-person address expresses a desire, failed in the end, to get beyond the prolonged mental distress of which Arnold warned. The lover cannot retain the impersonal viewpoint, though he tries repeatedly. The transition from an uncomprehending, forsaken lover to a knowing explainer is what lovers, especially old ones, should want to master. Without that mastery, there is only the deterministic drive of Riddle's arrangement—into the night, as Sinatra fans like to say.

I have tried to show that even sentimental song lyrics have been written with a clear sense of exactly the hazards of sentimentality that Eliot, Richards, Ransom, and Brooks described. These songs express sentiment, but as part of a story about learning lessons from loss: they pursue an intellectual objective. Ransom thought that sentimental poetry tends toward abstraction; it selects from the rich texture of experience only those elements that suit a single view. But the poems I am discussing are thick with narrative; they pull one into a story behind the few words of the songs. The third quatrain of Bob Hilliard's iambic pentameter lyric, "In the Wee Small Hours of the Morning" (1955), draws one to the view that feelings are governed by thoughts and ideas, that a life of feeling best answers to the needs of the mind, that sentiment alone is insufficient to romance and to art.

> When your lonely heart has learned its lesson
> You'd be hers if only she would call.
> In the wee small hours of the morning,
> That's the time you miss her most of all.

The phrase "you'd be hers" suggests that her desire for him has already been established; she wanted him in some contractual way, as a suitor for his hand might. He's ready to accede to her wish, to give her what she wanted, now that "his lonely heart has learned its lesson." (And he waits for her call, as a woman conventionally waits for a man's call.) The lesson learned? He did something that drove her away, though she had been asking for more. He has learned not to take her for granted. This was his chastening. The song is uttered through a stable second-person address, it is far from a sentimental moan.

The correction of lovers is a recurrent feature of the great sob-ballads. In 1947 Sinatra recorded a medley of, "The Gal That Got Away" (originally "The Man That Got Away," performed memorably by Judy Garland) and "It Never Entered My Mind." This last tune, extraordinary by any measure, is a revealing instance of a sob-ballad about a lesson learned.[28] Rather than discuss Sinatra's performance of the tune, I prefer to listen to Sarah Vaughan's unbeatable version. But I want also to make the point that there is no necessary gender-orientation to the recovery of sentimentality. Male sentimentality makes better stage action only because it resists a stereotype of masculine restraint. The real point, though, is the public expression of feeling, by men or women, which is why these songs often represent scenes of public statement—as at a bar.

Here is the text of Lorenz Hart and Richard Rodgers' "It Never Entered My Mind," (1940):

> I don't care if there's powder on my nose,
> I don't care if my hairdo is in place,
> I've lost the very meaning of repose,
> I never put a mud pack on my face,

Oh, who'd have thought   5
That I'd walk in a daze now?
I never go to shows at night,
But just to matinees now.
I see the show
And home I go.   10

Once I laughed when I heard you saying
That I'd be playing solitaire,
Uneasy in my easy chair.
It never entered my mind.
Once you told me I was mistaken,   15
That I'd awaken with the sun
And order orange juice for one.
It never entered my mind.
You have what I lack myself,
And now I even have to scratch my back myself.   20
Once you warned me that if you scorned me
I'd sing the maiden's prayer again
And wish that you were there again
To get into my hair again.
It never entered my mind.   25

This is a rare song of reasoned self-reproach. The lover understands something distinct about herself that she had earlier failed to understand. Her sense of sophistication and of proud well-being in social contexts depended on her lover's presence and devotion. She did not realize this simple fact about her own life; once her lover left, her previous obtuseness became obvious to her. Part of the song's strength derives from her cool self-analysis: she understands her own limits now. And she has adjusted painfully to a reduced life without her Beloved. The song presents an intelligent, candid—not pathetic—lover who has been forsaken.

The first strophe presents her change: she has lost her vanity and self-regard, or -repose. She has come to cold terms with her loss. The title of this poem is everything, but in the first strophe she is incapable of uttering it. Instead she sings a more general account: "Oh, who'd have thought . . . ?" No one would reasonably have thought that she would be so upset by the loss of her Beloved. But this misrepresents the situation she goes on to describe in the next strophe. What does seem true is that it would have been unreasonable for most observers of her self-confidence to predict that she would be in a daze if her Beloved left her:

she appeared not to need him or her. What is false is the suggestion that no one predicted she would suffer this way. Her Beloved did predict just that, as the next strophe says. She was a cool cookie before the Beloved left; then she was concerned about her own appearance, her makeup, her hair, her complexion. The last four lines say quite exactly how she has adjusted to her loss:

> I never go to shows at night,
> But just to matinees now.
> I see the show
> And home I go.

These wonderful lines tell a great deal. She is not utterly despondent. She still has a life; she gets out. But she has made this one small adjustment: she goes to daytime shows, because she can do so unescorted. To go unescorted to an evening show would entail a kind of social scrutiny she prefers to avoid. This is important, because the opening lines of the song describe her indifference to her physical appearance, but she is not indifferent to social status. She has changed, since her Beloved left, and her life is thinner now; but she can measure her loss, and it is not total. Her self-possession is still with her.

The second strophe is the richest. She describes a Beloved who foresaw her suffering and warned her that she had not fathomed the depth of her own involvement. She wrongly thought she was too cool for pain. Consider the ways in which her Beloved warned her. The Beloved may sound cruel, threatening to leave her, but actually he or she made the point about emotional distance in a witty manner. She was told that she would be playing solitaire, i.e. that the Beloved would not be easily replaced by another. The Beloved said she would wake early and order room-service for one. This is particularly revealing, because it establishes her composure as class-privilege. Working people lack the leisure to sleep late, not to mention room-service. She enjoys and displays an economic cushion. The literary-historical point is that she speaks from the milieu of Cole Porter, a kind of pastoral with hotel staff as nymphs and swains. Finally, the Beloved warned her that she would "sing the maiden's prayer," presumably for a lover. These are three ways to tell her that she would be alone if the Beloved left her. The last is an explicitly archaic, or literary way of saying this. (Only books spoke of maidens in 1946, when this song was written.) She is sophisticated enough to engage in ironic banter, and she is economically privileged. The Beloved knew that her cushion over the harder realities of life would not provide her sufficient comfort, without the Beloved, and she was told this in playful ways that might have encouraged her to try harder to keep the Beloved by her. Instead, she was accustomed to think of his or her presence as mildly annoying, to speak of the Beloved as getting into her hair. She had three gentle warnings, and she ignored them.

"It never entered my mind," she sings three times in this strophe. The first sense of the title is that this came as a complete surprise, though she had been warned of exactly what would happen if she lost her Beloved. The second sense is that the warnings never got through to her. This is a deeper and more self-critical realization. The point of the song is the difference between these two senses of the title. The title is marked as especially significant by virtue of its resistance to the poem's intricate rhyming schemes. Consider: Line 11 rhymes with the penultimate word of line 12; the end-rhyme of line 12 links to the end-rhyme of the next line. Two rhymes are binding three lines together quite tightly by this arrangement. Line 15 repeats this scheme by rhyming with the third word of line 16. The rhyme linking lines 11 and 12 is disyllabic; the one linking lines 15 and 16 is trisyllabic. This rhyming fit intensifies as the strophe proceeds. The end-rhyme of line 16 is linked to line 17, as lines 12 and 13 are linked by simple monosyllabic rhymes. Lines 19 and 20, however, are linked by end-rhymes, but by an extraordinary four-syllable rhyme. Line 21 has an internal tri-syllabic rhyme. Lines 21-23 are linked by a tri-syllabic end-rhyme. Lines 14, 18, and 25, as I said, are unrhymed, the only unrhymed lines in this chamber of emphatic echoes. The beauty of this obsessive form is that the reason for her own uncoupling is indicated in this repeated unrhymed line. I've said that this is an especially intellectual, analytical song. The elaborate rhyme scheme expresses certain, deft, resourceful control, entirely in character with the singer. But it also suggests that she is thoroughly ensnared by her self-presentation. This is the pathos of the song. She goes on to make rhymes and matinees. However distraught one imagines her to be, one credits her ability to make words serve her intricately. She is reduced, but not abject. She has her language by the throat. No syllable out of place.

As in poetry, so in song: the convention of sincerity is closely bound to the imitation of speech. Sinatra is the Wordsworth of popular song. He would not work without a proper microphone, a black one that would not be much noticed against his dinner jacket. A good microphone enables you, he said, to "sing as if you're singing in someone's ear, you can talk to a buddy at the bar, you can whisper sweet nothings to a woman."[29] His objective was to depart only inconspicuously from the appearance of intimate speech. His enunciation is especially clear and careful, so that he can always be easily understood. He learned from Tommy Dorsey to sing in long breaths, without an audible pause for breath within a sentence. He used to swim underwater to enhance his lung capacity. One should think that he really means what he says; Bob Dylan referred to "the truth of things in his voice."[30] Consider Sinatra's 1945 version of "These Foolish Things." He sings at a very slow tempo and without much volume, as though he meant to conceal altogether his effort to perform. Almost speech, from his mouth to your ear. His is an anti-theatrical style that continued to work for him for decades after this recording. But in the early 1950s he lost young audiences, and he was bitter about it (rock n' roll, in 1957, was "the most brutal, ugly, degenerate, vicious form of expression it has been my displeasure to hear").[31] Clyde McPhatter also performed "These Foolish Things," in 1953, at his last recording date with Billy Ward and the Dominoes; then he left Ward and founded the Drifters. Speech was one prominent co-ordinate of the doo-wop style, as one hears at the start; spoken monologues were a staple, but so too were the screams, the oohs and ahs—here: the bass moans following lines one, four, nine, seventeen, and twenty-two. This is body music, beyond social conventions. An appearance of sincerity and sentiment survived in the doo-wop style, but as theatrical pretense, or camp.

These are the words to Eric Maschwitz's "These Foolish Things" (1936):

> Darling, you've gone and left me.
> And now all I have left are memories,
> Memories like
>
> A cigarette that bears a lipstick's traces,
> An airline ticket to romantic places,   5
> And still my heart has wings.
> These foolish things
> Remind me of you.
>
> A tinkling piano in the next, next apartment,
> Those stumbling words that told you what my heart meant,   10
> A fairground's painted swings,
> These foolish things
> Remind me of you.

can claim this standard as a black achievement, a moment of pride. He assures the Beloved that he awaits her return (ll. 22-24) in a speech that is obvious hokum. The interesting revelation is that the possible return of the Beloved is a potential embarrassment to the forsaken lover. What the lover really wants can be heard in McPhatter's voice: the glorious consolation of art celebrating a religious sense of the material world.[33]

"I knew somehow this had to be," he says. An eager lover wants not happy circumstance, but a determined life. He had to be the lover, and now he has to be forsaken—"somehow." The determinative force is only incidentally his faithless Beloved. The real cause is mysterious, grand, and holy. All is in its place, even the Beloved belongs somewhere else, so that this music can ascend like a host. "Still," he says, "my heart has wings." One recognizes the gospel choral backing of doo-wop arrangements, but isn't it nonetheless stunning that McPhatter has transformed this sob-ballad into a religious hymn? He has gone to another level in the effort to learn from loss. He understood that the making of art is the thing. The Beloved is needed, for *sacrifice*: she must be lost, like Poe's dead girl, so that the spirit may climb higher. Sentimental song wants a sacrament. The song is more ritual than report. No need to say anything particular about the Beloved. This is the key to sentimentality: it leaves the thickness of contingency for an abstract set of concerns aimed at release, transcendence, transformation—the affirmation of the spirit.

I have been considering the modernist critique of sentimentality in connection with some especially distinguished popular songs, and three things have surprised me. First, the popular revival of sentiment after Cole Porter's ironic modernism began a good twenty years before U.S. poets pushed back against Eliot's embargo on sentiment. Maybe poetry is just more resistant to change; certainly the lucrativeness of the popular song leaves songwriters more responsive than poets to the appetites of audiences. Second, it is impressive that the best songwriters sought to find enlightenment in pain. Loving, losing, then thinking, and finally loving again. These aren't songs of kind lovers, but they are all thoughtful ones. They all take thought of themselves, and some give thought to the Beloved. However powerfully pain focuses one's attention, thoughtfulness, in both senses, is the issue. Third, songwriters, without any apparent awareness of the controversies among intellectuals, seem to have worried about the hazards of sentimental writing in just the ways that literary modernists had warned. That is enough to make one think that Eliot, Richards, Ransom, and Brooks had clear eyes concerning sentimentality. These lyricists sought correlatives, in Eliot's terms—some narrative context behind their words—for the feelings they expressed. I read them as *ballads*, poems that relate or imply a narrative. Sinatra admired Crosby, remember, as a troubadour who "tells a story in every song." Critics claim, though, that those correlatives are often ill-proportioned to the emotions expressed. And this is true, even in the great songs; but one sees too that disproportion may be inevitable, or even desired. Sentimental song moves easily toward religious ecstasy exactly because all that is material cannot measure up to the spiritual grandeur of the unseen. There is a point at which what one learns from loss is not judicious inference from human events but religious affirmation. Some great poems admittedly propose adjustment to the facts of life. But the genre evolved further: toward McPhatter's ecstatic refusal of justness or realism of any sort. Maybe there was a hymn inside the sob-ballad all along.

Notes

1. Will Friedwald, *The Song Is You* (New York: Scribner, 1995), 24.

2. Anthony Summers & Robbyn Swan, *Sinatra: The Life* (New York: Random House, 2005), 31.

3. Friedwald, 127.

4. Evidently Sinatra's press agent had coached a corps of young women to scream on cue, but they were able to provoke a large crowd response (Summers & Swan, 84).

5. Friedwald, 69.

6. Friedwald, 85.

7. Friedwald, 93.

8. I. A. Richards, *Practical Criticism* (1929; New York: Harcourt, Brace, 1967), 247.

9. T. S. Eliot, *Selected Essays* (New York: Harcourt, Brace, 1960), 248.

10. Cleanth Brooks, *Modern Poetry and the Tradition* (1939; New York: Oxford University Press, 1965), 37.

11. Ibid., 51.

12. T. S. Eliot, *The Sacred Wood* (1920; London: Methuen, 1960), 64-65.

13. Eliot, *Selected Essays*, 247.

14. Pete Hamill, *Why Sinatra Matters.* (Boston: Little, Brown, 1998) 127; see also Summers & Swan, 222.

15. Hamill, 26-27.

16. Summers & Swan, 93.

17. The critique of male sentiment, in particular, the notion that it is a shallow indulgence, is ancient. Socrates reminds Glaucon of the hypocrisy of appreciating poetic representations of lamentation and breast-beating and yet priding oneself on resisting such womanish expression in actual experience. Is it right, Socrates asks, to praise in poetry what is reprehensible in fact? (*Republic*, 605d-606a). Sentimentality, from this viewpoint, is insincere; a poet asks one to take pleasure in values by which one is unwilling

to live. One should not enjoy in art the pleasure of expressing overwhelming grief, so long as one means to move stoically past one's losses in life: this is what distinguishes sentimentality from honorable male comportment.

18. Summers & Swan, 225.

19. Pete Hamill, *Why Sinatra Matters* (Boston: Little, Brown, 1998), 96.

20. I am aware of two methodological premises that I want to express plainly here. My interest is chiefly in lyric poetry. I presume, first, that a poet achieves a lyric not by ending the line before the right margin, but by finding a music in the materiality of words. No musicality, no lyric. This genre of poetry is closely related to accompanied song. But popular songwriters try instead to find the words in a particular piece of music. I wonder what is to be learned about lyric poetry from an analysis of its obverse art. Second, I presume too that one's critical observations of poems gain validity to the degree that they correspond to the best poems within a class or kind. The songs I have selected for analysis are the best I know of their kind—the sob-ballad. Insofar as my assessments are off, I acknowledge, the validity of my observations is in jeopardy.

21. Philip Fisher, *Hard Facts* (New York: Oxford University Press, 1985), 105. To hear my musical illustrations, go to: http://humanities.uchicago.edu/blogs/vonhallberg. I have to presume here that my readers are familiar with the musical performances I cite.

22. Fred Kaplan, *Sacred Tears: Sentimentality in Victorian Literature* (Princeton: Princeton University Press, 1987), 3.

23. See Robert Pinsky, ed., *The Handbook of Heartbreak* (New York: William Morrow, 1998).

24. Matthew Arnold, "Preface to First Edition of *Poems* (1853)," (Arnold is surely alluding to Johnson in *Rasselas:* "Human life is a state in which much is to be endured and little to be enjoyed.")

25. John Crowe Ransom, *The World's Body* (New York: Scribner, 1939).

26. The song of a chastised lover is a sub-type of the forsaken-lover's song. See, e.g., The Five Royales, "Help Me, Somebody," for a doo-wop expression of the theme.

    I read sob-ballads as abbreviated narratives that invite skeptical interpretation. My sense is that this particular genre conforms to Michael Riffaterre's model of poetry as structured around a hypogram, or undefined center: "The significance is shaped like a doughnut, the hole being either the matrix of the hypogram or the hypogram as matrix." *Semiotics of Poetry* (Bloomington: Indiana University Press, 1978), 13.

27. Philip Furia interprets the breakdown of the second-person address as a sign of the forlorn state of the lover (*Ira Gershwin* [New York: Oxford University Press, 1996], 216). I should mention that Furia considers the poem an expression of "innocent longing," whereas it seems much darker to me (219).

28. Will Friedwald speaks of it as "one of the most subtle torch songs ever written," and credits Sinatra with its revival. (Friedwald 154)

29. Summers & Swan, 33.

30. Summers & Swan, front matter.

31. Summers & Swan, 234.

32. Paul Fussell, "Sentimentality," in *The New Princeton Encyclopedia of Poetry and Poetics*, eds. Alex Preminger, T. V. F. Brogan et al. (Princeton: Princeton University Press, 1993), 1145.

33. Eric Maschwitz's 1936 lyric, "These Foolish Things," is sung from the perspective of a lover forsaken only because the Beloved is *dead*. Thematically one might compare this tune with Hardy's *Poems 1912-1913*. Maschwitz's Beloved is truly a ghost. His lyric begins with Hardyesque lines that neither Sinatra nor McPhatter sings: "Oh! will you never let me be? / Oh! will you never set me free?" Lines 1-3 and 22-24 (the frame of the McPhatter version) were not written by Maschwitz.

Lee Upton

Purity: It's Such a Filthy Word

Look up *purity* in an Internet search engine, and you're likely to be brought to popular questionnaires that purportedly determine one's level of incorruption. One purity test option begins with "had a date" and ends with "committed bestiality." Another begins with "kissed someone" and concludes with "had sex on the astral or ethereal planes." Either way, we end up with the non-human. That's one of the less dangerous possibilities to which purity, at least on the silly level, seems to lead.

"Pure? What does it mean?"

Sylvia Plath asks the question in "Fever 103" and enacts a spectacle, an outrageous hallucinatory reverie that extricates her speaker from past identities and fleshly indentures: "I am too pure for you or anyone" (53). But it is an ascent, not an answer. In "Lady Lazarus" the purifying rays of rage overwhelm us as well. "I rise with my red hair / And I eat men like air" (9). Pure? To paradise Plath's speaker goes—where only the pure thrive. We can applaud Plath's satire, well knowing that it is foolish to think we are beyond the absolutism of purity. Billions of advertising dollars prove otherwise in attempts to repel time and function. And the fanaticism of many sorts that breathes down too many necks derives its power from conceptions of purity.

We know that the language of purity is connected to horrific violence, ethnic "cleansing," theories of "purity" in race and ethnicity and religious sect, and violence against women that proves ancient in its connection between "purity" and the honor of the group. One of the most contradictory and appalling phrases: Honor killing. The terrible history of purity goes on.

How do we most fully conceptualize purity? What can we make purity mean? Simplicity? Innocence? If so, it's lost to us in adulthood and probably earlier. Does purity exist as a relic in the mind? Is purity the devil's hot white hell and desert landscape and rock garden? There are some rational answers: purity can be conceptualized as positive, surely, if we're talking about food safety, but often the concept in action refers to destruction (cleansing, scouring, eliminating); or paralysis (unchanging, outside time); or exclusion, as an archetype belonging to some conceptions of an intolerant God. There's a clean mind and there's a clean drawer—and there's a difference. If we say "That's pure poetry" we're engaging in a cliché. If we say "That's pure fiction" we're engaging in an insult. We don't often use the phrase "a clean mind." The more popular phrase is "dirty mind." We speak of a "spotless" reputation. Of course reputation can't be controlled. There is, after all, the Internet.

What is my intention here? To ask Plath's question: "Pure? What does it mean?" mostly in terms of literary art, particularly poetry. Purity is a subject, surely one of the great subjects. It is one of the inescapable literary subjects. Yet the idea of purity may become a bitter antagonist, acting below the level of consciousness. How does a call for purity infiltrate whatever in the mind longs for rare shameless grace, and why should such imaginings turn bitter and lodge in us like viruses that replicate? Purity is not only connected in some minds to self-destruction, a violation of the mixed nature of what we are and will be, but purity may be experienced as a certain inchoate imaginative pull. Of course absolute purity is unattainable and thus belongs to the country of the imagination. But so much depends on the quality of the imagination.

The great defense against purity belongs to Pablo Neruda. In "Some Thoughts on Impure Poetry," he advocates "A poetry as impure as a suit or a body, a poetry stained by food and shame, a poetry with wrinkles, observations, dreams, waking, prophecies, declarations of love and hatred, beasts, blows, idylls, manifestos, denials, doubts, affirmations, taxes" (128). He concludes his impassioned defense: "He who would flee from bad taste is riding for a fall" (129). It is easy to argue for impurity now that Pablo Neruda has done it for us, but purity raises it stern face, glowing. The theme of purity is one that mocks us and yet provides its own volition. Its meanings accumulate.

Is purity Wallace Stevens's "Nothing that is not there and the nothing that is" from "The Snow Man," or Blake's "Little Lamb"? Or "Cleanness" from the Middle English Pearl-Poet:

Be careful, in coming, that thy robes be clean
and decent for the holy-day, lest thou meet with harm;
if thou approach that Prince of noble peerage,
he hates hell no more than men who are soiled.
(127)

Or consider Charles Lamb's "Cleanliness" in which "Virtue [is] next to Godliness." Not only that, but

Soil deliberate to endure,
On the skin to fix a stain
Till it works into the grain,
Argues a degenerate mind,
Sordid, slothful, ill inclin'd,
Wanting in that self-respect
Which does virtue best protect.
(364)

Or is the impulse toward purity best captured by James Fenton in "The Gene-Pool" from *Out of Danger*?

You are unclean!
Get out! Get out!
Out of the gene-pool, Gene.
(101)

Lives, including literary lives, are led in pursuit of the phantom of purity. And a study of that phantom, even in its minor dimensions, can make for literature. In her short story "You Should Have Seen the Mess," Muriel Spark gives us the point of view of a seventeen-year-old who forsakes all other values but cleanliness, rejecting even a generous, kind, and handsome young man because of the condition of his linens. This hygienic, self-satisfied little squirrel seems perfectly comfortable and benignly confident about her choices. She's clean, and she's stupid.

Purity? What does it mean?—as long as we have memories, given that our memories are both spotty and spotted? Unless I'm misremembering, it's recorded somewhere that Elizabeth Taylor is alleged to have said that she felt her virginity was restored after every hot bath. She forgot to add that it takes not only a bath, but a bad memory and a miracle. Of course a renunciation of the past, a purging of our histories, means memory must be deeply degraded if it is to be purified: Stuck a feather in his hat and called it—some kind of noodle.

In much literature, purity is both a necessary impulse and a dangerous thing. The impulse to purify is part of the literary art, its compacting, its extremes of selection, the prominence of the "telling detail," even the commonly-held conception that the work should create an illusion of inevitability from which no extraneous matter diverts us. The pressure to purify, to honor silence, to cut the line, the sentence, the stanza, is part of the literary instinct. We can never be or make the ultimately pure, and so the attempt may bear the mark of both ambition and rejection—including self-rejection. On the path toward a new voice, we fall into the ditch of wordlessness again, the destructive sword of purity hanging over our heads. Poets in particular are tempted to edit the past, expunging youthful errors or exuberances or indulgences, even those marks of individuality that amounted to originality. Of all literary forms, the poem, brought up on the most often declared impulse toward concision of any verbal art form, is endangered by the poet's proclivity toward a whittling that can purify it out of existence. Mallarmé sought to "purify the language of the tribe" and Pound, who admired Mussolini for far too long, echoed him. The language assigned to purity can exalt or condemn—or collapse the pillars of the creative act in retrospect. Marianne Moore's most famous excisions were in "Poetry," paring that trademark poem from just shy of thirty lines to a total of three, until the opening "I, too, dislike it" takes on even greater weight, given that the illustrative material is stripped away and reader after reader must note the loss of hands, eyes, hair, a bat, elephants, a horse, a wolf, a tree, a critic, a flea, a sports fan, a statistician, "'business documents and / school-books,'" "half poets," poets, gardens, toads, and "raw material."

When I was an eleven-year-old obsessed with poetry I confessed as much to a quick-sketch cartoon artist at the Ionia Free Fair. He drew my picture atop a tower of books. My legs became little dangly babyish things draped over the first couple of books. The legs were such an embarrassment to me, suggesting powerlessness and yet vanity and presumption where they dangled atop those books, with the name "Shakespeare" jotted on the spine of a thick volume. My great pure dream was reduced to comedy and hopelessness. Well, that's adolescence. Or pre-adolescence. Or adulthood. We are vast to ourselves, but miniature to others.

Sometimes the urge to purify takes a truly destructive turn. Writers who want to purify their work may ultimately want to purify the world of their work. Emily Dickinson requested that her writing be burned. Hawthorne asked that his drafts of unfinished work be destroyed. Patrick White claimed that he destroyed his drafts, but according to his biographer David Marr in the *Sydney Morning Herald* the reality was otherwise: "The old bastard. Patrick White told the world over and over that none of this existed. 'Don't bother hunting for drafts and manuscripts,' he snapped when I asked him years ago. 'They've all gone into the pit.'" According to Marr, the drafts were "Stuffed into cupboards and drawers in [White's] house on the edge of Centennial Park." Others who talked about wanting their papers tossed into the flames: Thomas Hardy, Nabokov, Philip Larkin. The connection between the corporeal body and the corpus of manuscripts is undeniable. The phenomenon may remind us of Oscar Wilde's famous putative last words, "Either that wallpaper goes, or I do." As fate would have it, the author always goes, but not always the paper.

In 2006 Helen Vendler visited the subject of the destruction of drafts in her criticism of Alice Quinn's edition of Elizabeth Bishop's uncollected poems and drafts, *Edgar Allan Poe & the Juke-Box*, accusing Quinn, according to the *New York Times Book Review*, "of undermining Bishop's legacy and of betraying something sacred, the poet's personal trust." Vendler is quoted as saying, "If you make people promise to burn your manuscripts they should" and argued that "personal fidelity is more important than art." She used as one of her examples the supposed request of Virgil to have his writings burned. Whatever our take on the matter of Bishop, using Virgil as our example, are we betraying him at this moment by calling to mind the *Aeneid*? Legendary last wishes aim for the ultimate purification. Nothing is more pure than nothingness. Nothing is more perfect than nothing.

A "rabbit catcher" is an old term for a midwife. Plath has a poem by that name that's about an actual snare as well as a psychological snare. But it wasn't rabbits she was catching. In the famous foreword to *Ariel* Robert Lowell narrates a metamorphosis of Plath into a heightened inhuman purity: she "becomes herself, becomes something imaginary, newly, wildly and subtly created—hardly a person at all, or a woman, certainly not another 'poetess,' but one of those super-real, hypnotic, great classical heroines." How pure, really, and in consequence how inorganic. He tells us that we hear "the pounding pistons of her heart" (xiii). She is "machinelike from hard training," with "her hand of metal with its modest, womanish touch" (xiv). The modest touch of the poet who wrote *Daddy*? His introduction to *Ariel* contains one of the most painful lines in any introduction: "This poetry and life are not a career; they tell that life, even when disciplined, is simply not worth it" (xv). To a machine, no. To an absolutist of the purest sort, no. But then it is purity that Plath is refusing to succumb to in her last work. When she turned and looked purity in the face and leaned away from the obsessive shadow of perfection, she wrote the poems that made her name. She chose a subject—purity—that could disable as much as liberate her gift. After all, a conception of artistic purity for the artist can be death to amplitude and instinct and an enemy of generativity. It stops us. If she seemed more streamlined, more machine-like to Lowell, her speakers became more humanly complex and vibrantly unfinished to other readers.

If once I thought that perfection was the mother of purity I have only recently realized that I got the generations wrong. Purity is older; purity is perfection's mother. Purity looks backward, to a prior state of being that was whole, unsophisticated, unadulterated. Whereas perfection, like most children, is not interested in the past as much as in the future. However unattainable, it is perfection, not purity, that at least harbors the notion of achievement after an apprenticeship. Perfection claims action for itself. Purity is a state of being, not an action. Once lost, purity may not be regained and cannot be sought in the same site. Purity, more elemental than perfection, takes its metaphorical weight from our perceptions of the body and what the body can bear. Both purity and perfection are allied conceptions, but purity is the more dangerous. Not least of all because we so seldom think about what purity might mean. More often we simply react, repelled at some level by some insufficiency that is beyond imperfect, that seems to attack our sense of wholesome physical integrity.

After my first daughter was born I experienced a period in which I felt one-dimensional. I admit that I come from a family where the failure thoroughly to clean out a can of tuna fish was held with the contempt reserved in other families for a member convicted of murder. But I recall a season after my first daughter was born when my resistance to previous shapes I made in poetry was so severe that I was in the grip of a tightening of possibilities. What was pure enough for my daughter? What could her mother make that might even approximate an awareness that came as if outside of language—who was this imperfect stranger I was? A loathsome purity came over me. The spaces in the work became more prominent, phrases pulled back upon themselves. I was treating my poems like the ancient Greeks treated women in Anne Carson's interpretation.

In "Dirt and Desire: Essay on the Phenomenology of Female Pollution in Antiquity," Carson quotes Hesiod: "Let a man not clean his skin in water that a woman has washed in. For a hard penalty follows on that for a long time." The Greek obsession with boundaries focuses on women, Carson informs us:

> Women, then, are pollutable, polluted and polluting
> in several ways at once. They are anomalous
> members of the human class, being, as Aristotle
> puts it, imperfect men. . . . They are, as social entities
> units of danger, moving across boundaries of family and
> house, in marriage, prostitution, or adultery. They are,
> as psychological entities, unstable compounds of deceit and
> desire, prone to leakage.
> (143)

Whether limning Sappho's fragments or writing her own poems, Carson troubles boundaries, puncturing pure form by crossing it, but also illuminating it. Carson's poetry achieved recognition precisely because of its resistance to genre purity and exclusivity, for its cross-breeding of scholarship and the lyric and, at the same time, its heightened attention to purity, silence, and abjection. As she writes of Sappho's transgressive poems, it is the image of "an irony of reference as sharp as a ray of light" (152) that she chooses to employ—sharpness, differentiation, even while she breaks the bulwarks between scholarship and lyric poetry.

In "The Glass Essay" Carson writes of an abjection that mixes human and animal categories and that takes the romantic love poem of longing in a direction that assails purity:

> Everything I know about love and its necessities
> I learned in that one moment
> when I found myself
>
> thrusting my little burning red backside like a baboon
> at a man who no longer cherished me.
> (12)

I can recall a performance by Laurie Anderson during which she quoted the above lines from Carson's poem. A gasp went through the audience.

Which brings me, oddly enough, to Plath again. Carson's baboon image opposes the organic metaphor that has most closely followed women in multiple cultures: the flower. The flower in its symbolic context creates an equation: flower, woman, poet—the ethereal and fleeting, fragile and lovely and pure. No baboon there. (For Carson's image to strike we have to bring with us a conception of women and purity that may seem retrograde. Change the genders and the baboon image performs in a wholly different way.)

In one of the more well-known photographs of Plath a hand reaches toward her with a carnation while Plath's own fingers linger on her scarf. She is looking up, in the other direction from the flower, her mouth open in a smile only partly realized. In another photograph—from 1953—Plath is holding a rose upside down and smiling as if in parody of the role she is supposed to be playing as "female poet." The sexual politics of the literary period suggested that the female of a certain class was somehow exalted but woozily embarrassing. As was poetry. The flowers are somewhat like fumigants. It is no accident that much of the drama of *The Bell Jar* is about reproduction and the control of reproduction, the "deflowering" of the protagonist. Once "deflowered" Esther Greenwood can't stop bleeding and must be exposed, her privacy violated, her interior broached not only in private but within the medical establishment.

In the lower left of the daguerreotype of Emily Dickinson a flower may go almost unnoticed. The flower held between Dickinson's fingers is at most an ornament, a blurry sign, a bow to convention more than a physical reminder of Dickinson's disciplined attention to her herbarium. And the book on the table next to her—is that a prop too? (We might have more images of Dickinson if she enjoyed having her image captured.) Flowers can be seen as purifiers in the way they have been deployed, whether the flowers are turned from lightly as in Plath's photographs or presented frontally in Dickinson's daguerreotype and yet overwhelmed ultimately by her steady human gaze.

That there is something "pure" about Dickinson's gaze in the daguerreotype is undeniable, it seems to me. She looks out of time and beyond time, and like other writers working with restraining structures (has ever the simplest hymnal form been employed so stubbornly for such radical advances?) she is imparting the lessons only a part-time purist is capable of. We go to Dickinson for the conception that is most compacted, in-drawn, and for breath work of the subtlest kind. We go to

Virginia Woolf to trace a style that illuminates consciousness as it moves about an absence, a silence that cannot be completely tainted. We go to Plath to scour the image clean in one tributary of her ambition. We go to Plath, too, to put the dagger in the heart, to understand Listen, bastards, she's through. And wasn't Hemingway a purist? It's a strange experience to read much of his fiction after we note how often he uses the word "and." Shouldn't such a word suggest inclusiveness, a non-hierarchical in-gathering of experience—isn't that a possible reading? Except that the coordinating conjunction is surrounded by the pressure of silence, by the untouched, unreal, the wound that can't show itself, the wound of the perfect man who must insinuate more than sully the moment of grace with ungraceful speech. Or think of Anita Brookner, with her repetitive plots, milling the same sorts of characters in the same quietly devastating situations, creating a literature as intricate and beautiful and pure in some ways as Matisse's palm fronds (as depicted by Elaine Scarry).

The age of innocence is getting a shorter life cycle. But there is a possibility of reckoning with the impulse to purity without being destroyed. Impurity may even need a conception of purity. And if we accept that there is at least a family connection between perfection and purity, a visual artist helps us.

The painter Agnes Martin, 1912-2004, born in Saskatchewan, is known for her spare paintings, many of them grid-like, composed of the most minute acts of attention, purposefully just shy of perfection. Not that she sought perfection in substance or execution. She sought the idea of perfection as stimulus: "I hope I have made it clear that the work is *about* perfection as we are aware of it in our minds but that the paintings are very far from being perfect—completely removed in fact—even as we ourselves are" (15). Or, as she explains further, "you get light enough and you levitate" (35). Her canvases resemble landing directions, fields that point toward a clarified state of mind. Her lines and shadings prompt a recalibration and refreshment of sight. Her pale washes of colors, her obligingly imperfect lines, make the purity of calmness and silence and emptiness palpable.

All the same, at first sight her canvases are, frankly, easy to ignore. They arrive in low-intensity, until we adjust and turn up our own intensity. I am fond of *Untitled No. 1*, "acrylic and graphite on canvas," (1993) with its egg shell tint so faint that the canvas makes us think of the Platonic archetype of paper. Other titles emerge as pre-Oedipal, suggesting pure feeling states before language: *Infant Response to Love*, *I*

Love the Whole World, Happiness—Glee, Little Children Playing with Love.
The art works remain somehow like surfaces to be written on, and yet curiously inviolable. Many look like unassuming writing tablets, the kind we used when we were children—the lines allowing us to form our first letters according to a template of perfection that we were meant to absorb. Indeed, Martin is the artist of the fresh-lined page, the page that is already art before we make our first mark. As she has written, "Seeking awareness of perfection in the mind is called living the inner life. It is not necessary for artists to live the inner life. It is only necessary for them to recognize inspiration or to represent it" (31).

Inspiration is, however, a difficult matter to represent—but, to beg the question, difficulty is an artist's inspiration. Nothing is more difficult than perfection—except for purity. We might turn to Gerard Manley Hopkins to see such inspiration at work as he writes of purity as if it were renewable perfection. He writes in "God's Grandeur": "There lives the dearest freshness deep down things." The freshness is dear. The freshness is deep. Such deep purity, in the same poem, lives with these lines:

> And all is seared with trade; bleared, smeared with toil;
> And wears man's smudge and shares man's smell: the soil
> Is bare now, nor can foot feel, being shod.

The poem is from 1877. At the time, Hopkins could say in the same poem, with confidence, as we cannot, "nature is never spent."

Pure? What does it mean? Plath was right, perhaps, not to answer, but to demonstrate what it means to be overwhelmed by an ideology of purity and then to be spurred into impure voice, acknowledging the power of purity as a cultural conception. When Neruda assails purity he ends with a threat to those who are overcome, raging in his defense of impurity because he knows purity's power, a power that even he, wily and defiant, could not ignore. Wrestling with the tenacious grip of the conception of purity, James Fenton writes, in more abstract terms in an untitled poem, "This is no time for people who say: this, this, and only / this. We say: this, and *this*, and *that* too." But then, purity is not human, nor is perfection, but both, we should keep reminding ourselves, are inventions of the human imagination. The products of the imagination demand their own life. Czeslaw Milosz, writing in *Unattainable Earth*, knowingly or not echoes Neruda when he tells us that the new poetry will include both "the rhythm of the body . . . heartbeat, pulse, sweating. . . . together with the sublime needs of the spirit, and our duality will find its form in [the new poetry], without renouncing one zone or the other" (33). Purity will take its place. We can't help but be disappointed if we long after purity in art or in life. But then, a great amount of literature, inevitably, must be made out of disappointment.

Works Cited

Carson, Anne. "Dirt and Desire: Essay on the Phenomenology of Female Pollution in Antiquity." *Men in the Off Hours*. New York: Knopf, 2000. 130-57.

———. "The Glass Essay." *Glass, Irony and God*. New York: New Directions, 1995. 1-38.

Fenton, James. "The Gene-Pool." *Out of Danger*. New York: Farrar, Straus, 1994. 101.

———. Untitled. In *Out of Danger*. 96.

Hopkins, Gerard Manley. "God's Grandeur." *Mortal Beauty, God's Grace: Major Poems and Spiritual Writings of Gerard Manley Hopkins*. Eds. John F. Thornton and Susan B. Varenne. New York: Vintage, 2003. 21.

Lamb, Charles and Mary. "Cleanliness." *The Works of Charles and Mary Lamb*. Ed. E. V. Lucas. New York: Putnam, 1903. 363-64.

Lowell, Robert. "Foreword." *Ariel*. New York: Harper, 1999. xiii-xvi.

Marr, David. "Patrick White's return from the pit." 3 Nov. 2006. *Sydney Morning Herald*. http://www.smh.com.au/news/books/patrick-whites-return-from-the-pit/2006/11/02/1162339990980.html Accessed November 20, 2007.

Martin, Agnes. *Writings*. Ed. Herausgegeben von Dieter Schwarz. Kuntsmuseum Winterthur: 1992.

Milosz, Czeslaw. "Into the Tree." *Unattainable Earth*. Trans. Milosz and Robert Hass. New York: Ecco, 1986. 30-33.

Moore. "Poetry." *The Poems of Marianne Moore*. Ed. Grace Schulman. New York: Viking, 2003. 135.

Neruda, Pablo. "Some Thoughts on Impure Poetry." *Passions and Impressions*. Trans. Margaret Sayers Peden. New York: Farrar, Straus, 1983. 128-29.

Pearl Poet. "Cleanness." *The Pearl Poet: His Complete Works*. Trans. Margaret Williams. New York: Random, 1967. 121-188.

Plath, Sylvia. *The Bell Jar*. New York: Harper, 1971.

———. "Fever 103." *Ariel*. New York: Harper, 1999. 61-63.

———. "Lady Lazarus." *Ariel*. 6-9.

Spark, Muriel. "You Should Have Seen the Mess." *Open to the Public: New & Collected Stories*. New York: New Directions, 1985. 141-46.

Vendler, Helen. Quoted in Rachel Donadio's "The Closest Reader." *New York Times Book Review*. 10 Dec. 2006. http://www.nytimes .com/2006/12/10/books/review/Donadio.t.html
Accessed November 20, 2007

Jane Alison

Bilbao

"This is not narrative."

Richard Serra on "The Matter of Time"

In a museum on the north coast of Spain you placed eight sculptures the size of fallen helicopters, made of sheets of Cor-ten steel. If whales weren't mammals but mollusks, and beached, the shells they'd leave on the sand might look like your forms; or if ancient glyptodons were bigger, your forms might be the rounded armor they left lying askew when they died on the plains. Enormous steel spirals, ellipses, a torus; we are to walk through each, one by one. Your plan is to lure us in.

Each form hulks on the floor and offers only one entrance. I stand at the mouth of the first, peer into the dark, hesitate a moment, then step in. Rusty walls graze my shoulders and rear high at either side. They tilt together to join above, cutting the light overhead to a ribbon, but five steps later they splay again and instead draw close near my feet, so close that I wrap arms around ribs and have to try not to stumble. Sometimes both walls tilt one way, so I tilt too, trying to keep balance, my fingers grazing the shark-hide Cor-ten, hoping things will get better. It's not possible to turn around.

Time passes as we each step forward, alone, along a dark, bending passage, holding a hand out to feel the way. Inside a spiral, the wall at my hand dissolves into black. Step after step in what seems a circle, although it's too dark to know; we listen to our feet scud the floor. Then we can't help it, each alone in the dark, and for company and control count our steps. But, hearing our breaths, we count them, too, so that as we walk in the dark the numbers, finite, rise silent in our throats, and gradually the dark passage we step through dissolves into the dark passages inside us, the ones bearing blood, breath, and words, and soon there's no telling the two apart anymore, and we panic, stop, and touch our own wrists to try to remember the difference.

"This is not narrative," you say in printed words behind plexiglass on the sunny museum wall. "It's not intended to make a point." But you say this only after you've lured us in and made us wander and worry through your dark spirals and whorls.

How is it not narrative? That's what I'd ask if you were here, if it were your face I met upon blundering from the last shell, and not just your words on the wall. Because this is what narrative means: to lead one along a path of words, space, or time; to pull from beginning to end.

"To narrate is to know," a man once told me. But he was a man I didn't trust; his cloven-lipped mouth alone made me doubt him, that and the stories he'd told me. So I checked a dictionary, and he was right. To narrate is to know—how it will turn out, where those words and passages lead, because you've traveled the tunnels yourself and now sit atop a wall looking down at us groping, or because you are only a few steps ahead, yet enough to turn back with a torch and say, "Trust me. Keep going. Come on."

You and your passages on the coast of Spain: you weren't the first. Another contriver also built twisting passages on a coast. He made a labyrinth in which people wandered, and wondered, and grew afraid, and sweated and wept as they walked forward in darkness, their damp hands pressing the walls, their knuckles bloody and scraping, their eyes wild for light, terrified of how those passages would end. He did other things, too. He created a living person from dirt. He drew a thread in and out of a conch. He taught his boy how to fly.

~

A story, a narrative, set in that labyrinth.

Once a girl lived there, in the famous house in which everyone got lost—really lost, no returning. There was only one way in and the same way out, but once you entered the mouth and began walking—the ground light and sandy at first, but then damper as the sand mixed with the old sweat of bare feet that had trod there, and with piss and runny shit that had slid down frightened thighs, and with the rotten pulp of old apples and cheese, things people had brought with them hoping to live, all that pulp now mashed into the sand, the air hanging heavy in the passage as well, air that was not even air but dead breath of so many who had been there before you—once you began walking you soon found the slick walls pressing your shoulders and the pitchy air harder to breathe, and discovered that after four or five turns you'd forgotten how to go back, could see nothing, and could only stagger forward, your hands scraping and slipping on the walls. At one of the bends, at one of the corners—sometimes it was like Venice or Naples: a knife, a quick goring. Or the ground would fall and you'd slip, be gone. Or from exhaustion you'd sink to your knees, press your head to the wall, and give up. The only way to survive was to get out. But no one knew how—except this girl.

She knew because she lived in the maze. Its passages were as familiar as each pat line on her palm, each tired twist of words in her brain. She paced it and paced it and nothing ever happened. Sometimes she believed she was immune to the maze because she wasn't really alive. It was her maze; it was *her*; they were laced together. In any case, she could go in and out, bump and skid against the walls like a skateboarder.

She might go in and out, but she couldn't actually leave. Sometimes she wanted to kick herself free, and sometimes she just went deep in and folded herself up, soothed in her darkness and smells. Yet on her sunnier days, she climbed the outer wall by the beach, stared over the sea to Africa, and believed with a passion that made her chest hurt that she *could* escape if she told her secret. It could only be to one person, though. This she understood. It must be the man she loved. Then he'd go in, come out, and cut her free, and they'd fly off into life, live forever.

One day a traveler arrived. He was sunburnt and smelled of old cloth and dirt and wore a baseball cap whose brim hid his eyes. He looked bored by the project, but she didn't believe it; she could see by the way he leaned toward her, how his breath stilled when she spoke, how he kept two fingers crossed behind him, that he badly wanted her secret.

"Take this string," she whispered, as they stood out in the wind, beneath the bright sky and cawing gulls, the sun glinting the little gold hairs of his thin arms. As she pulled a ball of string from her pocket, she thought of the blue string dangling between her legs, and how that string led into a passage within her that promised *real* life, a way out, if everything went as she hoped. She'd seen the inside of herself once on a screen, blue lines of ink fountaining out to either side. But she didn't mention any of this to her sun-spattered hero.

"Take it," she said, handing him the white string, "and once you've gone in you'll find your way out. Just tug. I'll tug back at the other end."

He nodded, took the string, and blundered into the mouth of the maze, the darkness, the smeared walls, the stink. Outside on the wall she waited. It was the outermost wall, butting the beach, littered with guano and shattered crabs. The string around her finger, at first loose, grew live and taut, and she pictured his steps and each bend in the dark. She shut her eyes and saw them. She waited, felt sick when the string went slack, thrilled when again it tightened. At last it began almost humming around her finger, so tight her fingertip went pale and numb. Then it pulled rhythmically, frictive, until it grew warm, and—a shadow at first, then an ear touched with light, at last he burst whole from the sooty mouth. A shine of coal lay on his thin arms; his feet were caked with shit. She kicked her own bare feet against the wall and shielded her eyes with one hand, the other clutching her sweaty string.

He looped the string around his wrist as he walked slowly toward her, looped it lazily around, until the length between them was short and tight and he stood before her. His hot stomach pushed her bony knees; his hand grazed her thigh.

Which was just what she wanted.

He looked down at her, his face lit with sun. He turned, spat hard, and laughed. Then, after yanking the string from her fingers and dropping the dirty tangle in the sand, he lifted her from the wall, carted her to the beach, and fucked her with gusto. He rolled over and lit a cigarette as she sat crosslegged and chafed, the blue string and its bloodied white head a few feet away in the sand where he'd tossed it, drawing flies.

Because here's what she hadn't counted on. She might have led him out of a maze and thought, fair's fair, now he'd free her, but she'd never once thought about *him*, about what he might have inside his own skin: his brain, for instance, his guts, his heart. That is: what he might want. He wouldn't need her now, why would he, he'd gone in and out and was invincible, and think of the opportunities! But what the hell, he'd probably thought as he looked down at her clavicle. Why not get started?

She looked up at him smoking. Tapping his jaw, he blew a wobbling ring, then let the rest of the smoke drift from his mouth. He was talking, too, saying some trash. His eyes, she decided, weren't there. As she gazed at him, she realized that the swirling smoke leaving his lips was mirrored inside in his bronchial passages, as a tree's branches are equaled by roots. And the words he was saying had a shadow form in him, too, and who would ever know if the words in the air were the same as those moving through his blood?

Despair bloomed, and panic. She would remain who she was, and what; she would never get out. No wanting would change this, and no hero. He—squinting away in the salty light—he was as much a maze or shell as she, tumbling alone his own way. It was only when they'd both held that string . . . The thought choked her, and she climbed to her feet and stumbled away, stumbled home, back safe to her maze.

⌀

When I first saw your Cor-ten shells, I was staying in a town with a beach called Playa de la Concha, which was formed by a deep curving inlet of the Cantabrian Sea shaped something like a scallop. But because the curve was so deep, the place sounded more than looked like a shell, the waves echoing and booming as they rolled in and crashed: the sea-sound you get with a conch to your ear, air swirling between the shell's whorls and your own. (The inner ear is called the labyrinth; to damage it will damage your balance, cause loss of *labyrinthine function*.) So I was already thinking of shells on beaches, the spirals of the ear, and labyrinths, when I walked into your steel whorls.

Shells are made mostly of calcium, like bones. The exterior skeletons of mollusks, like whelks, conches, or razor clams, shells only become shells when the resident creature dies. So the beach is a graveyard, a place of wet bones recently inhabited by soft flesh squirting and clinging.

Mollusks leave their shells only when they die, when the wet sensate part dissolves atom by atom into water, sand, and air. Whereas turtles, birds, and alligators instead leave their shells behind when they're born. As we do, more or less.

The word *shell* is what's remained after the words *scale* and *shale* have tumbled for centuries, their sharp parts worn away.

Cor-ten is a species of steel that, in air and moisture, creates a rust-like shell for protection. I don't know what the ancient labyrinth was made of. Limestone? Coral-rock?

⌀

Now another story on another beach, a sunny one in Carolina. Here a little girl, Gilly, is playing a game. She's imagining being blind. She's lying on her back, in her green swimsuit on the hot sand, with her eyes shut tight to block even the black glow of sun on her eyelids. Before lying down she arranged a ring of shells around where she'd lie, broken

68

orange scallops, slipper shells, pieces of conch. She has already noticed the similarity of the glossy snapped whorl of a conch to her own ear, has run a curious finger along one and the other. It seems important, a magic connection. So she made the ring of shells and placed herself in it, and is lying, eyes shut against the blazing sun, arms flung out on the hot sand at her sides.

What if I really lose my seeing, she thinks. She closes her eyes tighter, but this agitates the green dots of sun so she has to just pretend she can't see them. She thinks, *And what if I lose my hearing.* She concentrates on closing her ears but learns what she knew, that they don't close, but realizes it consciously for the first time. She pokes a gritty fingertip into each ear-hole. Inside, now, it drums. *Then what*, she thinks, her voice and breaths funnily loud in her head, *what if I lose my voice.* For the first time she becomes aware that there are a lot of passages in her head, little tunnels running one way to let the noises from outside in, and other tunnels running another way to let the wind fly in her nostrils and mouth, and even, it seems, tunnels to give the words she thinks enough room to echo in her head and make sound. This is a discovery, and weird.

Anyway, she thinks with an effort, *what if I lose my voice. Really!* she thinks, and hears the word in her head: *Really! So that I can't even hear my own thinking. Then what*, she thinks, giddy now and going for broke, *what if I lose my feeling?*

This last she thinks because it's how the game started: Gilly's mother, sitting in a striped lounge chair with her legs oiled and shining in the sun, had been talking over sandwiches with a friend about someone who had two children, twins, who had no sense of feeling. They hurt themselves all the time. They cut themselves and didn't even know until the blood got on their clothes or plates, and their mother couldn't bear it, couldn't bear to see them studying the bloody raw split in a hand, poking the rare lips apart to see what else was in there.

Gilly had wheeled like a plane around the women as they talked, fascinated to sickness. Then she'd looked back at the scuttles and soft white ditches her feet had left in the sand, and felt exquisitely the warm sand beneath her soles, and knelt down to feel it grinding her knees, and then in an ecstasy had thrown a glancing handful into the air.

So, Gilly thinks now, with her eyes screwed shut and ears plugged, *what if I lose my seeing and hearing and voice and smell AND a way to feel. What then?*

This is a child who recently did cartwheels up the beach, spinning, hair flying, hands and feet plonking into the damp sand, and even if her legs weren't all that straight, these were good, honorable cartwheels. Behind her was kicked up a wandering trail of handprints and footprints and occasional knee-prints in arcs that crossed over and into each other, as dizzy as she was herself. When she finally stopped, she lurched and swayed and looked back at her traces, then up the beach at her mother. She stretched out her thin arms and shouted, "I'm flying, that's what it's like! I don't feel like I'm on the ground at all!" And she tilted her head back and stared right at the sun with her pale hazel eyes until her mother cried, "Honey, I told you, don't do that! Now *quit*."

And this is the same girl who had come to her parents in tears at midnight. "I can't picture nothing! What does it look like? I need to know what nothing looks like!" And they had said, "Sweetie, it's just nothing, it's not bad. Go back to sleep."

In her circle of shells now, Gilly feels beneath her the booming of the waves, hears each of her breaths come and go loud and private, and even, she realizes, hears the throbs of her heart. Each breath comes in and goes out. As if she wasn't even there, or was just an open window and the air moved where it wanted. If she couldn't feel the breaths and hear them, would they still be breaths? Or would they really just be air or wind? Was it only her feeling them that made them be breaths?

She tries to make sense of this, and panics. *What if I lose my hearing, and sight, and smell, and a way to feel anything even that hurts. Would I really be nothing then?*

But if I was nothing, then how would I know?

·◇·

I picture you standing at the sphincter of a spiral, a dark form rimmed in light, waiting for us to stagger out, one by one. I wonder what else you have done. How much do you know? Have you modeled a child out of dirt? Taught a boy how to fly?

"This is not about knowing," you insist. "This is not narrative. I am making no point."

Our corollary to shell is bone, the hard substance that supports our soft flesh, but you could look at it another way and say that our corollary to shell is skin. Shell, shale, scale. Inside our skins, words and stories course like blood, each word a corpuscle pulling another behind it, a grammar of blood, of lifeblood.

70

Now another beach, and on it, this time, an older woman walking. Rosemary's sixty-seven, and she's had two husbands—one left, one died—and a handful of lovers. But she's said farewell to all that, she decides again as she walks into the morning. In fact, to hell with all that! She's enough, she's come to think, on her own. She's grateful. She's glad she's survived those passages of life and now feels something like peace. She walks over the yellow sand to where the frothy cold water tamps it, latches her hands behind her back, and looks to the hazy edge of the world.

Walking north, nodding now and then at fellow walkers in hats, she toes shells. She has bowls of spinnets and whelks and sand dollars at home, her home to which she's so attached that her children will never pry her from it. Her home, man-free, all her own things, her temperature and her colors. Suddenly she stops, staring down, and gives a cry, but there's no one near to share the moment. At her toe lies a speckled tiger cowry. And as if that weren't enough: inscribed upon it, in white gothic print, is what seems to be the Lord's Prayer.

Just a tourist-shop thing that made it back to the beach—maybe someone threw it as a joke from a boat. She rinses it clean, pinkish and spotted, and touches the wet white letters. She doesn't much believe in the Lord, although she sometimes looks up at the sky and wishes. But she does collect shells, and certainly ones like this, which she can put on her green-marble coffee table and point to, wine glass in hand and hostess eyes bright, and say, Just *look* at what I found!

Six years later: Rosemary again. Again she's outside bending to pluck something, but this time it's a golf ball. On this course not a month ago she found a tiny chipped porcelain lamb, and it was really too extraordinary; that shell and now the lamb. She squinted up at the sky uneasy. Then put the chipped lamb next to the cowry shell, because of course she had to.

Now, as she golfs, it's an electric gray Sunday in August, and she's been worried all morning about lightning and being exposed on the sloping huge green. But the sparking cloud mass has traveled elsewhere, and it's not lightning that strikes her; instead, it's a golf ball. It hits her shockingly hard near her ear. Although she staggers forward and her fingers splay deep in the grass, she doesn't fall. She straightens herself and with grace and effort brushes aside the perpetrator's apologies.

"Of course you didn't mean it," she says. "You're a terrific golfer but, dear, your aim's not *that* good!" She won't bother with a doctor, as everyone in the clubhouse urges when they peer at the place in her streaked gray hair that eerily shows nothing. She says she doesn't need a doctor. She just wants to get home.

All the way she clutches the steering wheel, squinting against the thudding in her skull. At home she drops her bag to the kitchen floor, lets her visor fall to the table, peels off her grubby gloves. She plugs in the kettle. She makes a cup of Rooibos and drinks it, eyes shut, hips against the sink, cold fingers gripping the edge.

There are no husbands in the house anymore and long since been a lover, even that last old fool who sometimes fumbled her name. The children are in three states, phone calls rare. A quiet house, except for a clock ticking and bonging the hour; a cowry shell on the green coffee table, a cat static against her legs. Her dear house, all the things in it that really are hers and feel like feathers she's nestled around her: the painted birds she's collected, the afghan pillows, each thing quietly alive when she pets it with her eyes, each humming its attachment to her. She lies down on the sofa, her fingers touching the rug.

But now with all her loved things in the house is something else: a strange feeling in Rosemary's head after the throbbing dies down. A feeling that grows the next day and that she wants to ignore. She shakes her head to shake it away, but with that shake comes the first sign of trouble: the windows around her, the big blue vase, the leaves of a philodendron, blur and smear just a little too long in her vision.

From then on, her hands begin to leave marks on the walls. First, just tentative whorls left by her fingers, and then, a month later, a flat handprint or two, but soon there are long helpless smudges and streaks as she fumbles and presses the walls when she passes, trying to steer herself straight. The walls of her bedroom, near the feeder where so many hummingbirds have sipped, the walls of the dining room that saw so much red wine and uproar: on all of them are smears and smudges because Rosemary can no longer navigate. She can no longer understand how to move through space; it will not be apprehended by her eyes or ears. The stuffed stool, the kilim, and the old gold chair loom up around her but spin away when she turns toward them, clasping, her world no longer solid but moving on without her, sliding too soon from her grasp.

·◌·

I walked into each of your eight spirals and ellipses, each time hoping that this one would be different, there'd be something promising at the end, some reason to have trusted you and stumbled on in the darkness. All I could do was measure time and space as they passed, as if that might make sense of them. In an ellipsis I counted steps, hoping that each inward curve was smaller than the last, that I was not moving in a circle but making some sort of progress.

But maybe I've misunderstood you? Maybe when you say, "This is not narrative," you really mean, "This is not knowing." That to be in those passages, those tunnels of time, we are just not knowing. But must keep moving forward, pushing forward in time.

᪣

A man now, who served in the war as a glider pilot and landed on a famous beach. He's old now and won't talk about it: modest, embarrassed, tired. He's color-blind, which made it hard to get into the war, but he's Jewish and was determined. He kept showing up at recruiting stations until they said, "You again? All right, you're in." They gave him a silk map so that when he landed on the beach, he could jump out and fight on land. Normandy, the Netherlands, Belgium. The map was silk so he could roll it small and stuff it into a pocket, grip it in a damp hand as he crawled.

But he wouldn't tell about any of this; you'd just have to look at the old wrinkled map and imagine things playing in his lids. Imagine finding your way through channels of empty dark air over dark water, and then, once you'd landed and staggered onto the beach, reading a map with muted colors you couldn't distinguish anyway. Running through woods, panting, into fields, toward farmhouses, looking for the Germans.

"All just old men," he said, the only time he spoke of this. He looked at me, lids hanging and gray eyes bloodshot. He shook his head, stared down. "Old men and skinny boys. Saddest damn thing I ever saw."

It's half a century later now, and he's tired, not well. He's had a good run, but he's had enough. Sometimes he feels as though it all spools behind him, a vapor trail of life—a branch of oak, a smell of fire, a car tire he's crouching near on I-95—and as he sits in the old brown leather chair in the rec room he becomes dizzy with this spooling behind him and feels he's falling helplessly forward. His body beneath his tired head plagues him, but he doesn't mention it any more than the war or the bone people he once helped free. It's a mess down there in his body. Heart, gut, and, worst, prostate.

Two days ago a doctor threaded a tube into his urethra. He shut his eyes as he sat in the paper robe in the cold room and tried to put his mind somewhere else. A long fine tube, meant to help somehow. Leading from his bladder to a sack on his leg.

The trouble is the pain. A word he doesn't use, it doesn't really live in his head, he has never found it worthy. But that's what the problem is, and it's growing. He tries to resettle himself in the leather rec room chair, flips from the Redskins to a movie about an old boat in the rain, rests a thick spotted hand on the mastiff's head, and tries to watch, to sleep, to do anything but feel this. He crosses his sneakered feet.

But sometime in the night, when the shows have stopped and the dog is snoring and outside it is so silent, so open, he can't stand it anymore. He grips the arm rests, pushes himself to his numb feet, and right there in the rec room shoves down the elastic waist of his underpants, and grips the damned tube by the throat. He tugs. The pain is indescribable, yet the thing doesn't budge. But it's the sort of pain that has to mean progress, this has to be true, and anyway he can't stand it, has to keep going now that he's begun. With one hand he grips the banister, and with the other he clutches the tube and pulls. But it's anchored somehow, like the grappling hooks at the ends of the ropes they had thrown up the cliffs. Some sort of hook has its teeth in his bladder. But it doesn't matter, he can't stand it, so he grips the basement door handle and pulls the tube.

Soon all his consciousness has focused on this hook. It's as if he is actually in there, up there in the dark, where his own tubes coil around each other, around the bladder, the prostate, that mess. He pulls the slippery rubber tube and it's like flames inside him. Pulls again, grunting, face shaking, hands sweating. Blood slides and drips down the tube, down his thighs. It is not possible to be anywhere else, anywhere but in that hot center of agony, and in there too rolling and flashing before him are all those old things, all those moments, the oily warmth between her breasts, that wormy scab on his brother's knee, his old Caddie with the ripped seats, and they are somehow in him but not there at all, not anywhere anymore, just gone.

He pulls, the hook tearing another quarter inch. He shuts his eyes. It goes on like this through minutes and hours that must travel their usual way through the night but don't seem to, they seem measured instead by the tiny portions of flesh ripped by that hook, by the drops of blood and urine that slide down the tube, by the smears his hands leave on the banister and wall, by the things he keeps seeing behind his lids, and at some point he begins to know that when it is out, when he has pulled the damned tube out, it will all be over.

☙

You and your passages. What's at their heart? What do we get when we reach the center? Empty walls, concrete floor, quiet. The glyptodon's all shriveled away, the bones lie dry on the beach. I stand there, the dark path spooling behind me, and hear the breaths and the words that had clung to those breaths, as if they meant something, led somewhere.

But maybe I've misunderstood you again? Maybe the heart of your passages isn't their center. Maybe it's what we find once we've come out again, once we've passed out of your last shell and into the light that bounces off the building's silver scales and brown glinting river, out into the blue air, where a little boy, breathing hard, body racing with promise, raises his thin arms above his head, pauses, then handsprings up the grass.

Geri Doran

Impedimenta

The hackberry blackens in the March rain.
The bur oak in the backyard waits—
we are all out of season, unkind
in our distrait.

So say you, spring. So you said
one evening, cool, damp as this,
but disguised by veils of Spanish moss,
soaked and heavy. Every night
the same dream: hairline cracks
in the plaster wall, a lover seeping in.

Impassive fences corral green-brown
lawns. Reluctant, permeable skins.
The orange tabby permeates.
Makes her buttonhole stitch yard to yard.
A robin-redbreast mounts one fence,
then another. He is dividing his fire.

·◊·

Out of season. April, perhaps, is crueler;
for now March is enough, these shoots
working up through hard layers.
The will is geologic: shale's density
commensurate with the desire
to withhold. Hardy crust, frozen
earth. Yet the tenderest green tips
nose into fissures and rise.

Out of this season comes the story.

Like no other. This is not rebirth,
nor the story of god and the devil
wagering at a barrio cockfight.
Especially this is not the truth.
It begins with a window, slightly raised,
that frames a barren tree,
home to a clutter of redwing blackbirds.
The birds which today are absent.

The window is a syllogism:
false logic on the nature of permeability.
If the window is closed it is impassable;
the window is open;
thus the soul disperses, fine-sieved
into black particulate with a small
red brushstroke on each wing.

〜

Earth says, *come home. Darling,*
come down. Home is sky's
imperfect hesitation: cohesion
lost to an uptake of breath. Such loose
configuration of love,
such delicate meandering—

Earth stretches up
her grass-stained fingertips.

〜

Or the blackbirds reinhabit the hackberry,
and the tree in rain begins to bud,
buds to leaf, green feathering
the tree so as to camouflage, finally,
all weatherings of the soul.
So, you say. *Spring.*

〜

There is no story, you understand.
Just foreplay in a dark March rain.

City

First morning, I woke
to the lying-downness of myself: my alabaster
arm and thigh more silken rampart,
my curves their hills, and in my dew-wet bed
of grass, I knew that my geography
would become terrain, and from terrain
sweet mappable streets. I am through-country
and settle.
They knew it, too—

men broaching my embankments, the toll
little enough: ruby trinket, coin.
So they paid, and in paying filled
their cups. Filled the cups
and stayed,

eager pigeons flocking to my line
and pecking, pecking.
No, if I call them city rats, then I am dirty
city, squalid city, teeming
along corridors of outer darkness.

Lies, it's lies. Venality's
no charge for beauty's exacting
recompense.

·⌒·

This my tribunal: a court of fire.
Jury of licking flames, white-hot judge
at poker.
He trails his verdict along my thigh
and chars my skin.

·⌒·

You call me Babylon, call me Whore—
I am Mystery and that name comes
before all other names.
If my accuser is a trinity, then so am I,
city, woman and the one that
is the three.

Talk, talk—you think that it reveals.
Talk is my privacy.
If I talk until oblivion do you think
you will know anything? Dear men,
you copulate.
After, you are as virginal
as the hundred and forty-four thousand
lambs, his bleating followers.
For these did not know women.

⌒

Remember
what I was? Sweet territory,
meadow of dahlias
full to bursting. I was summer.
The field that sprang
at the end of the street of the shoemakers,
beyond the leather-tanners' lane.
I was footpath
I was forest
I was love.

⌒

Easy, now. Rains are falling,
scattering dirty drops on windows.
City is a mottled view,
dabbed with pigeon scum and streaks
of paint.
One skyrise sees itself
in the windows of another.
So we look onto ourselves,
and what we see is glassy, bent.

·◎·

We needed no translators.
Birds chirping
in our thousand tongues.
All perched together
on the highwires, the curbs.

Now they name me *a hold of foul spirit*.
If I *am* befouled,
who will pity me?
Not the new converts. O rapture me,
they cry.

O seize my plain, pluck my
searocks for paving stones, dig
clay for wall, coal for fire,
diamond for selling,
root for knowledge.
I did not say: take all, except this fruit.
I said: take all, and take some more—

until I was bejeweled
with lampposts and iron pheasants
curving above shop doors,
marquees and limelight,
my alabaster arms
sheathed in silk

streaked now with char.

Debora Greger

By a Pond on a Muggy Evening

First came the *quaink* of a distant cowbell,
then the *quonk* of a plucked banjo string.
A cheep, a drowsy birdlike chirp,
the *basso profundo* of a *jug-o-rum*—

frogs of the duckpond, may I render
a rough translation? *I'm your kind of animal,*
you croak, *I'm big and handsome.*
I own real estate.

Where is the female to isolate your call
in the jubilant, desperate din
I can hear a block away? Love, stop the car.
Turn off the headlights and the air-conditioning.

Roll down the window—oh,
a policeman has pulled up beside us,
wanting to know why we're creeping along.
A pair of professors, old enough to be his parents

at the least, claiming that, on their way home
from teaching a night class . . .
he can only shake his head and drive on.

Death Takes a Holiday

Battleships melted down into clouds:
first the empire died, then the shipbuilding,

but cloud formations of gun-metal gray
towered over the sea that was England in June.

A scarecrow treaded water instead of barley,
gulls set sail across a cricket ground.

In a suit woven of the finest rain,
Death took the last seat on the train,

the one next to me. He loosened his tie.
His cell phone had nothing to say to him

as he gazed out the window, ignoring us all.
Had the country changed since he was last

on holiday here; a hundred fifty years ago?
Like family, rather than look at each other,

we watched the remains of empire smear the glass.
Had we met somewhere? "Out West last week

I passed your parent's house," he said.
"I waved but your mother didn't notice.

Your father must have had his hearing aid turned off,
in that way he has." In the rack overhead,

a net, a jar, a box, a pin: Death had come
for another of Britain's butterflies.

He rose, unwrinkled. "I'll see you later," he said.

Persephone on the Way to Hell

Over there, beside the road—
is that the letter I should have left you, Mother?
The shade of a scarecrow waves a blank page
as big as he is, but too late.

Blond waves of winter wheat roll up
to the knees he'll never have,
tempting his shirt to swash, to buckle
and set sail for some other myth—

and then he's just a white plastic bag
tied to a stake and stuck in a field
at the end of summer. What's left of a river
lies in a bed grown too big for it,

surrounded by rocks it carried this far
and then let fall. Mother seems smaller, too.
I saw you, my lord of the dark,
take her hand as it were just a child's.

The door of a room had closed in her mind.
"Where am I?" she wanted to know,
reigning from her old recliner. You knelt
and tenderly took off her shoes.

"And what is *her* story?" she said,
"That woman watching us,
who looks like my daughter."

Andrew Hudgins

Late to the Games

We slip along the lip of the ditch
and every time we come to someone
sitting, waiting for the games,
I grab chain link with one hand, swing
across them, grab the fence again,
inch down to the next spectator,
and do it all again. I hate
that moment paused face to face,
straddling strangers, afraid they'll shove me
down the steep concrete slope and out
onto the field. I've seen it happen.
Today, drunk men just jaw at us,
as we edge past. "Lotsa good seats!"
they shout. "Gonna be a great show!
I wouldn't miss this for the world,
would you?" Not me, I say. Below,
music, distorted to raw crisis,
quickens us. Smoke explodes. Engines
ignite. Steel chimes on steel,
and within ten minutes, the evening's first
blood drop flicks across my cheek.

The Circus

Yes, the girl sneezing pink froth and the woman fisting her eyes
each time another oldie crackles from the ceiling
look worse than I do. See them. And find, please, a dentist
for the man clutching two molars in a bloody paper towel.
And a CPA or lawyer—summon one for the man
squeezing the folder of gray paper to his chest and squeaking
grievously. But I have an *appointment*. I arrived two hours ago,
on time, a little early in fact, and someone must help me find
the Ferris wheel I hear looping in my attic and the tilt-a-whirl
lopsidedly unfolding and refolding in the basement.
Through the walls, I hear the oompah-pahing of a carousel,
and in dark windows and the gleaming facades of black appliances
I glimpse ascending and descending carved horses, real tigers,
elephants, and waltzing poodles. Whitewashed clowns ghost across
a TV humbling itself before beer, soap, laundry, and my armpits,
    muffling
the human cannonball's applause and the dumbfounded wow
when orange torches enter a human face and emerge unquenched.
The circus is not my fault or responsibility. Someone
must *write that down*. Someone must sell me a ticket.

The Unused Room

Through the sealed window, cars
sounded like the sea, the watery rote
of arrival and recession. When the phone
rang, we stared. Who? What?

Did we have towels? "Towels! Towels!" we laughed,
with ludicrous relief.
The second time it rang, a women said
she wouldn't have bothered you, really she wouldn't,
but she admired your work. She'd been crying
ever since you walked through the lobby with a man
who wasn't yours. Not
that she knew your husband. She could just tell
by the way you walked.
                    "Don't cry," you said
and started running. I caught you on the far edge
of the field, in a dirt circle
where big rigs turned. I grabbed your wrist.
A quick right filled my mouth with blood,
and calmed you, Love. From behind a U-Haul,
a boy, yelled, "I'm coming, I'm coming" and raced
toward a mother I couldn't see and a call we hadn't heard.

Abandoning the Play

They strode left and I slid out after
their disruption, and the woman's face,
I saw, was red—tears flicked
angrily away. The man, silent,
glowered, and then, heavily,
was gone. Her tears, now unhampered,
streamed down her face and long white neck.
Could I help? No, no, she was fine.
Coffee sometimes, talking sometimes
helps, and soon she was talking,
happy even, in the telling,
sipping coffee and then cognac,
my hands on hers, and then my mouth
on hers, and so on, till I was sitting
on the roof, home on slick slate, looking
through sagging phone wires and power lines.

I'd told her my mother had arisen
from her deathbed—I said "deathbed,"
I said "arisen"—to attend my wedding,
and I imagine Mother buried
in the hyacinth-blue suit she wore
that wasted, wintry day, smiling
when she had the energy to smile,
though—closed casket—I don't know.
For her story, she expected me
to tender passionate details
of course, and I offered truth so tired
that, for both of our nugatory stories,
it sounded like a lie.

D. Nurkse

Two Loud Bottlegreen Flies
at the Ananda Hotel

The lovers need a beginning and an end,
they require a universe and ask themselves
what happens beyond the last galaxy,
is it as fiery inside Aldebaran
as it is between their legs,
they imagine living forever
while they undress each other gingerly
trembling at the snaps and stays,
when they are naked they begin flying,
when they land it is dawn,
they are certain they are the same person,
they wonder if in a million rooms
in this huge city, lovers
are licking each other warily
in the sour heat of August—

but we the flies just zoom
in a shaft of light and all
our hundred eyes recognize
is the god of whirling dust.

The Island of the Ex-wives

There they play badminton
with their lover Charles
while the child watches
with bright eyes from the pines.

When they get tired
they doze in a hammock
with the gray-muzzled pug
twitching at their feet,

when they are hungry
they nibble tofu burgers
grilled on mesquite
at the first pinprick of Venus,

and when they grow lonely
they climb the granite cliff
to scan the dim whitecaps
for a smudge of mainland.

But no ferry goes there.
It is an eyelash on the horizon
between Cascade and Deseret.

If you ask the Captain,
he will grunt and shake his head
and coil the endless ropes.

Dice in Thuringia

after Tacitus

1

We wrestled, rolled in love,
and wandered home drunk,
straw stuck to our bellies,
kicking a little smooth stone before us:
light side, dark side . . .

We gorged on dark windfall plums.
In the tea-colored forest pools
trout nosed to our braced hands.

No need to dig, but if we stumbled on a pit
we graced it with a canopy of twigs
and reaped bear, bison, boar.

Our northlands were so vast
between the Rhine and the frozen ocean,
we had no word for frontier.
Romans rotted in our fever swamps.

2

Who discovered it?
Was it a stone or a number,
six choices or none?
Who stooped and marked it?

Nestled in the hand
it held a memory of childhood.
However tightly we gripped,
we felt only our aching palms.

3

Then we knelt and contended,
feinting like deathless warriors
though always with the same gesture:
letting go, followed by counting . . .

We gambled away our wives and children
while they watched open-mouthed,
our Samartean and Parthian ermine,
our omen-coins, the die itself,
the white horses of Mercury, that know the future—
a hostile slave led them away whickering,
glancing back with huge scornful eyes:
we staked our greaves and cuirasses—
strange to have no armor,
as if the body itself were an eye,
an eye that cannot close—

and we bow naked to the yoke.
Already our master kneels beside us,
cups his hands, and begs
mercy from the Unknown God.

Elise Paschen

Raccoon on a Branch

You want to face this illness on your own.
I take a plane to be nearby. Your physique,
still handsome, racked by coughs, by monthly chemo.

It's difficult for you to speak. I'm tongue-tied.
As I leave, walking down your block, ground trembles.
I meet another friend recovering.

She and I follow the reservoir path.
We've walked this trail before. Though you're not here,
you occupy the space that separates.

I tell my friend you want to be alone.
She says, "That's strange. After the operation,
I needed to be near all those I love."

We hear a scuffling in some fallen branches
scattered across the dirt. Crows caw above.
My friend stops, gestures: "Look, a young raccoon."

The creature stares straight at us. A dog barks.
The animal limps away, climbs a trunk.
He fumbles, ascends to a higher branch,

looks down, trembling, unfocused, blinks his eyes,
unaccustomed to the blazing sun. Leaving
behind the raccoon, clinging close to limb,

we understand he wants no company.
The light is changing now, but I'd stay planted
beneath the tree, waiting into the dark.

Feast for the Living

I dream my father is alive, preparing
the Ocean Drive house for a dinner party.
Together we walk down the aisles, my father

steering the cart, selecting favorite foods:
dark chocolate, crisp baguettes, smoked salmon,
buttery Chardonnay, chickens, romaine.

At home, he clips basil and thyme from garden,
pulls on his chef's apron and improvises,
reigning over the stove. Throughout our dinners

he would declare, "Let the wine flow," and we,
his family and friends, would travel down
a garnet river, bubbling, rippling, clinking

under the wind-blown stars, swapping the stories
of our shared adventures, the tales of places
he had navigated across the globe.

My father shows me how to poach, sauté,
and whisk, as he conjures from scratch this dinner
for his wife, my mother. "What's the occasion?"

I ask. While stirring he explains, to prepare
my mother for his departure,
so she will make new friends, once he is gone.

Outside the Tomb

Uproar of finch in olive leaves.
The angels spoke,

but I was blind. A gardener called.
If only pores

could drip with honey, bones would shine.
Let me explore

tuber and truss, tunic and whorl,
serve as your sole

translator: *miniature star, sun,*
dazzler, just wings.

You spoke my name, I understood.
Before I leave

this garden, climb clay path,
mountains of rock,

before I speak in parables,
appear again.

Warning Signs

The sky turns brackish green. I'm caught
outside and hear a rumble growing louder,
stomping the heart. Storm-clouds spit out the grit
of my indecision while I size up

the distance. Before I reach sanctuary
you strike, catch me off balance, then inhale
mortal flesh into air. *Cyclone, whirlwind,
twister, dust-god.* Above the cumulous

I hover. A scrim lifts: the world is radiant.
But you are done. You hurl me down with hail
among the living and the dead. I sprawl
against the dirt. Fish rain from sky.

G. C. Waldrep

The Toad God

There is a forest in Bulgaria
inside of which the largest boulders
                         have been hollowed,
niches the size of a man. Inside which
the ancients hung—
what? Or stored? Or stood
slathered in Slavic pigments, awaiting
a visitation from the Toad God.
                         This was in place
of the more cumbersome practice, i.e.
the consumption of their dead.
And in the swelter of summer the men
                         would stand,
and sometimes the women,
and even in the darkest days winter's
                         hand could not pry
the shivering bodies from their narrow,
lithic booths. And it was
a time of visions, the old stories say.
And the Toad God was a god of mercy
and of judgment. And they did not
                         build houses for him,
knowing that the earth was sufficient,
the cold earth, the damp soil,
their souls like the soul of his soul,
because this was the way of things
                         with the Toad God,

the way it had always been,
the soul burrowed down
to its place of sustenance, the body
in its chamber, piebald, trembling, awaiting
answers to its prayers, the way
                              a toad waits, patient,
in the hollow of a hand, in the hollow
of any blooded, human hand.

Lilac Poem

The lilac is not a thorny tree,
the lilac has no thorn.

The lilac takes the place of a
thorn, takes the shape of a thorn,

the lilac

dwells in the office of the thorn.
It is a holy office,

the office of the thorn,
next to the office of the nail.

The lilac

dwells in the office of the nail,
next to the office of the thorn.

It too is a holy office.

And for a time there is peace
between the office of the nail
and the office of the thorn.

And for a time there is peace
between the lilac and the pale
ladders of the destroyer.

In the shadow of a gatepost
a new office takes root.

It too will be a holy office.

The lilac

will take a hammer to the hand
of he who speaks its name.

Brian Henry

Crawlspace

The wind crosses
through the vents

stirs the spores
and cellulose debris

the rotting wood
the mites beneath

and then swoops
flees the house

and what's below
for the sun

knowing the sun
will level it

with its flame
of zero gaze

that bastard sun

Foundational

The sun slugs me in the arm
                and when I fail to flinch
    slugs me in the face
                  between temple and eye
        leaving something like a bruise
        or burn

The bricks I gather will help
              I tell my crumbling spine
     but know there is no way
              to keep out the sun
        once it makes you its baby
        or bitch

The mortar so dry it flakes
              when I stab at it
    with a stick I've chosen
              for a trowel
        and the bricks just laugh like bricks
        or boards

The sun sits on my chest
              its knees pinning my arms
    to drip a trail of mortar
              from between its lips
        spit mixed with blood
        or blood

The spit a burn
        bitch
    the bricks   the boards   a bruise
                    baby
      the blood   blood

Life's Better on the Porch

To visit, from the street,
a house you lived in as a child
is to strain to see the tops
of trees you once could vault with ease
before someone put up a fence,
that basketball goal, the ornamental
wheelbarrow on the once-white porch,
the railing of which you leapt
to chase down and pummel a friend
who ignored your command to keep off
the seedlings that, with water and time,
would establish this now-hardy yard,
struggling to catch when the kid tried
to undo what nature would have done
but was doing too slowly:
shape a half-acre into something
like a home, or what one driving by
would think to call a home
regardless of the air within,
on the other side of the still-black steel door,
which never stuck when it rained.

Lauren Watel

Cast Out

Spun through the revolving door, cast out
into the afternoon, indifferent
to the summer sun, we head uptown

to Grand Central Station, love-dazed, spent,
rug-burnt, and you touch my face, my hair
and I stare, seething in discontent,

at people holding hands and I dare
to take your hand and for a moment
we are a couple going somewhere

together, but we start our descent
underground, you let go of my hand,
you say "I love you" like a lament,

you hurry to the train, and I stand
on the stairs, praying you'll turn around.

Late Afternoon, Fort Greene

Across the river on Clinton Ave.
on a ripped sofa in a borrowed
walk-up I sat beside you and cupped
you in my palm and as you gazed at

yourself like a man watching TV
I gazed at you like someone watching
the sun set. It was late afternoon.
I wasn't ready for you to leave.

I tried to distract you with stories
that depicted me in the best light.
I fed you apples, almonds, salads,
and steaming bowls of stew. I'm afraid

I fed you more than you could stomach.
Forgive me. I couldn't stop myself.
You seemed to recede like a ribbon
of sand slowly buried by the surf.

I don't want to romanticize this
afternoon or any afternoon
I spent with you in that apartment.
Paint flaked off the front door like dead skin.

The windows were hung with torn paper
shades that kept the damp in and light out.
Hair in the sink. A rusted razor.
More things broken than in good repair.

And yet when I got down on my knees
and bowed my head, I vowed to myself
not to want, not to want, not to want
and we lost ourselves to the current.

My Love, I Am Here

(Eurydice in Hell)

My love, I am here, I'm waiting for you
to die and picturing the moment when
your heart stops hammering, your lips turn blue,

your fingers grow taut like the strings that won
over the gods of the dead in your bid
to bring me back, when our failed ascension

sent me back underground, though I feel bad
looking forward to your death and I wince
at my selfish desires and wish I had

doubts, but I want what any woman wants,
a lover who is willing to die for
her, because the thought of you alive haunts

me and I'm starting to fade and I fear
if you don't come soon I will disappear.

Addict

You can't take it away from me.
Everything is under control.
I wish you could get it for free.
You can't. Take it away from me,
give it to someone who can be
more restrained. When I'm on a roll,
you can't take it. Away from me
everything is under control.

David Wagoner

Ashes

In folk tales if you wish
for gold and dream of it
and search for it in the woods
or dig for it in the mountains
or sail to a strange island
       and come back or come down
       or come stumbling out
       holding your glittering
       treasure in your hands,
       it turns to ashes. You see it
blow away in the wind
and scatter into nothing.
And what do you say then
to those who watched for you
at the edge of the forest,
       who stayed by the campfire,
       who waited and waited
       on the near shore, wondering
       where you'd gone and why?
       Do you say to them (for the only
comfort you can imagine)
that even if gold hadn't changed
to what it had always been,
you probably wouldn't know
what to do with it now?

At Dawn on the Fifth of July

At the dead end of the street:
charred cones and cylinders,
no-longer explosive fragments
of spheres and nuggets, the pavement
covered with colored scars
from flashes and booms and whistles,
from all the Crackling Sams,
from Hopalong Knuckle Dusters,
from Grunts—an after-the-crazy,
the-hell-with-it banquet look—
and the independent birds
all gone now into hiding
till the end of the world is over.

Michael Chitwood

The Wind As the Figure of the Afterlife

They weren't getting where they wanted to go,
the turkey vultures, the death cleaners.
The wind knocked them off course, off the scent.
Such a wind. Pines shivered, cones came loose.

The turkey vultures, wanting the deer at the roadside,
rocked and sailed past, unable to stop.
They must have wondered where the ground was going.
They could smell the meal but couldn't make it stay still.

The deer, legs folded as in mid-leap,
didn't move and yet ran away from them
as they rocketed by, buffeted, ruffled, pushed
when they tried to turn. The wind wanted this one

left alone. Scraps of paper ran like rabbits.
Tall weeds brushed over like fur.
What could not be seen was having its day.
The ground threw grit. Old leaves got up and jigged.

The turkey vultures, the death cleaners, latched themselves
to a powerline pylon. They seemed to caucus.
Why the sky conspired against them was their subject.
Folded, wind-proof, they were judges in black robes.

From their lofty bench, they presided,
unable to rule. The law, such as it is, did not apply.

Finish Work

Of his table saw I will speak,
but not his wood plane
displayed now on my bookshelf,
its shape too elegant, its cut too precise.

·❦·

A male cardinal has come
to my windowsill.
Over and over he thrashes
against the glass,
battering his own enemy reflection.

·❦·

He worked in a small shed out back,
dust climbing the sun slats.

·❦·

During mating season
the finches' butter yellow brightens to sunburst,
once a year.

·❦·

He was a furniture maker in his day job too,
mostly for Bald Knob Furniture in the days before safety regs.
He was missing the ends of eight of his fingers.
When he took me to Moran's Store to get a Brownie,
a cold chocolate drink,
he would hold my hand as we walked across the parking lot.
What I felt was what wasn't there.

·❦·

In his hand, a boat.
It sailed across the made world.
That's near to breaking my vow.

·❦·

He made a bedroom suite for my parents,
chest of drawers, vanity, nightstand,
and, of course, the bed.
All walnut, rich, dark, fine-grained wood.

~

My father was an only child.
I first heard the phrase as lonely child.

~

I picture the wood curls at his feet
as he worked,
blonde locks of a beautiful woman.

~

During mating season,
our suburban deer herd goes crazy.
One buck wound up crashing through the plate glass
of a downtown shop.
Does slam into cars in their headlong flight
running from bucks.

~

He breathed his creations,
inhaled the fine blonde dust.
Then he'd go out to the over-turned bucket
and put fire to the Lucky Strikes.

~

I don't know why she felt she needed to tell me.
I can still see the curve of the off ramp we were on.
I can feel the centrifugal shove the curve gave the car.
It was the middle of the trip.
We'd been talking about nothing much.
It was just the two of us.
"Your grandfather cheated on me."

~

What he made in his spare time,
his pieces, grace many houses, homes.
Even mine.

∽

A pair of cardinals at the feeder,
he, scarlet, selects a sunflower seed
and feeds it to her, drab olive, sitting beside him.

∽

In his mind, before it was done,
he knew where everything went.

∽

He, third grade education. She, seventh.
In the days before birth control was common,
and never discussed, an only child.
When he died they had been married thirty-eight years.

∽

Before he made the first piece,
he made the table saw,
its guides and stops.

∽

We, the three grandchildren, took turns picking what we wanted
after Grandmother died.
I took a little cedar chest he had made.
She had saved letters in it.
There was one from my Dad, not sure the occasion.
In part it read, "Mother, I'll take your hand and Dad's
and hold us together."
I wonder how many pieces were already missing from that hand.

∽

Grain. It continues.
It does not end where the piece has been cut.
You have to understand that.

∽

Snug, square, trig, true,
As far as I know he made only one bed.

∾

Dust climbing the sun slats,
the ache of that.

∾

The bed was in the spare room at my parents.
It was where my grandmother stayed when she became ill.
She died in it.

∾

He ran his hand along a finish to know that it was done.

William Virgil Davis

An Affair

When he discovered it
he discovered almost
immediately that everybody
already knew about it.
But nobody had told
him—not surprisingly,
he thought. He knew
he would not have told
anyone either, if he'd
known about something
like this, not even his
best friend, not even his
wife. Indeed, he wondered
how one, really, *would*
go about talking about it?
In this case, wouldn't it
be obvious that (if not
everyone) some at least
would have already
known and, therefore, it
would seem that they
would have assumed
that he knew too—and
thus not tell him—because
(they'd also assume)
either that he knew—
and was trying to ignore it—
or, if he didn't, that he
wouldn't *want* to be told?

They must all, he thought,
have thought that he knew,
thought that he was being
adult about it (not, surely,
that he didn't care, but
just that he didn't care
to discuss it). Even she,
he thought, must have
thought he knew, since—
after the first few months—
she never made any attempt
to hide it from him. Even
so, she must have wondered,
as time went on, when *he*
might mention it, how he
might bring it up, under
what circumstances, where
they might be at the time.
Knowing him, she imagined,
if he *were* to bring it up, it
would, inevitably, be at the
most unlikely moment,
and under the most awkward
circumstances. Early on,
she'd even thought about
what she would say, how
she would defend herself,
even if she would deny it all
outright (in spite of all the
obvious, incriminating,
evidence), or—if she'd been
caught off-guard—might
attempt to throw the blame
back on him, accuse him
of having forced her into it
(even subconsciously)
for some sort of strange
psychological need
he had, and had,
perhaps, repressed.

·❧·

But, as time went on,
and he didn't say, or do,
anything, and because she
couldn't really be certain
that he really didn't know—
unlikely as such an assumption
was—she stopped thinking
of possible excuses, stopped
inventing various, almost
plausible, scenarios to
cover herself, or even, she
thought, to *protect him*—
if it came to that. And,
therefore, the new became
old all over again, became
a justification for both
of them: he, waiting for her
to get bored with her lover
and come back to him,
to confess—contritely,
he hoped—and be forgiven,
so that they could make
up, and take up where
they had left off; she,
for him to say something,
do something, take some
sort of action, hint at least
that he knew—or, at least,
suspected something—
even, she thought, take
up with another woman,
and thus give her both
an excuse for continuing,
something to throw up
to him—if it ever did
come out and she needed
(as she knew she might)
some excuse. But both
of them, no doubt, knew
that neither would do
either—or both both.

One of the things, finally,
that most intrigued him
was the way he had,
apparently, *permitted* it all
to happen, the way he
had pretended to himself
that it wasn't really
happening at all, that
she was not away,
so many days, on some
trumped up trip, but
actually upstairs, in bed,
asleep, or, even, waiting
for him to come in and
surprise her—even to
make love to her. Had she
noticed, he wondered,
how often he had,
apparently purposely,
chosen to miss something,
overlook an obvious
clue left unaccountably
behind, failed to initiate
a comment or make an
accusation when there
seemed to be an obvious
opening or an
unaccountable gap in
one of her accounts (an
hour or two here or there
left out and open to
question), when she had
given him an almost open
invitation. It was as if,
she thought, that he had
almost *forced* himself
to be deceived—even
as if he wanted to be
finally.

They had,
of course, both thought
it all through many times,
and they had both come,
independently, to the
same conclusions, again
and again, so that all that
ever surprised either of them
now was that they couldn't
seem to get back to
any kind of beginning
beyond this end.

Call

You know, she said,
he used to call me
maybe six or seven
times a day, interrupt-
ting anything I was
doing, he didn't care,
and it was always
something small he
wanted, to ask a
question or to tell me
something he was
thinking about, or
what he had heard
on the radio he
listened to all day
long, and I got angry
with him often and
once I even said
I didn't want to hear
about it, or from him,
again, I'm tired, I said,
of listening to what
you want to tell me,
why don't you do
something, or call
somebody else,
even though I knew
he had no one else,
and that he often
called me because
of that, that he was
lonely, although
he never said so,
it wasn't his way,
maybe he didn't even
know it himself, or

think about it that
way, it made me
wonder, and I do
wonder what he
did all day long,
sitting there in his
chair, all alone,
listening to the radio,
and maybe thinking
how he might call
me, just to hear
a live voice, just
to talk back to
somebody, and
then maybe he'd
think he shouldn't
call again so soon,
and then wonder
when he had called
the last time, and
not know for sure,
and put his hand
on the phone and
almost dial the full
number, and then
put the receiver
back on the hook
and plan to wait
at least another
hour and then,
when he did call,
he must have heard
the disappointment
in my voice and
maybe he even
imagined all kinds
of things about
himself, or me,
and wondered,
when I told him

I had things to do,
or somewhere to
go, whether I was
telling him the truth,
because he knew
what my life was
like, that I didn't
do very much,
and rarely even left
the house myself,
but we never talked
about that, we never
really talked about
much of anything,
we talked talk, and
then we hung up,
often with some
excuse neither
of us believed in,
and now, every
day, I sit here
alone, and I wish
he would call.

David Kirby

The Ninety-nine Names of the Prophet

Turn That Darned Thing Down!

A little more than halfway through the last century, millions of Americans turned on their radios to hear, not Mitch Miller's spunky march through "The Yellow Rose of Texas" or Andy Williams' hyperglycemic version of "Autumn Leaves" or some other forgettable single from the 1955 hit parade but a jungle cry that may or may not have been "A WOP BOP A LOO MOP A LOP BAM BOOM!" No chords served as warning; no hup-two-three horn section or soothing violins announced that a song was underway, just this savage scream. And there was more to come: "Tutti frutti!" shouted some crazy guy, and then "Aw, rootey!" or "rutti" or even "Rudy." Who the hell is Rudy? And isn't "tutti frutti" a kind of ice cream? The music charged ahead, too fast for most people to follow, and from time to time that nut would scream that "A WOP BOP!" noise again. What the hell's going on here? What the hell does any of this *mean*?

A couple of years later (on December 11, 1957, to be exact), ABC television aired an episode of the long-running series *The Adventures of Ozzie and Harriet* called "Tutti Frutti Ice Cream" in which the patriarch of American's ideal (read: hopelessly square) family goes in search of the eponymous foodstuff, though when someone asks him what tutti frutti is, Ozzie's reply is "Well, it's kind of hard to explain." I'll say. But then life in America has never been easy to explain.

Okay, it has and it hasn't. Sure, there's an official explanation for

America: Columbus landed in 1492, the Pilgrims came along a few years later, the cowboys tamed the west, people drank a lot of cocktails during the Jazz Age, we kicked Hitler's butt, hippies smoked a lot of pot and then became baby boomers. But, um, there's a little more to it than that, beginning with the country's very name. "Strange," Ralph Waldo Emerson wrote, "that broad America must wear the name of a thief. Amerigo Vespucci, the pickle-dealer at Seville, who . . . managed in this lying world to supplant Columbus and baptize half the earth with his own dishonest name."

So while it'd take more space than is available to write America's unofficial history, one can make a start, beginning with the fact that the man who gave his name to this country was, as the first line of the best book about him says, a pimp and a magus. Hero and villain, salesman and sorcerer, Amerigo Vespucci was, according to Felipe Fernández-Armesto's *Amerigo: The Man Who Gave His Name to America*, possessed of "quicksilver tongue, featherlight fingers, infectious self-confidence." The term "pimp" might be a little harsh; the author himself backs down at one point and says "procurer" might be more accurate, since Amerigo acted as a go-between for certain friends who had amorous interests.

But as a Renaissance Florentine, he certainly practiced sorcery— what great man of the time did not? As a navigator, he wielded the quadrant and astrolabe that other mariners used, but Fernández-Armesto points out that these would have been of limited use on the long voyages he took to the coast of South America between 1499 and 1502, that they were "conjurer's toys, useful . . . for cowing impressionable sailors and conning impressionable historians, but of no practical use except display"; handling them, Amerigo was merely "a stage magician distracting his audience with his props," thereby proving that if you act the role convincingly, the audience will buy it.

So how did a poser get an entire continent named for him? After all, Columbus both beat him to the land mass and was the first to identify it as a new continent. But effective public relations work will always trump fact. Convinced by accounts of Vespucci's voyages that were later discovered to be fabrications (not by Vespucci but his followers), in 1507 cartographer Martin Waldseemüller produced a map on which he gave the new continent a Latinized version of Vespucci's given name. Waldseemüller came to doubt Amerigo, and in a subsequent map labeled the new continent Terra Incognita instead. It was too late, though; the "Vespucci industry" had triumphed. There's no greater force in human affairs than effective branding.

But even a successful ad campaign will fizzle if there's nothing behind it. It took a century to get things going, but the America we know today was built from scratch by a motley gang of jackleg entrepreneurs with little interest in the continent's indigenous peoples and every desire to pursue what would later be called, without a shred of irony, "life, liberty, and the pursuit of happiness." Here is Richard Kluger's capsule summary of America's early settlers (from his *Seeking Destiny: How America Grew From Sea to Shining Sea*): "Crafting their own destiny with whatever tools were at hand, they gained a continental expanse by means of daring, cunning, bullying, bluff and bluster, treachery, robbery, quick talk, double-talk, noble principles, stubborn resolve, low-down expediency, cash on the barrelhead, and, when deemed necessary, spilled blood."

And there was an increasing number of people with just these survival skills in Elizabethan England. In his writings promoting the settlement of the Americas, Richard Hakluyt advised the enlistment of Elizabeth's unhappiest subjects: in Kluger's words, "the growing masses of displaced farmers and urban poor, soldiers mustered out of service and left without other work, debtors, petty criminals, religious dissenters, and separatists," not to mention second and subsequent sons of landholders and merchants who, thanks to feudal inheritance laws, would never come into wealth. England would be better off without these marginals, reasoned Hakluyt, and it might even be enriched. The colonizing process might lead to a discovery of undiscovered resources and, were a shorter passage to China be discovered, lucrative two-way commerce. Everyone stood to win: "whether a jobless Midlands father of a hungry brood, a redundant Berkshire yeoman seeking gainful farm work, a Puritan bootmaker reviled by his London neighbors, or the besotted fourth son of Lord and Lady Periwinkle in quest of respectability," says Kruger, "scarcely a prospective settler in the new British America was short on motivation."

When they arrived, many of these new settlers found themselves embroiled in the peopling of a continent that was less a grand pageant, says Kluger, and more of a series of shaky land deals. Masking their assertions in the rhetoric of manifest destiny and divine providence, France, Britain, and Spain each made preposterous claims to ownership based on imaginary rights as well as the minutiae of boundaries that changed overnight, surveying errors, and disputed historical rights of every kind.

To thrive on the new continent, then, the voyagers who survived the journey over and the initial period of adjustment quickly translated themselves into the daring, cunning, and bullying go-getters whom Kluger places at the center of our national identity. As opposed to the European model of personal identity, this American type defines itself not through the stasis of ancestral history—God forbid others should find out that Uncle Bob was a horse thief!—but by means of a fluid creation-in-action, a constant reinvention described brilliantly by Tim Parrish in *Walking Blues: Making Americans from Emerson to Elvis*. Taking his title from the Son House song about a man waking up in the morning feeling around for his shoes and knowing by that "I got them walking blues." The song rolls out of the motion; in fact, there won't be a song unless the singer hits the road, which makes his shoes as important to him as his guitar.

Thus the bluesman echoes Emerson, says Parrish, who writes in "The Poet" that "all language is vehicular and transitive" and therefore meant for conveyance, as ferries and horses are, rather than homesteading. You don't settle into language the way you do a farm or a house; you slip it on like a pair of shoes and get going. No wonder so many blues songs begin with the words "woke up this morning," writes Parrish, when the time for corpselike sleep is done. Yet even the dead move: in "Me and the Devil," Robert Johnson says you can bury his body "down by the highway side / So my old evil spirit can catch a Greyhound bus and ride." Just because you're dead doesn't mean you can laze about all day (or all night); in Robert Johnson's America, the dead, too, have places to go and people to meet.

As far as being alive and well after being dead and gone, of course, Johnson may have had a jump on the rest of us. The stories of his signing a pact with the devil are legion, but my favorite version is the one recounted in Greil Marcus's *Mystery Train: Images of America in Rock 'n' Roll*. Here Johnson is seen as a pest, bothering House and the older bluesmen for a chance to play with them and being brushed off. Months later, Johnson shows up again, as bothersome as ever. Finally, the journeymen musicians take the air, leaving Johnson alone in an empty club. Then from inside, House and the others hear, in Marcus's words, "a loud devastating music of a brilliance and purity beyond anything in the memory of the Mississippi Delta."

What exactly happened at the crossroads is between Robert Johnson and the Lord of Night is not known to the rest of us; the best I've been able to come up with is a third-hand account quoted in Peter Guralnick's *In Search of Robert Johnson*. Here bluesman Tommy Johnson's brother LeDell is telling researcher David Evans his brother's experience in the school of Satanic licks:

> If you want to learn how to play anything you want to play and learn how to make your songs yourself, you take your guitar and you go to . . . where a crossroad is. Get there, be sure to get there just a little 'fore 12:00 that night so you'll know you'll be there. You have your guitar and be playing a piece there by yourself. . . . A big black man will walk up there and take your guitar, and he'll tune it. And then he'll play a piece and hand it back to you. That's the way I learned to play anything I want.

In the thermodynamic of higher learning, every great university has a rival of equal and opposite potency—Harvard has Yale, Auburn has Alabama, the University of Florida has Florida State—and as far as the musical curriculum goes, the devil's school meets its match in God's. "Wherever rock 'n' roll is played," writes Camille Paglia, "a shadow of its gospel roots remains," an echo of the "ecstatic, prophesying, body-shaking style of congregational singing in the camp meetings of religious revivalists from the late eighteenth century on," from "open-air worships services in woods and groves." Indeed, "gospel music, passionate and histrionic, with its electrifying dynamics, is America's grand opera," and "the omnipresence of gospel here partly explains the weakness of rock music composed in other nations—except where there has been direct influence by American rhythm and blues, as in Great Britain and Australia."

Our American voice pours out of nature rather than buildings, and it may just as well be said to come from the spirit-filled camp meeting as from the devil at the crossroads. This dichotomy is a well-known one, and we see it most starkly in the cases of artists like Jerry Lee Lewis and Little Richard, both of whom sang in church as youths and came to denounce rock as Satan's music after it had made them their fortunes. Other singers, though, including Mavis Staples and Sharon Jones, say that all music is God's music, that any music which makes people of every race, gender, color and age get up and dance together can't be bad. Other, more secular writers, such as Greil Marcus, author of *The Shape of Things to Come: Prophecy and the American Voice*, approach rock 'n' roll as though it is something like inspired utterance, that is to say, revelation.

What tools, then, do our electrified prophets use as they reveal to us the secrets of our minds and hearts? Writers are always told to be concrete, to appeal to the senses, to use imagery. That's good advice. But every true axiom has its equally true opposite; compare "Absence makes the heart grow fonder" and "Out of sight, out of mind." If the concrete is good, then the vague must be just as valuable. In *What Good Are the Arts?*, John Carey argues that one of great literature's chief virtues is actually indistinctness, as when Shylock speaks of "a wilderness of monkeys" or Caliban of the "noises, / Sounds, and sweet airs" that fill the isle or Macbeth of the "Good things of day" versus "night's black agents." Carey praises "nonsense" language: Carroll's "the slithy toves / Did gyre and gimble in the wabe" and Dickinson's "The doom's electric moccasin" and "Like rain it sounded till it curved," though I prefer "Diadems—drop—and Doges—surrender—/ Soundless as dots—on a Disc of Snow—."

So much for poetry. Do not most songs rely on indistinctness? When Johnny Cash sings

> At my door the leaves are falling
> A cold dark wind has come
> Sweethearts walk by together
> And I still miss someone,

who does not see the lonely man looking out on an autumn evening, the light almost gone from the sky as lovers hurry by arm in arm, the leaves crunching under their feet as they hurry off to dinner or a party or a bedroom as he sees in the shadows the half-forgotten face and figure of someone he can barely stand to think of, someone whose name he can't utter for fear of the pain he can only hint at?

We don't know what happened to the man, the woman, the relationship; we don't know whether he done her wrong or she him or whether their love foundered because of one of the hundred ills that human pairings are heir to. But do we need to know? In *Will in the World: How Shakespeare Became Shakespeare*, Stephen Greenblatt says *Hamlet* was a breakthrough for the playwright because, whereas he'd written tragedies before, here he used "a new technique of radical excision. . . . Shakespeare found that he could immeasurably deepen the effect of his plays, that he could provoke in the audience and in himself a peculiarly passionate intensity of response, if he took out a key explanatory element, thereby occluding the rationale, motivation, or ethical principle that accounted for the action that was to unfold. The principle was not the making of a riddle to be solved, but the creation of a strategic opacity. This opacity, Shakespeare found, released an enormous energy that had been at least partially blocked or contained by familiar, reassuring explanations."

So we don't know why Hamlet behaves the way he does, just as later, we don't know why Iago hates Othello so much or Lear and Cordelia behave so perversely. And far from being a lapse on the author's part or a problem for the reader, that lack of knowledge is an indispensable virtue, a necessity for artistic enjoyment. Do these omissions not establish what Wolfgang Iser calls the "fundamental asymmetry" of all successful art works, an imbalance created by the artist who leaves gaps in the work so that the reader can have the pleasure of filling them?

If it sounds as though we have strayed too far from rock's quick and dirty shouts to the farther reaches of abstruse literary theory, consider this passage from Ann Marlow's memoir *How to Stop Time*:

> Rock is about not having enough time to think or find your bearings, certainly not enough time to procrastinate or rationalize. This is one major reason it's been condemned as mindless music, assuming the equivalence of the superego and mindfulness. But Western philosophy began in haste, with the simulation of rapid-fire argument in the dialogues of Plato I spent so much time analyzing in college and grad school. And most of the philosophical writing I like shares with rock qualities of brevity, speed and directness. Descartes, Wittgenstein, Nietzsche, Adorno and Plato were never easy, and rarely unambiguous, but they went straight to the point. They have a quality of motion shared by every great rock song.

Brevity, speed, directness are essential tools for both the near-sighted scholar dipping his pen in an inkwell and leather-clad punkette with a guitar slung almost to her knees, as they are for a painter like Jackson Pollock or just about any playwright except Eugene O'Neill. The creator throws down and moves on; the audience finishes the job.

Consider Bob Dylan, arguably the most enigmatic though, at the same time, the most successful songwriter of our time. Even when he's making sense, he doesn't, as a leisurely amble through *Bob Dylan: The Essential Interviews* reveals. Interviewer after baffled interviewer tries to pin him down, but Dylan prefers to gyre and gimble in the wabe: "I have an idea that it's easier to be disconnected than to be connected," says our greatest master of reinvention, which is why, after one questioner begins by noting "I don't know whether to do a serious interview or carry on in that absurdist way we talked last night," Dylan tells the simple truth when he replies, "It'll be the same thing anyway, man."

It'll be the same thing because Dylan is, like all the great songwriters, is a true reincarnation of the Sibyl, that prophet or witch revered by the ancients for her powers of divination. She gained her power, of course, by *not* dealing from the top of the deck: the greatest of this sisterhood was the Sibyl of Cumae, who, as Virgil tells us, would set down her utterings on oak leaves and spread them at one of the mouths of her cave, to be picked up and read or scattered by the winds to be seen no more, whichever came first.

It is she who tried to sell the nine books consisting of her gathered sayings to King Tarquin the Elder, and when he scoffed at the price she demanded, hurled three of them into the fire, and then three more when he turned her down again, until finally the King's advisers told him he must meet her original price, even though there were only three books left. The three books revealed that the sibyl could indeed predict the future of Rome, so the king begged her to rewrite the other six. No, she said, you've chosen your destiny; I can't change that.

Heeby Jeebies

American pop music, in all its variety, does not reflect American life so much as it refracts it, concentrating the diffuse light of daily existence into the concentrated radiance of art. From the beginning, the American pop song reveals a sense of personal displacement that is presented more as a fact of life than a misfortune. If you read the headlines, you know that not very many of us out there seem to feel at home in our own skin.

The political founders of America, men like Thomas Jefferson, Benjamin Franklin, and John and Samuel Adams, were followers of Locke and other Enlightenment figures and thought humankind capable of tolerance, democracy, and reason. They were right, of course, if only partially so. The mindset that we encounter in pop music accounts for everything the Enlightenment overlooks: perversity, strangeness, a sense of not knowing where one is or how one got there.

That sense of dislocation explains why the best pop songs *can't* make sense. Take Sam Cooke's "A Change Is Gonna Come." The quintessence of Cooke's art and life, "A Change Is Gonna Come" is ostensibly a protest song he wrote during the civil rights turbulence of the early sixties. Like all of his songs, though, the simple, three-chord arrangement and elemental lyrics—"I was born by the river in a little tent"—reveal more than they seem to at first, especially the verse where he sings, "I go to the movies / And I go downtown / Somebody keep telling me / Don't hang around." Who tells him, though? A girl? A cop? Himself? Cooke once told protégé Bobby Womack, "Bobby, if you read, your vocabulary, the way you view things in a song—it'll be like an abstract painting; every time you look back, you'll see something you didn't see before." You can listen to "A Change Is Gonna Come" a hundred times, and it'll never sound the same, because a good song is like a painting in which you see new meanings every time you look.

When the first all-girl punk band the Slits say "Fuck you," they're really saying "Why not," as Greil Marcus writes in *Lipstick Traces: A Secret History of the Twentieth Century*. In rock's secret meanings lies its power: when Malcolm McLaren, who would later manage the Sex Pistols, heard a fellow student sing "Great Balls of Fire" in a grammar school talent show, he recalls that "I'd never heard anything like it—I thought his head was going to come off." And here's how Pete Townsend of the Who characterizes the power of rock:

> Mother has just fallen down the stairs, dad's lost all his money at the dog track, the baby's got TB. In comes the kid with his transistor radio, grooving to Chuck Berry. He doesn't give a shit about mom falling down the stairs. . . . It's a good thing you've got a machine, a radio that puts out rock and roll songs and it makes you groove through the day. That's the game, of course: when you are listening to a rock and roll song the way you listen to "Jumpin' Jack Flash," or something similar, that's the way you should really spend your whole life.

No wonder the grownup world worried about Elvis: if, as Greil Marcus says, real life meant "the pleasurable consumption of material goods within a system of male supremacy and corporate hegemony," the kids wanted something else entirely—or thought they did, which was good enough to get rock 'n' roll out of a few scattered clubs and into every American living room.

What do the kids want? They don't know: any pop musician can say, as blues singer Johnny Shines did, "The public don't know they want it, but they know there's something that they want from me. Otherwise they wouldn't be climbing onto me. . . . I know it's the next thing. I got the thing that they want. They just don't know what it is."

One of the most powerful lyrics in rock history comes in the first verse of Smiley Lewis's "One Night of Sin," where the repentant vocalist confesses that "The things I did and I saw /Would make the earth stand still." What are those things? A fourteen year-old kid wouldn't know, but from an adult perspective, it sounds as though the singer was involved in a scene of Old Testament pagan proportions: an orgy, maybe, or at least painful and violent sex fueled by booze or uppers or just the take-no-prisoners savagery of the id. Now a teen wouldn't say any of that, but he might say the song makes him think of something like freedom. No wonder, in Elvis's version, where "one night with you" is substituted for "one night of sin," the evening in question is what the singer is "praying" rather than "paying" for, and the joyful horror of the first verse is wiped away when he says that "The things that we two could plan / Would make my dreams come true."

At its best, rock's too big, too magical, too scary to go unsupervised. When the sloppy garage-band anthem "Louie Louie" broke into the top ten in 1963, the song was banned on many radio stations because of the supposed profanity of lyrics which graphically depicted sex, according to the kids who, like me and my friends, "translated" the band's mumblings and passed them from desk to desk in study hall. The FBI even became involved, though the agency's thirty-one-month study concluded with a report that investigators were "unable to interpret any of the wording in the record."

So what is Little Richard saying when he shouts "A WOP BOP A LOO MOP A LOP BAM BOOM!"? The same thing the Slits are saying when they shout "Fuck you!" In the seventies, of course, four white girls from London could say what couldn't be said in the fifties by a gay black cripple in Georgia. According to the Macon meistersinger, "I was washing dishes at the Greyhound bus station at the time. I couldn't talk back to my boss man. He would bring all these pots back for me to wash, and one day I said, 'I've got to do something to stop this man bringing back all these pots to me to wash,' and I said, 'A wop bop a loo mop a lop bam boom, take 'em out!'" In other words, why not?

Peter Johnson

Bad Behavior

When will the cops, asleep or gliding down asphalt pavements, get the call? When will children be taken away? . . . A little thing, an episode: many drinks, a few pills, a bit of playful grappling. Later, they made love when she was half-asleep, or maybe unconscious. He's not sure. This confession, over a mean cup of java in an understated coffee house, when we should be at the zoo, watching our children mimic a penguin's walk. "She's my ex-wife," he says. "We'll laugh about this later. She may not even remember." He let himself go when he moved out, abandoning his Bowflex and West-Coast diet books. No more barbecues in the backyard where we'd all drink wine and watch four-year-old boys lunge at each other with Styrofoam swords. No more roasting marshmallows over a jerry-built brazier. I want to tell him I'm not the concierge, nor do I have the key to the secret garden. And I'm still waiting for the *Grammar of Marriage* book to arrive. And yes, she'll be angry, though mostly at herself, and every time I see her, I'll look away, or stare into my Palm Pilot, which is really my palm, hoping for directions on how to behave, or how not to.

The New York School Poem

I had a favorite poet until he kept writing about his friends, Beau and Binkie, how they got drunk and tweezered hair from their noses, then thought they discovered a new way to make love, not realizing the Neanderthals had invented it. Yeah, I liked this poet until he described how Gloria got knocked up by Chrétien, who mainlined heroin into his temple while "Walk on the Wild Side" blared in the background, and how Chrétien survived, so Rashid wrote a song about it, which he'd chant at the end of Chrétien's readings. Boy, I would have liked this poet more if he hadn't felt obliged to write about Mahi's depression memorabilia, which he stole from scenes of real suicides, or about how Joanie, after a near-death experience, believed the best part of her had come back as a car alarm, or if he'd just been happy to be another Bukowski, a drunk who didn't care if anyone read his poems, and who despised his friends and ex-girlfriends even more than his friends and ex-girlfriends did.

Julie Suk

Each Day the Hand

Each day the one hand washes its brother,
fingers finding a momentary link,
though we live one place, and dream another—

maybe to escape what we might uncover.
I didn't mean to! the man shouts at the sink,
one hand washing blood from its brother.

Aim, shoot to kill, is the given order.
The second round is easier than you think
if you live one place, and dream another.

Say, in our lives we prefer to wander
without thought of the ruin left in our wake.
Night comes, and each hand must wash its brother.

Once by default I lost a son and daughter,
lost heart during their prodigal way back.
I lived one place, they dreamed another.

Each day I reason with nightmare and order,
ranging here, there, in a world out of sync.
Each day one hand washed its brother
while I dream one place, and live another.

Therefore, Mortal, Prepare
for Yourself an Exile's Baggage

Ezekial 12:3

Hard words, old man.
I want to hear what I don't necessarily believe.

Tell me the life I'm leafing through now
has a spectacular end—pushed out ablaze,
weeping and wailing on shore, my final words sizzling.

Never mind that the living turn toward tomorrow,
Hurry! The day's on the table, and getting cold.

Tell me scraps of memory last
longer than the people who pass them on.

Tonight the moon hangs so close I swear
it could drop into my arms.

This heart still fibrillates despite the rational ribs.

I don't want to hear what I know is true
that Voyager, with a capsule of me and you, wanders
in a fathomless sea, no handouts, no drawing ashore.

The stars with no one on board have nothing to lose.

I do.
My luggage was packed soon as the world took me in
touching everything mine I believed I owned.

Judith Hall

Lost Songs

Once was a song—and you know a dozen, noise,
Zealots demanding a head in the sand,

      Born-again badges
      And gadgets and baggage—

Who knows a song for agnostics?

         ∾·

An out-and-out doubt shout?

      Go find uncertainties
      In perpetuity—to flout—

      And rosters of scoff
      And incredulity?

         ∾·

Who knows a song with a skeptical tree,
A willow that laughed caustic and saucy?

      Unknowable willow!
      A wallow of old

Reliable doubts. A song for agnostics?

The Crowded Tree

However, whenever whispered, whatever said,
Prayers blow out the windows
And tangle on
The way to heaven in a tree.

Some sound like leaves: Brittle: Wishes: Please.

Some boast, swinging on a golden pail
Among the lightest, scentless fruit.
No reason why.
What is above the head smells divine.

Most never rise above a tree. Demands,
Woven whatnots, green the
Grief, white, denial,
Snag in, why not, lavender nests.

Not yet: Tedious begging twig embedded.

Hope against hope against crows,
Shiny as officious chimeras,
Possibilities,
Going nowhere: So far.

Annie Boutelle

Passage

How could they know how far to the gate?

Or how near, earth unsteady under their bare feet?

It had something to do with light, slicing the branches.

How to see sky with so many leaves in the way?

How to trust it was there?

She complained about her ankle. Puffed up, as if an adder
    had bitten it.

And the leaves chattering among themselves, passing on the news.

He wrapped it in ferns, tied it with vines. All night he stroked it.

Juice

She used her fingernails, peeled peaches, bit off chunks, and fed them to him.

He was suspicious of all fruit.

She rained tears.

He thought he would always remember how they fell, determinedly, as if to punish him, as if they'd never stop.

They made rivulets down her dusty breasts, and when they dried, her body was a map.

She hated that he felt nothing.

Birds sang the same old songs.

It annoyed her intensely.

Even if she died, he wouldn't shed a tear.

Cartoon

They stumbled now, nothing but names to guide them.

His nose stuffed up, allergies kicking in.

And how could a red nose and a swollen ankle find a gate?

Cartoon characters in stupid fog.

Strip off a name, and what's left?

He used names as markers, a way to control the day.

Light trembling on thorns, sliding along the branch.

Fish meant quickness.

Worm meant laughter.

Stone meant justice.

She wearied of his voice.

He could go on forever.

She didn't give a hoot about the names.

Future

Something about the way the light would change.

Something about how the darkness would marry it.

He pitied her. He thought he pitied her.

There would be a gate, or perhaps a tunnel.

An entrance, or an exit.

Her swollen ankle would take it in stride.

His eyes bent away from hers, reflection in a river,
  hovering close.

He didn't mind finding new ferns to wrap and tie.

She thought it would be an exit.

First, light.

Then nothing but dark.

He made a grass pillow for her.

He thought it would be an entrance.

She supposed it meant he loved her.

River

They lack direction.

A few tentative steps forward, then the predictable faltering.

How hard, after all, to let gravity and physics dictate?

Who can teach them to be liquid and pulled?

They are so stolid, so determined.

A bank can be a useful thing: it sets limits.

They look inside their own space.

They should be looking out.

No matter how often I call their names, they never answer.

They need to acknowledge they are not that important.

Tirelessly I whisper the background music of each dream.

They think they have the answers.

It is because of me that they sleep well.

Kristen Tracy

State Lines

Geese fly and refuse to honor them.
White-tailed deer graze unequally
on both sides of the boundary. But I've
had to decide, time after time, and declare
a street address, a spot I am now
stitched to by my never-ending mail.
I owe so much. Envelope after envelope,
a steady flow. I understand why some
delinquents blow the box up. Dead flames
send me letters and their clumsy sentences stick
to my thumbs. How many times can you leave
the same woman? That question doesn't
shame me. Even in heartbreak, it's not uncommon
to crave abundance. Luckily, I think I've found
my next speck of hope. New state after new state.
My heart a fist of twine. I can't surrender.
The clock ticks. Empty suitcase, where have I
stuffed you? Forget grace. The rabbit darts
over the open road. Rain clouds gather. A man
sits in his kitchen overlooking a seacliff,
eating a piece of toast. Who wouldn't go?
Who wouldn't risk tossing herself into the brick
wall? What woman wouldn't drop her whole life
into a basket, plow into the dark, and run?

Manuscript

First, I tried building you out of bees.
Everybody said, That will never work.
But neither their doubts nor the tremendous
buzz could deter me. Then bees throughout America
began dying out—wild bees, rooftop bees,
bees in fields sealed in white boxy hives—and I thought
it best to change course. I pursued
elephants. No, not as a metaphor. I went
after the actual great-trunked beast. The zoo
became my home. Peanut shells surrounded me.
My mouth filled with salt. And soon,
the zookeeper, a rule-breaker, led me
behind the rail. They plodded right in front of me,
rubbery and gray. I could have burst.
But then I was told that I could never touch
the elephants. Lawsuits. And I got bored.
Book, you became a snooze. I could have
burned you. But I'm not a cliché. Besides that,
I was absent any decent flame and I was hopeful—I had
a loaf of bread. So I ate it underneath the moon
and discovered, like a seizure, my new aim.
Pluto. We think it's a planet, but it's not
like that. It's something lesser. Something
gassy. I pecked for days. Weeks. A bird outside
my window broke its wing. Peck. Peck. Months.
A year. A lot of my meaning hinged on
circumference. I surprised myself by what
I found next to Pluto in my own
black holes. But Pluto is so cold and
distant. At times, circling well beyond
Neptune. Even through a telescope, it's one
of many measly dots. Book, I thought
I'd never make you. I considered learning
to play the harp instead. Because that
would take every finger I had and possibly
my feet. Pluck. Pluck. Feel like cream. I almost

scheduled a lesson. But then came help.
A famous poet. Who had written many
good books about childhood and what came
after. I taped you up in a box and stuck you
in the mail. Week after week. I thought of you
fanned across his khaki lap. When his letter
came, it said that he was uncertain about
where my lines broke, and he had more serious
concerns about where they ended altogether. He didn't
mention the bees or the elephants or any
of the multiple planets I'd so aggressively explored.
His letter was brief. It closed: Call me. Oh book,
I thought everything hung in the balance. Your fate.
My ego. When I finally called, there was polite chat
about boisterous ping-pong games being held
in his garage. And how both of us were looking forward
to our separate trips to Canada. All that open space.
Then, book, came you. He said: The poems are
a little glib. I said: Maybe there's a market
for that. He said: We're talking about poetry here.
And I said: Right.

Peter Cooley

A Kind of Chinese Aubade

For Zoe Yu

The Seven Wonders of the World are here
in every one of us awakening
as I am, these lines coming to me fast,
then slow, like clouds of the opening dawn.

My friend sent me this postcard of a print
by Changfen of the Great Wall of China.
In the foreground the wall runs like a road
as if the photographer had stood
where heaven descended to catch the rock
not as enclosure but revelation.
Behind it all, a sea of thunderclouds.

Telling you this—it's brought me to my feet.
My palms lift, upward. What should I do next?

Poem Written by Me after My Death

Against the light, Death crossed the street with me
mid-June, New Orleans blue afternoon.
After the downpour a few minutes back
the sun began a second kind of rain:
radiance, transcendence, a second chance
such as we have within this earthly life
again and again. I had an ecstasy
trembling head to foot, my body all light.
And then, just as I started to jaywalk,
no traffic in sight, the way cleared for him,
I saw Death, smiling at me from his side,
the street between us, empty as I said,
everywhere. He looked exactly like me
as you last saw me, reader, my last day, yesterday.

Bruce Beasley

Valedictions

little missives against your going

—Oh Xenos
oh Nowhere-Near, who knew we'd be divisible

so evenly
with no carried-over

remainder

—The wheels retract and newly
de-iced, sleet-
hit wings
shiver now into the arc
of your casting-out,

thy going unenough

—I am to you a currency
devalued, then defunct
then collectable among
cabinets of curiosity, some
access-forbidden archival vault

—Insomniac, what aubadal
song when you don't wake

having unslept

what shred
of snatching-you-
back-from-night

clung in my hand

—Have you continued to feel
filaments of chill

Are the utterative possibilities already exhausted
Do even questions leave

not any more their mark

—What is this thing
between us, its
morph and drip and fang

its escape and stompings-yon, its
ill-understood
agon and undemise

—You are to me as what's made
in love is
to the humdrum means of its production

—If we could make ourselves some housed
and inhuddled figurines, prayer-
poised toward each other, some
shrine we haven't figured
out yet
how to erect

148

—Little uncancellable voice of four A.M.

A permanent intermission
will follow this closing act

There will be no further announcements. Listen, hard

—Away
from speech, *apo-*

logize, are we
now at apogee

that orbit point
most recoiled

from what draws in

"*Apo-* marks things

detached or separate"
so cast

away from me, abide
with me: let's each

apologize, all disattached
(as we must be now)

from speech

—Death-sentence me

like the lichen splotched on fir limbs
that spells out the wood's inner
irreversible process of decay

—Are we like the blistered surface of a crepe
as the batter
settles to the quiver and shrink
of the last wet white at the core

—Some Documents of Separation
unfileable, uncertifiable
their edges singed, their broken
contract language melted inward, word
ashcrumbling over charred word

—Half hymns, these, a quarter snarl, an eighth at least
the shrilling pitch of gnat and gnat
and gnat lost someplace deep inside your ear

—You were to me as trout-mouth
was to lure, to temporary air

You *are* to me   caesural

—These missives you won't read
missals

we don't pray
Let's write this

divisibility

off, as
if our losses

were only on paper

—Still the little wintersquall-
scuttled ferryboats between us

Do not forget to shutter the storm windows
Do not forget to gather
what children there
still are
in

Erica Levy McAlpine

The Sandhill Crane

When he decided to weather the early frosts,
and outstay fallen leaves all turned to mulch,
and graze our lawn in paces with his neck
looped back, his head protruding forward,
both wings flapping over every step as if he were
a farmer driving a herd, shuffling stray things
into place, and always with his beak upturned,
like when a stifled feeling rises in the throat,
and one claw tucked up in his down at the sight of us
to pluck and preen and give his crown a shake,
we called it luck, his staying on to nest
among our pines (the dogwoods were out of season
but the pines were evergreen), so when he later
disappeared one cold December morning
filled with snow and ice, our best defense
was holding on to what we call migration,
that what is beautiful and gone has merely flown.

C. Dale Young

The Bridge

I love. Wouldn't we all like to start
a poem with "I love . . ."? I would.
I mean, I love the fact there are parallel lines
in the word "parallel," love how

words sometimes mirror what they mean.
I love mirrors and that stupid tale
about Narcissus. I suppose
there is some Narcissism in that.

You know, Narcissism, what you
remind me to avoid almost all the time.
Yeah, I love Narcissism. I do.
But what I really love is ice cream.

Remember how I told you
no amount of ice cream can survive
a week in my freezer. You didn't believe me,
did you? No, you didn't. But you know now

how true that is. I love
that you know my Achilles heel
is none other than ice cream—
so chilly, so common.

And I love fountain pens. I mean,
I just love them. Cleaning them,
filling them with ink, fills me
with a kind of joy, even if joy

is so 1950. I know, no one talks about
joy anymore. It is even more taboo
than love. And so, of course, I love joy.
I love the way joy sounds as it exits

your mouth. You know, the *word* joy.
How joyous is that. It makes me think
of bubbles, chandeliers, dandelions.
I love the way the mind runs

that pathway from bubbles to dandelions.
Yes, I love a lot. And right here,
walking down this street,
I love the way we make

a bridge, a suspension bridge
—almost as beautiful as the
Golden Gate Bridge—swaying
as we walk hand in hand.

The Argument

To T.G.

There is an inky darkness in certain old paintings
used, for lack of better technique, to add depth.
Of course I would notice it. Of course, you would
notice that I notice it. It wouldn't be the first time.

It is a fault. I am certain of that. But I can only hope
that recognition is the first step toward correcting this.
One could whine here and state, for the record,
how difficult it is to see the gold light clinging

to things when one lives a life attending to darker
things. But you, old friend, will not let me whine,
will not accept such a facile response from me.
So, let us agree to disagree about my faults.

There is a moment in the early morning when
the sun is not yet visible but the light is visible,
a tint of it, perhaps, advancing down the hillside.
It is my frightened hour before I don the white

lab coat, before I enter the halls of the hospital.
Always there is relish and dread at the same time.
How can I explain this to you who believe I am
incapable of tenderness in my art? I could lie

but I won't. I see darkness in the timbre
of your voice, even when you are excited,
even as your face lights up with the story of
serendipity, of how Whitman's *Leaves of Grass*

found its publisher. The shadow? I cannot help
but trust it more than the object itself. One sees
what one is meant to see. And darkness is,
I fear, an older friend. Let us leave it at that.

In the frightened hour before I don the white lab coat,
anything is possible, anything. I could return upstairs
and refuse to get dressed. I could refuse to check
with the answering service. And that, my friend

would be darkness. Tenderness? How would you
define that? I define it this way: the care to address
another's concerns with the same exacting care one expects
for themselves. And is this not dark? It has always been dark.

Tony Barnstone

The Trinity Test

We all came out to Trinity
(the name was Oppenheimer's bright
idea—for some fellow's poem,
Batter my heart, three-person'd God,
that one) and right by base camp we
lay in the dirt, ten miles from ground
zero, and watched the shot through dark
glass like they use in welders' helmets.

I couldn't look at first but felt
heat on my temple. When I turned
at last, through the dark welding glass
I saw ballooning up a flaming
planet that glowed inside dull red
and folded in upon itself,
like bread dough in a mixing bowl.
It held to earth by a dark stem.

Somebody said, "My god!" and we
all felt relief. We cheered and went
about and shook each other's hands.
And then the ground shock hit us hard,
and the sound echoed off the hills
back and forth for a long time.
A hush. Someone said, "Well, it worked."
And then we talked of other things.

(Scientist, Trinity Test, July 16, 1945)

Holocausts of Water and Fire

You can't say I liked killing kids.
I told myself: treat beasts as beasts.
It's most regrettable but true.
Think of Pearl Harbor and their murder
of prisoners. The A-bomb spoke
a language they would understand,
I reasoned. But I fear machines
have outpaced morals; when this race
is done there'll be no reasons left.
We're termites in the planet's crust.
We bore too deeply in the earth
to find its secrets. There'll be
a reckoning before we're done.

The Hebrew visionaries said
the world would die in holocausts
of water and of fire, first rains,
and Noah and his fabled Ark,
and then the world would die in flames
and spin through space inert and dark.
The fire holocaust has come.
We made a bomb more terrible
than any bomb in history.
It was the worst thing ever made.
Monstrous. But it could be of use.

(Harry Truman)

Enola Gay

1. The Pilot's Tale

In the plane's glass nose the whole sky
lit up the beautifulest blue
you ever seen, bright blue, but I
didn't react when the bomb blew.
Not right away. Then I turned round
and saw the cloud of boiling dust
bubbling upwards from the ground
where I guess Hiroshima must
have been, and felt the silver fillings
in my teeth, shocking me. They sent
the chills all through me, boots to hair.
We wiped 'em out. And as for killing
the ones they say were innocent—
that's their tough luck for being there.

(Pilot, Enola Gay)

2. The Bombardier's Tale

I called out "Bomb away," but didn't know
what kind of bomb it was we dropped that day.
A minute later the shock wave rocked the plane
and then Paul banked us so that we could see
the ground like boiling tar, a mass of rubble
that flowed in all directions outwards to
the docks and mountains. I'm awful sorry
lots of people died, but it was war.
I don't feel guilty. Through nine miles of sky
no one could tell a soldier from a child.

(Bombardier, Enola Gay)

Milk Run

We thought it was just a milk run
but we hit black flak once we shed
our load and watched it drop like rain,
and I saw Al's red chest and dead
white eyes and jumped as the plane spun
off. I was the youngest one, a babe
in arms. That's why I tried to run.
But that was all a hopeless stab
in the dark. See, where could I run
that wouldn't be Japan? They caught
me in some kind of old-style ruin
and I gave up. Should I have fought
them all? Come on. Then later, in
the camp I was in a wood cell
right next to Cap, God bless him,
and we whispered all night to tell
what news we knew through the bars. Hey,
where's Tom? Where's so and so? I asked.
It kills me what he had to say:
it was just me got out the back
of that damn plane. We lived with lice
and open sores that wouldn't heal
and only little bites of rice
to eat, with giant rats, and holes
that let in light and rain. They made
us piss and crap in a wood pot.
They beat us every day. We faced
our deaths because we wouldn't talk.
The officers would threaten to
slice off our heads with samurai
swords. I don't blame them, much. To do
what the Japs did—it was the times.

But gee whiz, when the A-bomb set
us free it was, *hip, hip, hooray!*,
hats in the air and no regrets.
Yessiree, that was one grand day.

(American Prisoner of War)

Rosie the Riveter

I do recall the atom bomb,
and I recall how glad we were
that day. Because the men were gone
to war, me and the gals repaired
planes at the base. Some days we'd rivet,
or else we'd clean the glass and blood
from out the cockpits, knowing that
it could be from a friend or loved
one—that was hard—and then we sent
them out again. How did I feel
about the Japs? Well, by the end
of that big war I could of kneeled
them in a row and shot them all
myself. That's why we all were dancing
when that bomb dropped. That's why we all
threw parties. Everyone was dancing.

(Riveter, American Airbase)

The Pit

The men who volunteered to cut off heads
were shocked by Hiroshima, and by the burned
cities. I helped because my wife was dead.
She burned alive. The captured pilots earned
this death. In a blank field, stripped to their shorts.
they watched us, blear-eyed. I think they knew it
before they saw the hole to hold their corpses.
We put on blindfolds, kneeled them by the pit.
I killed four, with a borrowed sword. To strike
just right is difficult. The neckbone stops
the blade. But Satano in one fast stroke
cut his off clean. We tried Karate chops
on them for practice, buried head and trunk
below the shallow dirt. Then we got drunk.

(Japanese Officer, Western Army Headquarters)

The Man Who Won the War

Grandfather never spoke about the war
but people say he won it, worked for Boeing
inventing ways to speed production for
the flying fortresses. The young men going
to die in planes could be replaced, but not
the planes, not fast enough. He didn't choose
to be the man who won the war. He taught,
"Believe in Jesus, just in case." He used
to quiz us, "Why did Xerxes cry?" We said,
"He was the greatest king alive, but knew
within a century he would be dead
and every living person would be too."
Like the young men who went to die in planes.
Like grandfather. He gardened in the rain

in his great backyard jungle, grew tomatoes
large as melons. I always wondered what
he put in them, this millionaire with clothes
he bought at Goodwill, this Harvard man cut
from Southern, racist cloth, who yet refused
to give them one red cent because no Jew
would be let in. He went so blind, he used
a magnifying glass to peer into
our faces, asking with his awful breath,
"Which one are you?" And yet he still would drive
with all the kids and swerve around our death
while we yelled, "Hit the brakes!" "Watch out!" We lived.
He never flew in planes. Not out of guilt.
It was because he knew how they were built.

(Young Woman, Yacolt, Washington)

Fred G. Leebron

The Idiot, or Life in Wartime

I.

It was hard to wrap the chains around himself as he sat in his car in the parking garage, and even harder to account for the baby. He hadn't planned on the baby; the baby had been the great invention of his unconscious; and now as he turned it around and around he could see the many ways the baby would work to his advantage and the definite ways he would not.

He thought of how prisoners were sometimes shackled like this, twined around both groins, encased at the waist. It was an art he had had to study just so that he could walk.

He levered himself from the car. He must now weigh thirty more pounds, but he'd lost thirty pounds for this (how thin you're getting, his wife had said. For you, he'd replied, and kissed her.). And he'd stood in front of a mirror and practiced with sissel rope while downstairs the baby napped.

"Oh, honey," he said, gently reaching in and unbuckling Sam from the car seat. "It's time to go see the White House."

"Mommy coming home?" Sam said. It was what he always said whenever he woke from a nap.

"Soon," Carl said. After all, if he said five minutes or five hours, the response was always the same—the baby howled. But soon—soon always worked.

He'd allowed enough space to fit the baby within the chain metal net, and now he dipped him in. Sam was snug against his chest. He could feel the rapid heartbeat against his sternum, and Sam's head sunk deeply into his shoulder. It was only yesterday that, inexplicably, as Carl sat on the couch reading the newspaper the baby had climbed up into his lap and started kissing his face, like a moment of conviction, as if he'd finally decided he loved him even if he wasn't Mommy. Where would they be in ten hours, in twenty hours, in twenty months?

Up in the waning light of late afternoon, he clanked along with the baby, his oversized winter coat making them look like a harmless genetic mistake huddled against the cold. Sam was an act of genius. Without him, no doubt, Carl would have looked like he was carrying a bomb.

He was careful not to bump into anyone on the wide sidewalk of Pennsylvania Avenue. The White House fence went on and on. On one hand it looked like he could stop anywhere, and in an instant change everything for himself for once and for all. He gave a frantic tug on the loose draw, tightening his attachment to the baby. Sam whimpered but did not raise his head.

"Okay, baby," Carl soothed him. "Okay."

They passed the east entrance, moving as naturally as the two of them could move. He concentrated on staring straight ahead, past the concrete dividers and the thick metal pylons, to the next section of continuous fencing.

Somehow, thirty years ago, this kind of gesture had seemed significant, it had had an impact, but now he was beginning to see it as empty, futile, self-indulgent. Here was the fence, here was he. The problem was, he knew, he wasn't politically astute enough. Whenever his daughter, now thirteen, proclaimed that she was going to be President some day, he'd wonder, "Whatever would you want to do that for?" "Because I'm going to," she'd say, glaring at him as if not only were he simple but weak. He sighed heavily and leaned back against the fence. How ironic the ease with which he did this, right here on Pennsylvania Avenue.

The truth was he didn't want to threaten anyone.

But power without the threat of violence wasn't power. It was nothing. That was what the whole problem was about. He was nothing. For years he'd accepted that he was just another professor at just another small college in the hinterland, while his brother had gone on to become a nationally renowned intellectual and his oldest friends had left him behind for Hollywood and Wall Street and Capitol Hill. Even now he didn't mind that he was nothing. What he minded was the war. He was sick of the practically casual and apparently acceptable violence, he was sick of watching some of his students go off so willingly into it. He'd sat with them in his office and watched them say that they wanted to go, that they were all for it, that it was a duty, an honor, something that they understood might happen from the beginning, before there even was a war. There always was a war, but he knew what they meant.

Tracy had been one of his favorite students. She had talked in class. She had handed in work before it was due, just to get a response and have a chance to make it better. She worked at the one bar he sometimes went to. She was six months from graduation. She changed the color of her hair every few weeks, it seemed. Even her boyfriend tried to persuade her to somehow resist. What was there to resist? Half of Tracy's platoon was going, and if she was in that half, that was absolutely fine by her. She was twenty-one years old. Now she was gone.

And then, just this morning, there was the kids' swim teacher from the Y, a skinny red-headed guy who looked fifteen or sixteen, but when Carl heard the news of the helicopter crash off the African coast, he instantly had a sick feeling in his gut, and at noon when he drove through the town square the flag was at half mast, and in the grocery store someone told him it had been Tim on that helicopter. Tim who had coaxed Max into the water when nobody else could, Tim who had put the tentative Elissa on his bony shoulders and engaged in a tender chicken fight during free swim. Damn that kid had been a nice kid. Carl hadn't even known he'd gone to war.

Goddamn it he was crying. What kind of man was he to stand here tearful and chained. A nonviolent man in a violent world. An idiot—a private person, a person without political affiliation—in a world where everyone had chosen sides. He'd never believed in choosing sides. He'd believed that there were always more sides than could be chosen. He'd always told his students in writing their papers that there were no rules, only principles, and every choice they made as arguers, as writers, involved weighing the principles against each other. Tracy had nodded her head at this. He liked being attracted to students—it gave him energy—but he'd never felt attracted to her. Now she was his first thought when he woke every morning, and his last thought when he tried to fall asleep each night. You couldn't stop her. You couldn't stop anything.

"Sir?"

He looked up. It was an officer in a white military cap with a black brim.

"Sir, I know the baby's sleeping, but you have to move on."

Goddamn they were so polite, goddamn they were so civil while they were off killing and being killed.

"I understand," Carl managed. He tried to smoothly separate himself from the fence but the weight saddling him—the weight of the baby, the weight of the metal, all the weight he'd been feeling for these last long goddamn years—gathered itself around him and pushed him back against the fence. He heard the odd mechanical sound just as the officer did. The brim turned surely back upon him, and just as surely Carl whipped the padlock from his pocket, caught the draw chain in his other hand, and as if he had practiced his whole life for this one meaningless gesture, locked himself into place on the White House fence.

"Sir!" the officer said sharply as something dull and black stuck its long snout at Carl. "Move away from the fence."

For the first time all day, all week, all month, all year, Carl felt absolutely clear-headed. He could see her again. Her hair was henna. He could see his wife in the kitchen, standing over the sink, wondering where the hell he was. Upstairs his daughter lay in her bed in her willfully chaotic room, reading a Tamora Pierce book with an iPod attached to her ears. Across the hall his son was playing Star Wars on PlayStation, his back tensed, his anger ready to launch itself against any intruder. Carl imagined he wouldn't be hearing that awful game for a long, long time. He loved his children, but he wasn't crazy about tending to them. Maybe he thought he'd get a rest in prison.

"Sir!" the officer commanded, and now there were a half-dozen officers with him, and Carl supposed he was to raise his hands or shout something vile or blow himself up. He looked for fear, in himself or in the young officer within three feet of him or within his colleagues grouped to either side of him, but there was no fear anywhere, even within him, which surprised him, though soon he imagined he might feel quite lonely and depressed. Soon he would feel worse. But not now. Not yet.

"I can't," he said.

There were sirens in his ears and sirens in his eyes, there was the baby's sleepy breath against his neck, there was all this metal he'd trussed himself up with. He was rooted to the spot. Everything felt a little tight. He tried to measure the baby's breathing. He was breathing fine. Nothing was too tight, nothing was too loose. It was just as he had planned and not as he had planned at all. He could have said, The war is wrong. He could have said, The President lied. It was more complex than that. It was better to say nothing and stand there and not see the cordoning off of the sidewalk and the leveling of the revolvers (revolvers? guns? pistols? automatic weapons?—he had experience with none of them) and the heated glaring of all the personnel so freshly descended upon him. He was going to be in a lot of trouble, he was in a lot of trouble. If he said anything—I'm not going to hurt anyone, I don't have a bomb—they could mishear him or not believe him. They might shoot him to save the baby, but the baby was right over his heart. A stroke of genius, the baby.

They were shouting things at him. He stared blankly at nothing. He could imagine what his mother would say. He could imagine how his brother might defend him. He could hear the exasperation of his one sister and the indifference of his other sister. At least his in-laws would probably be pleased. Hadn't his mother-in-law been screaming and throwing tomatoes right before she had gone into labor with his wife? He allowed a smirk to play on his lips. Perhaps it was the President's own smirk. Anything he said could be used against him. Anything he said could be misinterpreted. Anything he said would be reductive.

A military dog sniffed at him with disinterest. A long wand approached and swept him.

He was a pacifist, a peacenik, a protestor, a professor.

"You're in a heap of shit," someone said.

"Evans," someone else said.

"Is this a hostage situation?" said a third soldier—or a cop. You couldn't tell who was talking. There were too goddamn many of them.

He's my son, Carl wanted to say proudly. But he knew it was better not to talk. Now that he had acted, there was no need for talk. He was done talking, yet he had never talked. The fact that Sam was his son would mean nothing to these people. It occurred to him he should have made a sign. What would the sign have said? Stop the war. Too basic. It had all been said by everyone else. He felt himself slipping into nihilism. Not a good sign. There were no good signs now. Why had he done this?

"Daddy," Sam said. And from him wafted an instantly recognizable odor. "Want a fresh one."

Maybe the baby had not been such a good idea after all.

"He's clean," a smiling officer said. It wasn't even dark yet. It should have been nightfall, but it wasn't. He hadn't lasted ten minutes on this fence.

"You'll get one soon," Carl whispered to the baby.

"Now!" the baby whined. "Need one now."

I have made a very bad decision, Carl thought. It was like precipitating a car accident—the one last maneuver you shouldn't have taken—yet apparently so much worse than that. What had he meant to accomplish here? Across the street a few bright lights flicked on.

He could say, It's about the war. He could say, Bring our men and women home. He could say, Stop the lies. It had all been said. Was there no more eloquence?

"Daddy," his baby cried.

Was there really nothing to be done?

"Please," Sam said. "I want a fresh one."

"That's a good sentence, Sam," Carl murmured. "A really good sentence."

Hands were upon him. They'd moved in. "Give me the baby, pal."

"I can't," Carl said.

"Damn, he's locked in good."

They just wanted to sweep him away.

"You have the right—"

"Not now, you dumbass. Just get him off the fence, for Christ's sake."

"Daddy," Sam whimpered. "Please, Daddy."

"That's real nice, what you've done to your son there."

Carl tried to look past him. They were so in his face all he could see was skin and shadow.

With something like shears they snipped at his parka. It fell at his feet. The baby shivered.

"What about a blow torch?"

"Locksmith?"

"It's a combo."

"I bet you don't know the combo, do you?"

"That's correct," Carl said, trying to warm Sam with his breath and wincing at how professorial he sounded.

"Mr. Rivers?" His wallet was held to his face. "And this would be . . ."

"Sam," Carl said.

"Isn't that just perfect," someone said.

"Cold," Sam said.

"Fucking bolt cutters."

"Language!"

"Get those damn media people."

"We got 'em. We got 'em."

"No one's ever gonna see your face, Carl."

Carl just breathed with the baby. Behind him they commenced pounding and sawing at the lock and the chain.

"We could take him with part of the fence."

"Don't be so damn absurd."

Someone tucked a military blanket into Carl and the baby.

"Kid needs a diaper."

"No kidding."

Carl's teeth vibrated with whatever they were doing. The baby shivered and chattered.

"You guys getting anywhere?"

"Nope."

"We could tent him."

"Now there's an idea."

"Then we could . . . uh . . . proceed in . . . uh . . . privacy."

There was general laughter.

"Now don't you believe everything you read, Carl."

Somehow a yawn escaped him.

"You bored, Carl?"

"I can guarantee you Carl is not bored. Carl is scared."

A wall of canvas sprung up in front of him, around him.

"Welcome to Camp Fence, Carl."

"You boys knock it off." A guy in a tie stood eye to eye with him. "I'm Agent Wright, Professor Rivers. You have committed a crime on Federal property in the District of Columbia. Without a doubt you will be arraigned on several charges. Is there anything you wish to say?"

"The baby," Carl said.

"Oh the baby," Agent Wright said. He stroked his moustache. Carl hadn't thought facial hair was allowed. "Your wife is on the way down with your other two kids. And your mother-in-law should be here shortly. With any luck the baby will never see our custody."

"That's great," Carl said.

"Great?" Wright said. "Are we off our meds today, Carl? Or perhaps trying something new?"

Carl gave up a laugh. He wouldn't mind something new right now.

"You are aware, Carl, that this was all begun on our soil? You are aware that we didn't choose this conflict, that it chose us? You are aware that not five miles from here innocent people perished in a fireball?"

Behind him, at the fence, they continued hammering and cursing at the padlock and exposed chain link. His whole head reverberated with the pounding.

"I'm not reading your rights until I know exactly what I am arresting you for," Wright said. Then he read him his rights anyway. "Have you figured out what you want to say?"

"God no," Carl said.

"No one will ever hear it anyway." Wright glanced beyond Carl. "Any progress?"

"Hell no."

"Excuse me?"

"Hell no, sir."

"I was Navy," Wright said. "I fought in the first war."

"Thank you," Carl said.

"You're most welcome." Wright shoved his hands into his pockets. The baby was eerily quiet. "That is one scared kid."

Carl nodded.

"You realize how much simpler it would be without him?"

"Nothing is simple anymore," Carl said.

"You remember that when you registered back in seventy-nine you wrote C.O. on the little card?"

"Well—"

Wright pressed his nose practically up against Carl's cheek. "Wasn't that enough, Carl? Don't you know how much you're costing us here? Right now something dangerous could be happening somewhere, and you've gone and tied up twenty or fifty of our guys. That to me is the real crime, Carl."

That was not the whole point, but a good point, Carl thought.

"You think Sam here is ever going to forget any of this?"

"I hope not," Carl said.

"And what do you think Tracy's parents will have to say about this?"

"Nothing good," Carl admitted, trying to hide his shock at how quickly they already knew everything.

"Our intelligence is sometimes outstanding," Wright said, noting the surprise in Carl's eyes, "but of course that isn't always the story." A muscle swam in his face, close to his ear piece. "Your mother-in-law's here." He grinned at Carl. "Don't worry. We're not letting her in."

"I'd appreciate that," Carl said. His mother-in-law was okay, and he was grateful she was here to take the baby, but he didn't need to see her.

"I don't have a lawyer," Carl said. "Not really, anyway."

"Not a problem," Agent Wright said.

"Just some guy back in Pennsylvania who did the closing and our wills."

"But this wasn't spontaneous, was it, Carl?"

"I guess not," Carl said.

"Bingo!" one of the soldiers said, and the chains loosened around his groin.

Wright tugged gently at Sam, who began shrieking. "Get the mother-in-law," he barked.

She was brought in by two guys with white MP helmets. Carl could now see it was dark outside. For a moment bright lights splashed into the tall narrow tent.

"Grace," Carl said.

"Oh Carl," Grace said. She reached and Wright handed her the baby. "I—"

The MPs shuttled her from the tent.

"Visitors come later," Wright said.

They snaked the chain from his waist and chest. He was gripped very firmly and far more heavily than all that metal had.

"Drape him," Wright said, and they hooded him with a sheet of his parka. When he tried to move his hands they were already cuffed. "Time for a ride."

Carl heard Wright throw open the tent, and the light pierced what was left of his coat. He heard voices, people calling at him as if from a distant shore, half-phrases and nouns that he tried to make out as he was partly lifted and partly stumbled over the sidewalk to the curb.

"Why now?" a woman shouted.

"Look over here," a man ordered.

"Faggot!"

"Asshole!"

"They're loving you up," Wright said, as his hand cupped the top of Carl's head and ducked him into the back seat of a car. "Now scoot over so we can ride properly."

The fabric fell from his head as he banged against the far window. Lights flashed and he kept his eyes shut. They started out Pennsylvania in what seemed like a three-car parade. The window was wet. When had it started raining?

"Just what were you hoping to accomplish back there?" Wright asked, looking at his watch as if no answer would make any difference to him.

"I'm not sure," Carl said. "It was just a gesture."

"The best you could come up with?" Wright sighed. "Moral conscience needs more imagination than that."

"The march wasn't any better," Carl tried.

"Too many goddamn channels, is what it is." Wright gave Carl an apparently friendly elbow. "You can avoid seeing anything you want to avoid seeing, and usually you don't even know it's there." He nodded his head backward. "You'll probably end up on YouTube, for goodness sake."

"That wasn't the point," Carl said.

"But here is the point, Carl. This could have been the living room-bedroom-kitchen war, what with all those embedded personnel and all those televisions everyone has. But with seven hundred channels it's like the war's not happening. Just like we're living lives that aren't happening," Wright said.

Carl stayed silent.

"You don't take meds, do you?" Wright said.

"I drink," Carl said.

"He drinks!" Wright cheerfully acknowledged the driver up front for the first time. "Think we can slap you with a D and D? And can't we add an ex post facto DUI?"

"Not today," Carl said.

"All this courage and you're sober? You should have been a soldier, Carl."

The car swung down a steep grade and entered an underground lot.

"Well, we're almost home, Professor Rivers. I meant to ask you: You get good evals, Carl? I mean, if I looked you up on Rate Your Professor, what would I find?"

Carl just looked at him. The car squealed to a stop.

"I see our time is about up," Wright said, launching himself from the car and swinging back to pull Carl with him. Carl straightened himself under yellow light outside an all-window white-walled office. "I could say good luck to you, but I wouldn't mean it."

He led him into the basement office where three gentlemen stood waiting, apparently just for him. "These guys will take you through the rest of the night, and perhaps in the morning everything will be significantly clearer. Travis?"

Travis took him and Wright quickly stepped into an obedient elevator. "Lots of paperwork," he sighed, as the door closed on him.

"This way, Professor Rivers." Travis opened a door and he was led ever downward along a sloping windowless extremely well-lit corridor. Travis was so young he had that kind of acne, and his nose was glistening from a cold that he mopped at with a handkerchief in his free hand. Carl could have asked where they were going, but it wouldn't have made any difference, and Travis didn't appear nearly as talkative as Wright. The corridor seemed to go on and on.

"Your mother-in-law get your son all right?" Travis finally said.

"I believe so," Carl said.

"That's a good thing."

"It is. It is."

"You wouldn't want your son to be stuck in here with us. We really don't have the facilities."

"It was poor planning on my part," Carl agreed. He wished he could recall the excitement he felt when he first thought of the scheme, first envisioned himself chained to the gate, but back then he saw himself singlehandedly blockading the whole White House. Back then he saw it as an act. It was only an infinitesimal gesture. He'd known that, these last days, but he hadn't admitted it. He might as well have taken a dip into a pool of invisible ink and then given a speech in sign language. That's what the guys had meant when they'd said no one would see him. He'd made himself disappear.

"Here we are," Travis said, opening another door.

Inside were the requisite photographic equipment and observation rooms and a half dozen people milling about and no one bothering to look up. He was almost entirely irrelevant.

"Have a seat," Travis said, and sat him on a cold metal-framed chair.

Travis sat at a desk opposite and looked at a computer screen. He nodded behind Carl. "We'll get you into a room as soon as one opens."

"Sure," Carl said. So this kind of stuff happened all the time. Of course it happened all the time. And it was all swept under some giant textile of competent security and indifferent public reaction, unless there was some kind of celebrity or mystery or twist to it, preferably horrific or grotesque.

"Do you need a sip of water or anything?"

"No thank you."

In the silence he tried to hear what was going on behind him, above him, anywhere. He heard nothing. He wanted to ask some questions but he wasn't sure he'd like the answers—if any would be given. It was better to wait and not know. He thought there might be more hope in that. In an odd way, he still had a lot of faith in his country and he didn't think he had done anything truly terrible. He might be ignored but he doubted he'd be imprisoned, at least not for long. His whole point was he wasn't a threat. Now anybody could see that.

He sat there so long and became either so relaxed or so exhausted that he fell asleep. When he woke he was sitting in a different chair in a small room.

"You know where you are, Carl?" a new man said.

"Vaguely," Carl said. He wanted to rub his eyes of dust but he was still cuffed.

"Do you think you've been depressed lately? Do you have feelings of inadequacy? Any trouble sleeping?"

"All of the above," Carl said.

"Have you entertained thoughts of killing yourself?"

"God no."

"Why not?"

"The kids," he said. "And for the most part I like what I do and where I live and who I live with."

"Then why'd you throw it all away?"

"It was a statement." Carl shrugged. "A not very effective one, apparently."

"What are your thoughts about the President?"

"I try not to think about him."

"The Vice President?"

"I *don't* think about him." Although over Christmas he'd driven down to see where the Vice President lived. They had barricades that looked like monster snowplows, and men on bikes perched along the fence, smirking into walkie-talkies latched to their shoulders.

"Sure you don't." A scrap of glossy paper was slid across the desk to him. He felt ill before he even looked. It was a photograph of him staring intently as he drove past—they both knew what he was driving past. "You wouldn't believe our database," the agent said.

"So I'm not allowed to drive past the Naval Observatory?"

"Not looking like that. Not considering that you've done what you've done. You know what this shows, Carl? A pattern of behavior. A pattern of behavior that is of great interest to a lot of people."

"But I didn't *do* anything."

"You trespassed on Federal property. You breached Presidential security. You held a two-year-old child hostage. That's a lot, Carl."

"I want a lawyer," Carl said.

"This is a different kind of thing, professor. You should know that."

"What do I have to do?" Carl stared at him. "What do you want?"

"We want what's good for the country," the agent said. "What do *you* want, Carl?"

It was like dealing with an unhappy child and trying to figure out what would appease him.

"You know why laws exist, Carl?"

He hated that the agent always used his name. And of course he didn't know the name of this guy at all.

"To protect you, Carl."

"I know," Carl said.

"Why do you think you broke these laws that were meant to protect you, Carl?"

"Because I'm an idiot," Carl said.

The agent looked at him. Now Carl felt sufficiently awake to take in his handsome blandness, his non-descript, unremarkable features. The kind of face you wouldn't recognize again because it looked like everyone else's. His suit was navy blue, his shirt white and crisp, his tie red and blue stripes.

"Are you crazy, Carl? That's one question everyone is asking. Do you hear voices? Do you have a martyr complex? Do you feel people pay you too much attention or no attention at all?"

"I did something foolish and futile and inconsiderate. That's all."

"What were you thinking about when you drove by the Vice President's?"

"I don't know," Carl said. He suddenly was hit by a headache. It bloomed above his right eye and instantly stretched in a tight band around the inside of his head. "Is it still today? The rule is . . ." he tried to think through the pain. "The rule is seventy-two hours."

"In cases like this, there's a school of thought that thinks there might be no such rule."

"Have I been drugged? I've got a terrible headache."

"Goodness no."

"Sleep deprived?"

"Actually, you did sleep," the agent pointed out.

"Starved?"

"You haven't been here that long, Carl. How long do you think you've been here?" The agent looked at the window. "You'll get something to eat soon."

"What do I need to say to get out of here?"

"Come on, Carl. You committed a crime. Or two. Or three. It doesn't work that way."

"I hate the Vice President," Carl heard himself say.

"Okay."

"That's not against the law."

"It's a free country," the agent agreed.

"I don't own a single weapon."

"You own baking soda. You own vinegar. You own detergent. You own several tool kits. You have two cars. A garage full of newspapers and flammable liquids. A basement with four jars of terpentine. A stockpile of bottled water and canned food—"

"—We were told to!" Carl said.

"9/11," the agent said.

"9/11," Carl eagerly agreed. "My wife bought that stuff."

"What do you think of 9/11, Carl? Do you think it was our fault?"

"My first reaction," Carl admitted, "was that they wanted us to experience what life in their country every day was like."

"And?"

"And after the plane hit the Pentagon I realized it could be seen as an act of war."

"You agreed with Afghanistan."

"I agreed with Afghanistan. I have a student there."

"—Mitchell Phillips."

"Mitchell Phillips. He's all for it. But what happened to the football player was disgraceful."

"So you're not for Afghanistan anymore?"

"I don't know. I'm probably for killing Bin Laden."

"You want to kill him yourself."

"I've never killed anybody," Carl said.

"What's the closest you've ever come to doing somebody real harm?"

Carl shut his eyes and tried to get past the headache. "Drunk driving," he finally said.

"Drunk driving?"

"The driving that I've done while drunk could have been considered or could have resulted in real harm."

"And that stuff with your wife."

"That stuff with my wife is between me and my wife and wasn't even when we were married," Carl said hotly. "And the fact that we got married shows it wasn't even anything."

"Everybody's got stuff with their wife," the agent said encouragingly.

"I didn't say that."

"And everybody's got stuff with the President."

"Come on," Carl said.

"And everybody chains themselves to the White House fence with their two-year-old. My goodness, Carl, you could have smothered that kid."

"Please," Carl said.

"You consider Sam a patriotic name?"

"It was my father's name."

178

"Why don't you think your father liked you?"

"I don't know." Carl looked at the floor. It was the whitest linoleum he had ever seen. There weren't even decorative specks for depth perception or why ever they had them. "He never understood what I was doing, and I was a pain in the ass as a kid. Essentially I don't think I ended up being worth the trouble. You wind up not connecting with the kid who gave you the most aggravation, and there's going to be some unexpressed hostility. How's that?"

"That's very good," the agent said drily. "Where do you think you really are, Carl?"

"At the bottom of some federal facility in Washington, D.C., where I'm not going to see the light of day anytime soon."

"Carl." The agent looked at the window and smiled. "Carl, Carl, Carl. What does Carl stand for, by the way?"

"My mom always said it stood for Caustic Abusive Recalcitrant Loser," Carl said.

"Now we're getting somewhere," the agent laughed and gently slapped Carl on the back as he lifted him to his feet. "You didn't see anything on the floor, did you, Carl?"

"Like what," Carl said.

The agent opened the door into a bare-floored room with just a few green desks staffed by military-looking people that looked out onto deep blue water as far as Carl could see. Instantly he felt the heat and noted the lazily whirring overhead fan.

"Guantanamo Bay," Carl said.

"It's a shorter flight than you think," the agent said.

II.

Carl stood there dazedly. For a moment he couldn't see anything. Hysterical blindness, he thought. Then, gradually, he could make out a series of structures—barracks and prisons, he assumed—painted in a military khaki.

"I guess this is the end of the line," he said sadly.

"Do you think you're a danger to anyone, Carl?" The agent held him lightly by the arm. "Do you think you might be a danger to yourself? What do you think makes people act?"

"They can't speak. They can't articulate. They aren't heard or they feel they aren't heard. Then there's nothing left to do but act."

"You never said anything, Carl. I mean, of course you muttered things to your colleagues and even your wife—"

"*Even* my wife?"

"You don't tell her everything," the agent said.

"Telling somebody everything is never a good idea."

"But if somebody told her . . ."

"*If* somebody told her," Carl said slowly, feeling more ill with each word, "then she wouldn't care if I came back."

"I don't think anybody would care if you came back, Carl."

"I deserve this," Carl said.

"It's just a chip," the agent said. "Just a chip."

"You know how hurtful total honesty can be? I don't want to know everything about her. I don't want to know everything about anybody."

"That's a very sane attitude," the agent agreed. "Tell me about that piece, 'Why Haven't We Marched Yet.'"

"Obviously, I never had to finish it."

"It might have been a good piece."

"But I never had to finish it. They marched. It was pathetic."

All this time nobody even looked up from their desks at him.

"'I want you on this wall,'" Carl muttered. "'I need you on this wall.'"

"Easy, Carl." The agent turned him firmly around. "Shall we go back inside."

Again they sat across a bare table.

"Does your brother's importance diminish you, Carl?" the agent asked.

"I don't think so," Carl said wearily. The whole thing was like being stripped naked and then feeling like they kept stripping you beyond that, like they could see inside your balls and all the way up your rectum. "Probably," Carl said.

"You're feeling it," the agent said, each word working to make obvious that the it was all-encompassing.

"I'm feeling it," Carl said.

"That's important," the agent said.

Carl tried to think about something concrete—his children, his work, his wife—but it was all slipping away. Soon it would be as if his life had never happened. It was liberating and terrifying at the same time.

"What about your sister? You know, Evelyn."

"Evie," Carl said, and for an instant he could see her photograph atop his dresser. She was wearing something red, sitting next to her husband. It was well after the diagnosis, but it didn't look like it was after anything. She looked stunning. "I failed her."

"Everybody was going to fail her," the agent said. "That's the way those things play out."

"Whatever," Carl said, and now he could see himself taking his sister for a colonic, taking his sister for an MRI, taking his sister for chemotherapy, taking his sister for a drive, and in the carefully labeled metal cannister taking his sister's ashes home. "How many people have died here since 9/11?"

"Tracy," the agent said.

"Tracy didn't die here," Carl said.

"Of course not," the agent said. "I was just thinking about her since we were talking about death."

"She loaded airplanes."

"You basically begged her not to go."

"I thought she really didn't want to go. I thought if someone was forceful with her that she would act on that impulse."

"You offered her money."

"I did."

"I think that's illegal."

"You could see she was marked," Carl said. He tried to wipe his hair from his eyes as if to see her better, tried to wipe sweat from his head as if to think more clearly—had they turned off the air conditioner—but he was still handcuffed. Oddly, he felt hunger. "You could see she was going to get killed quickly, and she did."

"Everything is about luck and timing," the agent said. "If you hadn't been approached at the fence, you might not have done what you did."

"That's obvious," Carl said.

"It was almost a gesture of self-defense."

"It was," Carl agreed too eagerly.

"There are a lot of ways we could support a lot of different scenarios," the agent said. "That's life right now."

There was a knock on the door. The agent muttered something. Carl thought it was *too philosophical* but maybe that was what he wanted it to be.

"Time for chow," the agent said.

The door opened. Carl tried to glimpse the sea again. Seeing the sea would help him, he thought. From his angle, all he could see were walls.

The agent nodded at a tray. Carl saw something resembling chicken tenders and fries. A straw gleamed from a carton of nonfat milk. The agent patted him on the shoulder.

"The only thing Max eats," he said. "Enjoy."

Left alone Carl stared at the plate. They hadn't bothered to uncuff him. Carefully he bent his head and mouthed a piece of chicken. It was hot but not too hot. He raised his head and chewed. His throat felt unprepared to swallow. He moved the piece of chicken around in his mouth and kept chewing. When he thought there was room in there he bent to the straw and sipped. The milk was cold, and it began to open his throat. Through the straw he gulped. Finally he was able to swallow the chicken. The milk was almost gone. He felt sleepy and full.

If he dozed, when he woke, would he be in Abu Ghraib?

He descended in a slow swoon, and in his dreams saw nothing. In sleep he searched for the non-dream. Where was his wife, where were his children, where was the house with the roof that needed to be replaced and the garage door that could no longer close and the basement that took on water from under the center of the floor and all the other million little things that irked him and he had thought were driving him crazy, pulling him down further from any capacity to act? Where was the mailman who often left them someone else's mail and the station wagon that sucked up a grand just to fix an oil leak and the backyard that had killed off all the grass and the damn puppy that had just gotten her period and leaked blood all over the kitchen and dining room and the two cats who needed dental work which he was in no way going to pay for and the big screen HD LCD TV he had bought for a football season that had turned into a disaster and the fireplace that seemed to not like anything burnt in it and still they lit their Duraflames and afterwards the basement smelled like a bomb had gone off and even the cats waddled up stricken and teary? From wherever he was now or was going to be when he woke or they woke him he tried to reach back and grab hold but it was like reaching after something that dissolved just as it came into focus, as if it were an image mirrored in a pool of water or generated from the hot asphalt of a desert road. How many days had he been gone?

Whoever woke him was someone else and he was on a cot and for a moment he thought his hands were free but when he went to move them, each laying on its respective side of the bed as if neither knew the other, he found they were strapped securely to the frame of the bed. He checked his ankles. Still liberated.

"Carl," the person said.

He made himself look and saw sunglasses and a deep tan, a desert camouflage shirt not tagged with any name, a five o'clock shadow around the lips and coating the chin.

"Yes," Carl said.

"Do you know where you are?"

"Guantanamo Bay?" Carl tried.

The soldier laughed and Carl stared at the ceiling, too tired to raise his head and look around. "That must have been some dream," the soldier said.

It wasn't a dream, Carl knew. "Yeah," he said.

"You're in a secure facility on the eastern seaboard of the United States."

"Right," Carl said. "Which state again?"

"It is my job to orient you into the transitional incarcerated population," the soldier said.

"I'm here temporarily?" Carl said.

"That's right, sir. Three square meals, one hour of yard time, shower every other day, brief stints of labor."

"North Carolina?" Carl guessed. He raised his head, and saw with disappointment three walls and a series of bars where the fourth wall could have been. "Delaware?"

"Panic won't get you anywhere," the soldier said.

"I'm not as far from home as I thought," Carl tried to reassure himself.

"No sir," the soldier agreed.

In his chest he felt an absolute emptiness, as if everything in his system had been used up, pumped from him, exhausted.

"All this for chaining myself to the White House fence," he said.

"You violated three Federal statutes, two District statutes, and a temporary statute, sir."

Carl let his head sink into the pillow. "Oh," he said.

"It's time to get up, sir." Swiftly the soldier unlocked the wrist restraints. "You are free to sit on the side of the bed."

Free to sit on the side of the bed. That had a definite and clear limit. Just sit on the side of the bed. Very carefully, he swung his legs down and pushed himself up and sat on the side of the bed.

"I am so tired," he said.

"You've been interrogated in accordance with the guidelines set out by the Geneva Convention, sir."

"You guys have been starving me," Carl said.

"On the contrary, sir." He pointed to a small dot on the back of Carl's hand. "You refused sustenance, and we had to feed you through a tube."

That didn't make any sense, but he wished he hadn't said anything.

"Are you good to stand, sir?"

"No." Carl shook his head, and even that slight gesture nauseated him. "I'm not good to stand."

"One more minute then," the soldier said.

In the silence Carl thought, where am I really? He bit his lip. He felt as if he'd been boiled down to nothing.

"Sir?" the soldier said. He began to lift him by his arm.

"Okay, okay." He recognized his daughter's impatient plaintive tones in his voice, or was it the other way around and had she taken on his? He hoped there was as little of him in her as possible.

He rose in a brilliant orange jumpsuit and synthetic slippers. His legs felt as if they hadn't been used in weeks, and he imagined them as bony stalks under the bright color. He imagined he must have lost at least another ten pounds. He no doubt weighed less than when he graduated from college twenty-three years ago. He had other observations, but he and the soldier were moving now, the floor seeming to shift under him like a conveyor belt. They passed five empty cells and were buzzed through several thick and heavy doors until they stood in a small yard overseen by a piece of sky bit off by barbed fencing that ran along the top of tall cinderblock walls. In one corner, under the shade of the wall, was a rusting stationary exercise bike, in another corner a stunted basketball backboard and netless rim under which sat—as if out of a still life—a bald, practically brown ball.

"How long will I be here?" Carl asked.

"One hour a day, sir."

He breathed in deeply. The air seemed dry and wrung of any scent; the sky was very blue. He thought it still had to be February. He wondered if he had missed Valentine's Day.

The soldier motioned him back inside.

"What's the date?" Carl said.

"Your meals are served in your cell," the soldier said, leading him through the several doors. "Your labor is executed in your cell." Past the five empty cells they walked, each without any apparent inmate. "Tomorrow is your shower day."

He was locked into his cell and sat on his cot listening to the soldier's retreating footsteps. The place was like an aquarium filled only with water—you couldn't see anything when you were inside it and yet you moved against some kind of resistance and you had no depth perception until you hit a wall. Perhaps he was in northern Florida or South Carolina. Alabama and Arkansas were not on the "seaboard," but he could be anywhere. There was no mirror and he felt his face for growth. It seemed about three days' worth, but they could have shaved him. He took off his slippers and looked at his toenails. He examined his fingernails. He felt the length of his hair, but at forty-four that didn't grow so much as recede. What other clocks were there? If you took away time and setting, what was left? Weren't those the two variables that determined everything? There was only himself left. That wasn't at all pleasant to consider. He looked around the spotless cell. A stainless steel toilet without a real seat, a stainless steel sink with only a cold-water tap. The cot he sat on. He stood and went to the bars. He could see only the wall and off to either side of his cell a few feet of corridor. He pressed his ear between the bars. At first he heard nothing, then after a while a humming came to him. A very low droning tone. He looked up and above the outside left corner of his cell he saw one of those mirrors that sometimes appeared at the end of tangled driveways to gauge oncoming traffic. Of course someone could see him. He looked closely at the mirror. Still not close enough, but he was sure he could see something. He pulled the cot over and stood on it. In the mirror was a little boxed image. A television! On the television was an orange-jumpsuited man. Of course it was him. But it wasn't him at all—the man was blindfolded and kneeling, he saw as he got ever closer to the mirror. Around him were masked and hooded men pointing rifles and guns and a bright silver sword at the blindfolded man's head. Now he knew what he was looking at. He stepped down from the cot and tugged it over to its original place. These guys had thought of everything. He rested his head in his hands and tried to think of how lucky he was.

Stephen O'Connor

White Fire

So the first thing is I get out the gate and there's this big crowd. Mostly it's women and kids. But also there's. I mean. Parents. And signs. And everybody's yelling and everything. And. You know. Welcome back! Our Hero! Stuff like that. So I'm looking for Trudy, and it's like there's so many people, and everybody's jumping up and down, screaming. So for a long time I can't see her. Then all of a sudden, there she is. She's. You know. Just like all the rest. Her hands up in the air. Her mouth open. Like this is after some football game, and we're the victorious players coming out the locker room. Like we won the championship and everything. And when I get closer, I see that she's crying. That her cheeks are all shiny with her tears. And. Well, here's the thing. I just hate her when I see that. I just. Well. Hate her.

And she comes running up to me. She doesn't even say anything. Just. You know. Throws her arms around me. And she's squeezing herself up against me. And finally she whispers in my ear, "Oh, Davy, I'm so glad you're home!" So I put down my bag and I wrap my arms around her too. And I'm squeezing her and squeezing her. "Me too," I say. And then I say it again, "Me too." Because I am, you know. I really am glad to be home. And I think if I just say it, it'll start to be true. I'll feel it, I mean. I'll feel it like it's really true. Something in me will just. I guess. Open up. But it doesn't. And I got my arms wrapped around her ribs. And. Even though I already seen how she lost weight and everything. Been running herself ragged, like she said in her e-mails. And she looks good.

Practically like she did when we was in geometry class. But all I can think is how she's like this big bundle of. Like organs and everything. Bones and muscles and. Well, meat. That's when I have to let her go. And I'm like, "I love you, Trude. I'm just so—" But the words cut off in my mouth. I just can't say them.

So now we're standing apart and everything. And she wants to hold my hand. So I let her. But at the same time I bend down and pick up my bag, hoping that maybe. You know, she won't notice. But she does, of course. She knows me too well. So then there's like this big kind of silence. And I'm like. You know. I want to tell her I love her. Just say it. Cause I can see she's all like, Aw fuck. Like when we're just about to have a fight. And I can see her tears. She's wiping them off her face with the end of her sleeve. I know she isn't crying just because she's happy to see me. I know that she's, you know. That she's fucked up too. That she's been going through her own thing while I was away. That I'm not the only. But the thing is, I just don't care. You know? I mean, I know I should be compassionate and everything. That I should feel her. What she went through too. But I was just. Well, what it really is, is. Well. Shit. You know? Just shit.

So finally I'm like, "Where's the car?" That's all I can say. I mean, I noticed Ashley and Clarry aren't there and everything. But I can't even say, you know, "Where are the girls?" Just, "Where's the car?" And she's got this worried kind of hopeful little bad dog smile on her face. And she's like, "This way," she says. "This way. Over here." And then she reaches up her hand and puts it along my cheek, and she's like, "It's okay, ma-honey." And she's. I mean, she's really trying. And I can see how. Well. We had our problems and all. But I can see how we were right to. You know. Married and everything. Kids. But I don't say anything. Just silent. A rock. I mean, how can a man tell his wife he can't stand the feeling of her hand on his cheek? How's a man gonna say that?

In the car it's better. Mostly I pretend to sleep. That way I can give myself a talking to. You know: This is a whole different situation, man. You're *home*. Ain't nothing can happen to you here. Shit like that. Turn over a new leaf. And after a while. I don't know. Maybe it just starts to seem like it's true. I mean hope and everything. The only thing is when Trudy says, "Do you have to do that?" And I'm like, "What?" "Your leg." And that's when I realize I been bouncing my leg up and down like it's the end of diving board after somebody jumped. So I'm like, "Sorry." And I stop it. But after a while it just starts up again. All by itself. I can't do anything about it. So it's like this really long time and she's not saying anything. And I'm pretending to sleep. And finally she just says it like we been smack in the middle of a conversation. Just, "I don't want to hear about any of it until you're ready to tell me." That's what she says. But I know that what she really wants is for me to start talking right then. You know? Like, "Explain to me what the fuck's the matter with you." So I just don't say anything. Just pretend like I didn't even hear her. Asleep and shit. And then there's this other big long silence. Until finally she's like, "I only want to know why you stopped calling. Not even any e-mails." I just let that set there in the air for a little bit. Then I say, "You just told me you didn't want to hear about it." And that's pretty much it for the rest of the drive. Maybe an hour after that.

Trudy already told me my parents were there. Pick up the girls from school and everything. Taking care of Jimmy. So I'm like prepared for it and all. But still. You know? I mean, *man!* So, anyhow we're not even in the driveway when the door pops open, and there's little Clarry running down the steps, that white-blond hair of hers flapping around her head like the color of spaghetti. And I don't know what Trudy is. You know: *doing.* Cause she just swings around into the driveway and doesn't stop. And there's Clarry running right in front of us. And I'm like, "Trudy!" And she's like, "Sorry! Sorry!" And I'm like, "What the fuck!" And the car's already stopped and everything. You know: The dust we drug up the road is already blowing past us. And Trudy's got her head down on the steering wheel and she's like, "Sorry." But Clarry's just standing there shouting, "Daddy! Daddy!" She don't even know how close she come.

So I get out the car and I say, "Hey there, Clarabelle! You got to watch out little Ding-Dong!" And, I don't know. Maybe that's the second Clarry figures out what nearly happened. Or maybe it's just. You know. Finally seeing the real me. Too much for her, I mean. Anyhow, she just suddenly gets all quiet. Looking down at her sneakers. And I'm crouching down. Gonna. You know. Take her in my arms, give her a real hello. Then boom! Something hard hits me from the side. All I can see is like this spidery blackness. And I'm like. It's like. You know. I mean it just nearly sets off something inside of me. I almost.

And then I see it's Ashley. And I just let myself be knocked right over. Just fall down flat on the dust and gravel. And Ashley's all, "Daddy! Daddy!" And I'm just lying there looking up at the sky. Thinking. You know. Until finally it's like Ashley's voice gets a little funny. And I see Trudy just standing there looking at me. So I hold up both my arms and say, "Ash-Trash! I fooled you, hunh? I fooled you!"

And she throws herself on top of me, just like she rammed me from the side. She's only five, but she's all muscle and bone and wiggle. And her headbone knocks my cheekbone. And I'm like, "Whoa! Watch it there! Gonna have to call you Ash-*Bash* from now on! You watch what you're doing." So I get up on my knees and I scoop her up. And then I scoop up little Clarry. And I'm like walking toward the front steps. And, you know. That really does feel good. Makes me feel like I'm a real father. I look over at Trudy. And she's just standing there. Still looking at me. And I give her this smile. And she gives me this smile back. And then my parents are all over me. Dad's got this Abraham Lincoln thing going. With the beard. Trudy wrote me about that. And Ma's face. It's just like a plum exploding with its redness. It's just like tears exploding out from her eyes. And she says, "Look, Davy! Look! Little James!" And she holds up this blanket that's all wrapped around this other exploding red thing.

What it looks like to me. I mean, I know he's just having a poop and all. But what it looks like to me is a heart. A human heart. Only it's more like raw muscle, just kind of twitching around itself. You know? And my ma is like, "Look, little Jimmy! Meet your daddy! That's your daddy, little pea!" Then she's holding up the blanket for me to take. And I'm like, "Hold on a second, Ma." And I bump up the two girls I'm already holding. My arms're full and everything. And she's like, "Oh." And I'm like, "Let's go inside."

So I lead the way and there's. I should have known it. But still, it's like this shock. I mean. First there's this big sign going all the way across the living room. It's like all Christmas colors and everything. Every letter cut out of a different piece of red or green paper. My mother must have done it. Not Trude. That's not her. You know. And it's like, WELCOME HOME DADDY. And hanging off of the H and the O are these two drawings. One's just an orange and black scribble. The other's got these blue stick people holding hands. Three have skirts on. And the other one's holding what looks like a broom with a trigger on it. And they're all crammed up into one corner. In the other corner, way down at the bottom. There's like this red stick figure, lying on its side. A big red dot for its mouth. Two little dots for its eyes. And there's this smoke coming up from its mouth. Just like these two letters over and over—WAWAWAWA—going right up to the top of the page. But that's not the shocking thing. The shocking thing is in the middle of the table. There's all like these glasses and silverware on it. Set up for lunch and everything. And then there's this photograph of me in my National Guard uniform. In this shiny brass frame. And on the top it says AMERICAN in these like sort of like fat psychedelic letters. And at the bottom it says HERO.

So the first thing I do is put the girls down, pick up the photograph and stick it in the drawer where Trudy keeps the dish towels. And everybody's like. I mean. You know. But nobody says a word. So then my mother. Her face is like she got this really bad news for me. And she's holding up little Jimmy. And I'm like, "Hold on a second. I'm all dirty. You know? Better go wash up." So then I'm walking out the room and I hear Trudy saying in this soft voice, "Dave's kind of tired. Long flight."

I get to the bathroom. And. I mean, I don't even know what I'm doing there. Don't even have to pee. So I pee anyway. Then I wash my hands. Just. You know. For the hell of it. And that's when I notice how much I changed. I look in the mirror. And. Well, I'm twenty-six. But that dude in the mirror there. He's forty-six. All bones and sunburn and these little lines and everything. Stubble. Sweated off every drop of fat in that 120-degree heat. You know? And that awful food. So I been seeing that face for months, of course. But this is the first time I *really* see it. I mean. Like in my own bathroom mirror and everything. With those same old purple flowers on the wall behind me. This is the first time I see how much I changed. And what I'm thinking is that what I got is the face out of a mug shot. You know what I'm talking about? You know how those faces always look a little tilted? Like the bones don't line up exactly. And there's always something off about one of the eyes? That's how my face is looking to me. So I decide, Fuck my hands, I'm gonna take a whole damn shower. And that's a good idea. You know? Feels like a cleansing or something. Finally getting all that sand out of me. Out my ears. Out my hair. Out my asshole even. That sand's not like real sand. It's like this dust. Gets in everything. It's in your spit and your snot, twenty-four seven. So I wash my hair three times. Even rub in some of

Trudy's conditioner. Then I use her armpit razor. All my shaving stuff is still. You know. In my bag. In the living room.

So then I get out the shower and I can hear Jimmy's wailing. But not just like normal crying. It's like some kind of cosmic. I don't know. Rage. And then I'm thinking, Oh shit. I bet he's colicky. I bet that's what Ashley's picture is all about. The red baby going WA and everything. Shit, you know. Trudy didn't say anything about that. But shit. Fuck! That's all I need. So then I'm turning around in circles. And finally I just stuff my uniform into the hamper. Thought about burning it. Wanted to burn that motherfucker. But. Well. So now I'm out in the hallway in my bath towel. And Jimmy's still crying. But not. I mean. All the time. It keeps being interrupted by that Three Stooges noise. You know? That *gnargnargnargnar* babies make when they're feeding. So I go into the bedroom and there's all my clothes hanging in the closet, all neat and skinny. Like Trudy sent them to the dry-cleaners while I was gone. You know? And my underpants are all folded up in stacks. And my T-shirts. And it's like she did all this work for me. Like she put in all this effort. And I'm thinking I got to thank her for that. I got to remember to thank her. But what I like best about what she did is that they don't seem like my clothes anymore. It's like they're the clothes of a different me. A better me. The me I would have been. If. I mean. So, I put on a pair of black jeans and a black Pantera T-shirt. *Pantera*, man! Home.

By the time I get out there, everything's quiet. And everybody's just sitting at the lunch table. You know, waiting for me. "Jimmy got tired," Ma says. And I'm like, "I know. I heard him." And Trudy's like, "Perfect timing!" She's up by the stove, putting the chicken on people's plates. "He'll be down for at least a couple of hours," she says. "We'll all have time to talk." And she looks at me. But I can't really tell what's on her mind. So, anyway. There's my usual place set for me. At the head of the table. Between my mother and my father. And soon as Trudy sits down, my father. He takes hold of my left hand. And my mother grabs hold of my right. And my father's got. You know. His deacon voice on. And he says, "I think we all need to say a special grace today. Cause the Good Lord's seen fit to bring our Davy back to us." And soon as he says that, it's like my head starts to pounding. Cause I know just what he's going to say. But I don't say anything, cause Trudy fires me one of these looks. Like, *Just you hush!* And I figure, you know. She had to make her own kind of peace with these people. With them helping her out and everything. And me being away. So I'm just like, I can sit through this once. Just once. What the fuck does it matter anyway? What the fuck does it matter?

And so, of course, my father says everything I knew he was going to say. Talking bout fighting terrorists and everything. Saving the country. And of course he's like, "American Hero" this, "American Hero" that. Even my mother thinks that's. You know. She just does this little thing with her breath. But he keeps at it. The usual God-bombing that he's always doing. In that Abe Lincoln beard of his. And I just keep my mouth shut. Don't say a word. But also I don't say Amen when he's finished. And he gives me this. You know. Like this glance. Like he used to do when I was little. The kind that meant, *Just you wait!* And sure enough. Soon as we're all eating, he's like, "I hope you was talking to Jesus when you was over there, Davy." And I just keep chewing on my chicken, even though it's making me sick and I can hardly swallow it. "Cause you know, that's the time a man needs His guidance most. When the bombs're falling and there's an enemy on every side." My mother hisses, "Henry!" And my father puts on this boogle-eye look that's supposed to be all innocence and everything. Like he's *shocked*, you know. Just *shocked!* But really it's like that's almost his most angriest expression. And he's, "What! What did I say?" And my mother's like, "I just think maybe Davy doesn't want to talk about such things his first day home." And my father's like he's more shocked than ever. "Can't a man even talk about his son's mortal soul? Can't a man talk about things that matter? Davy knows what I'm talking about. He knows how a man can get so confused in the heat of battle that he can't tell what's what and what's not. And how, 'less he asks for Jesus's help, he can carry that confusion home." Trudy sees what's was coming, and she tries to stop it. She's like, "Grampa, there's a time and a place—" But I had enough. I had all I can stand. So I'm like, "The thing is, Dad, you don't know what you're talking about. You don't know one blessed thing about what happened over there. So I think you should just keep your mouth shut and let me eat my chicken." And my dad's working himself up to be shocked all over again, but my mother won't let him. She's like, "Give it a rest, Henry. Give it a rest. We should just all be happy we're together again." My father's mouth opens and closes a couple of times. Finally, he just starts gnawing on his chicken bone and doesn't look at anybody. My ma pats my hand. And I look at Trudy, who's got a headache on her face, but seems relieved. Ashley's looking all big-eyed over her chicken leg like she been hiding behind it. And Clarry's waving a thighbone in the air. You know, conducting an orchestra and everything. Trudy grabs her hand and presses it down to the table. "No."

So after a while the girls can't stand it anymore. And Ashley's like, "Can we go outside?" And Trudy's, "Sure, honeybun. You just take care of your sister, okay?" And I sit there a little longer. Trudy and Ma talking about how Tiffany Delgado made so much money last week selling baskets to the neighbors. How her son's, you know. Biggest pothead around. And my father's just chewing on his bone, staring into space. Like he's having this private conversation with Jesus. And Jesus is telling him, "Don't you worry, Henry. They're all going straight to hell. I got it all worked out. Just straight to hell." Finally, I stand up. Bring my plate to the sink. And I'm like, "You know, I think I'm gonna go outside. See how the girls're doing." And Ma is like she thinks that's a great idea. You know: Spend some time with your children. Her head going up and down. And Trudy looks at me with this like, Don't abandon me! But I can see how she's re-signed to it. You know: Spend time with the children; that really is what he ought to do. So, I'm, "Don't anybody touch those dishes. Okay? I'll get to them myself when I get back inside." And, of course, my ma makes this kind of click in her nose like that's ridiculous.

Soon as I'm out the door, there's. Well, it's like this big noise cuts off. Like a motor or something. A car alarm. Then suddenly there's just this quiet. It's like the quiet's this *thing* suddenly. You know? And you can appreciate it. Instead of it just being. I don't know. Just another kind of nothing. And the air. Well. It's like that's the very second I take my first breath of American air. Fresh. Cool. And since as it's about halfway between Thanksgiving and Christmas, the air's not. You know. So hot anymore. And there's this smell of grass. Peat moss. Trudy's planted these four skinny trees at the edge of our property. Put peat moss all around them. I never realized how much I like those smells. And water. You can *feel* the water in the air. Soft on your skin. Comfortable. Not like that sandpaper air. You know? Like the wind out of an oven. Not like that. So I just stand there for a long time. Just. Well. Breathing. And I'm thinking, Maybe this is how it will begin. You know? Me, I mean. I don't know. Normal and shit.

Ashley's like jumping up and down on this itty-bitty trampoline thing she got for her birthday. Trudy told me about that. Like a truck inner tube with this cloth across it. Like a rolled up condom is what it is. And I'm thinking. You know. About this girl there. Another soldier. From Florida. I suppose I got to tell Trudy about her. For a while there things started happening. But. I don't know. That's all over with. That girl got. You know. Fucked up. This guy's brains all inside her mouth. Sniper. Maybe I don't have to. You know. It's all over with. So anyhow. Clarry's just sitting there in the sandbox. Bucket between her knees. Shovel in her hand. But, not doing anything. Just sitting there. Like somebody turned her off. And Ashley's just going up and down, up and down. Ash-Trash. Both of them are looking the other way. So neither of them knows I'm right behind them. Watching. "Hey you two!" I shout, like they're in trouble. That makes them look around. Ashley just turning around slowly, one jump at a time. Sort of like she's one of those spin-around ballerinas on the top of a kid's jewelry box. "You wanna go to the playground?"

Normally we drive over there. But this time I just feel like walking. Of course that means I got to carry Clarry most of the way. Half a mile. Playground's over to the new middle school. Behind the ball fields. Where the old Armitage place used to be. And while we're walking, it's already getting dark, you know. Gray sky. It's not even four. But there's already like this definite change going on inside the clouds. You can feel how there's just a little more darkness in there. And a few minutes later there's like. A little more. Night comes so early this time of year. So, even before we get to the school, I'm thinking this is a mistake, you know. Walking home in the darkness. Cars going so fast and everything. But the girls just love this playground. Swings. They got this whole jungle gym there. Made out of tires and such. Chains. Really, it's like this mountain of tires. All made into tunnels, rooms. Some of them hanging off like swings. One time I spun Ashley around so much on one of those tires she got sick.

So anyway. We get there, and the place is like. Deserted. First thing is the girls run straight over to the regular swings. And I'm, you know. Pushing them both at the same time. Pushing them really high. Like, "Can you touch the sky? See if you can put your feet right up against the sky!" And I never really pushed Clarry this high before. But I'm watching her hands. And I can see she's holding on just fine. She's like three and everything. And she's loving it. Laughing and laughing. But then they had enough of that and they're off to the tire mountain. I sit down on one of the benches there. And I'm wishing I brought along a basketball so I can shoot a few hoops. Cause one thing I already know is it's no good when I got nothing to do. Got to keep my mind *occupied*. Just do stuff, you know. All the time. So after a while I hear Ashley calling out, "Daddy! Clarry's going on the top." "So what?" I say. And she's like, "She's not supposed to go on the top." "Don't be such a spoil-sport," I say. And she's, "But she's not supposed to." "You're just jealous!" I say. And at that very instant I see Clarry's little blond head stick up from the mountain. You know, like she's this little burp of yellow lava coming out a volcano. "Hey, Clarabelle! Look at you, big girl!" And. I don't know. Maybe she was going to wave at me or something. But soon as she looks up over the edge of that tire, her head disappears. And Ashley starts screaming. "Daddy! She fell! She fell!"

And what really scares me is I can't hear Clarry crying.

I'm up those tires in half a second. And it's, you know, like basic training. I'm ready to dive in one of those holes soon as I know where she is. But I don't see her till I'm right at the top, looking down through the hole she disappeared in. And she's just lying there on her back. Six-eight feet down. Not doing anything. You know. Her eyes all filled up with blue and just staring at me. And she's maybe twitching her hands a little bit. And I'm. You know: Fuck! Shit! It's like for a second I just die there. I go all weak. Can't move. Fuck! Shit! My little baby! And then it's. I mean, boom! Kicks out her foot and starts crying. You know, like she just got the wind knocked out and shit. So then I'm down there hugging her. And I'm all quivery and everything. Way overreacting. Like I'm gonna faint. So Ashley helps me get her out. And then we're all rocking on the bench and I'm saying, "It's okay little Clarissa-pie! It's okay my little Ding-Dong." Her little fluffy head right up against my chin. And I don't know. Even though she's a big girl now. Her head's still got. Especially when she's all crying and everything. Hot. It's still got this *baby* smell. That's the most beautiful smell there is in the world. I always loved that smell. But I don't know. This time. Somehow. She's still crying and I say to her, "There, there. Got to stop crying now. Be brave. Got to be brave like a soldier." And that's when it starts.

I don't know why I say it. Sort of like I can't help myself. But I know exactly what I'm saying. So, I'm like, "You know, where I just was, the little kids were soldiers too." That does it. Her tears stop just like that. She's all ears to what I'm saying. Ashley too. I can feel it. So I say, "It's true. They were soldiers. Just like the grown-ups. Only thing is, they were *enemy* soldiers. And sometimes they stepped right in front of your truck. To make you stop. So that their daddies. Or their brothers. Could shoot you. Or blow you up. That's what they wanted. That's why they would stand in front of us. And. So, you wanna know what we did? We just ran them right down. Like they weren't even there. Their mamas too, sometimes. And. Well. We just had to. If we didn't, they'd shoot us. And we would die." I stop talking then. I can't say anymore. And it's like the whole world. It's like God takes this big deep breath, and he's holding it. And he's not going to let it out. It's. You know. Like long as he's holding his breath, nothing is going to happen. So then I say, before either of the girls can make a sound. "Ice cream time! Let's all go home and have some chocolate ice cream! You girls haven't even had dessert yet. You all deserve a treat!"

I watch the girls as we walk home. And mostly they're pretty much normal. Maybe a little quieter. I have to carry Clarry most of the way. And she falls asleep on my shoulder. When we get home my parents are just leaving. So there's goodbyes and everything. Then Trudy doesn't want the girls to have ice cream. Says it's too late. But I say I promised. You know: a special treat. Daddy's home. So she gives them both bowls and puts them on the floor in front of the TV. *Pete's Dragon*. Ashley's favorite. Soon as they're settled, Trudy goes to the cabinet over the refrigerator and gets out the china bowl with the rolling papers in it and the weed. "Thank God," she says. "That was a torture." I just shrug my shoulders. "I swear," she says. "For a while there I wanted to hit Grampa over the head with my fork. I'm serious! Wanted to stab him in the cheek." "He's a trip," I say. I don't want any marijuana, so I go to the refrigerator and get myself a beer. Tecate. My first real beer in six months. I sit down at the table opposite Trudy. She lets these jets of smoke out her nose and smiles. "So now you're really home," she says. I raise my bottle. You know: sort of a toast. She reaches across the table and rubs the back of my hand. "You doing okay?" I shrug. "Don't worry about it," she says. "I been talking to Lucile Gordon. I told you about how Pauly's come back? Only one leg? She been telling me what it's like and everything. Said there's this wives group I could join if I want to. You too. They got all kinds of groups for soldiers." She takes another long toke. When she lets it out she says, "We'll get through it." Then there's this sadness on her face. She looks like her mother. Then she smiles. "Come with me!" She takes my hand.

196

Just before Jimmy was born, my father. He's always been like a handy-man. He builds this wall in the girls' room. Right down the middle of the window. You know. So both rooms have light. Air. So, anyway. Jimmy's room is hardly bigger than a closet, really. Just big enough for us to squeeze in next to his crib. And his changing table. Trudy takes a last toke on her joint before going in. Puts it down on the bathroom sink. And then she's like, leaning over the crib. "Look," she says. The room's all. You know. Baby-breathing, diaper cream. So then there's this little guy lying there with his butt up in the air. His cheek's all pressed down against the sheets. And he's got no nose worth mentioning. Know what I mean? So Trudy's like, "That's our son. We *did* that! That's our little boy." Then she points again. "You see that? That's your ear! That's exactly what your ear looks like." And I'm like, "Oh yeah," even though I don't have a clue what my ear looks like from the side.

So then, you know, most of the rest of the evening's not so bad. Normal mostly. Me and Trudy have time for another beer and a joint. Then Jimmy wakes up. And I get to feed him a bottle. I'm holding him. And it's just like when I used to hold the girls. I can do it, you know? What was I so worried about? And then I'm changing his diaper too. Which isn't really like changing the girls, of course. I realize, smack in the middle of it, that this is the first time I'm like. Touching somebody else's dick. Which is. You know. But anyhow, it's just this little pink thing. So then there's dinner. And more TV. And then the whole family's in the bathroom. The girls are having a bath and everything. And I hold Jimmy out over the water. And he's kicking it with his little pudgy feet. And the girls are all laughing and. You know. Loving it. And I'm think-ing. Just. I mean I'm thinking. Maybe. Just maybe. You know?

Then finally, the day's over. It's like ten-thirty. Me and Trudy are sitting on the couch and she's opening up her shirt. Getting ready to give Jimmy his last feeding and everything. But then Clarry calls out from the bed-room. She's like, "Mommy! Mommy!" And Trudy's like, "Go to sleep! You should have been asleep hours ago!" And Clarry's like, "I can't sleep. Ashley's crying." So Trudy gives me like. This look. And she puts Jimmy in my arms. And she's, "Hold him for a second. I'll be right back." But this time I can't hold him. I mean I can't stand to. I just got this. Like this whole feeling in my body. And I guess he can tell. Or maybe it's just he's hungry. So he starts wriggling around the way babies do. Cranking his head around. Looking for titty. His arms working. You know. All spastic. His legs peddling back and forth. And he's getting all red again. And I can tell he's just about. You know. So I'm like, "There, there, little Jimbo. There, there, little man. It's gonna be all right. Mommy's coming." But he's not having any of it. And I don't know what I'm going to do if he starts to scream. Crying and everything. So I stick my pinky in his mouth. And for a while, that's okay. For him, I mean. That satisfies him. But me. I'm starting to get that feeling. I'm shaking all over with it. You know. What I can't stand is how hot the inside of his mouth is. How slippery. Wet. How he's just sucking on my finger.

So, finally I pull it out. And that's when he starts to cry. It's just a little at first. Just cranky. And I'm, "Shhh, shhh." But it's no good. And then he's wailing. You know. Screaming. And that's it. I just can't stand it any more. So I get up. And I don't know what I'm going to do. I'm just. You know? Walking around the room. So that's when I see his playpen. And I put him down inside it. And then I go out the back door. I just have to get out. Get some air. Get away. But even outside I can hear the crying. Jimmy in the living room. And now Clarry *and* Ashley in the bedroom. I don't know. Maybe Trudy too. The whole house is just full of noise. So I don't know what to do. And I'm running around in circles. Then finally, I just grab on to one of those skinny trees Trudy planted. And I'm like trying to rip it out of the ground. You know. Then I'm trying to break it off at its roots. But I can't. It's just too strong. Too green. So then I just sit down on that trampoline. My back to the house. And I'm trying to cry. Trying to make the tears come out my eyes. But I can't do that either.

That's where I'm sitting when Trudy calls my name. She calls it again but I don't answer. I don't look around. She goes back inside. Jimmy's still crying. But then he's quiet. And the girls are quiet too. And now I can hear this one cricket doing his deedlydee next door. And in this big old black oak tree at the corner of the yard, a squirrel makes that kissy-laughing noise that I always used to think was a rattlesnake when I was little. And far, far away. Like it's coming from everywhere. Like it's the sound of the whole world. There's this big, quiet. Like roar. From traffic on Route 57. Maybe Route 36 too.

After a while the back door opens again. And I hear Trudy walking toward me. Fast. Like she knows exactly where I am. I don't turn around, but she keeps walking till she's standing right in front of me. *"What did you say to those girls?"* She says that in a whisper, but it's like the sort of whisper that rips out your mouth. At first I don't answer. Then I say, "Nothing." And she's like, "What did you say? They wouldn't make that up! Why did you say that?" "I don't know what you're talking about. I didn't say anything." I was sitting down when I started saying that, but now I'm standing up. And that's when I notice she's carrying Jimmy. You can hear these like. These little cat noises he's making. But I don't know whether he's sucking or just dreaming. It's too dark. All you can see is like these sort of gray clouds. You know: Faces. Shoulders. And then Trudy makes this noise deep in her chest. It's like the closest to a growl that a human being can get. And she says, "David, I'm willing to put up with a lot. I figure it's my duty. As your wife. But I am *not!* Do you hear me? I am *not!* Going to let you do *anything* to harm my children!" "Shut up!" I say. "Just shut the fuck up! I didn't do anything! I don't know what you're talking about!" *"I will not let you harm my children!"* "Oh, Jesus, Trudy! Jesus Christ!" And then she says it: "It's *true* what they said. That *is* what you did. You *did* do it, didn't you? You *did* it!"

And that's when there's like this explosion of whiteness inside my head. The whole night sky lights up with whiteness. The house. The trees. Everything. Everything burning in white fire. And it's like. You know. I'm not there. Or I am there, but it isn't me. And I don't know what's happening. Or what's going to happen. But I know it's going to be. You know. Very bad.

Murzban F. Shroff

A Matter of Misfortune

I was there the day Amay died. He fell from a height he was unable to handle. The ground it seemed was extra slippery. Too much varnish for his Bally shoes. Before I knew it he'd plunged to his death. Gone—without a warning, without a whisper of an exit imminent. And now he was still, so very still. A cutout of a memory you could do nothing about. Except carry it sheepishly to some dark corner of your mind, wondering how much you had to do with this untimely death, this amputation of youth, this severance of childhood roots. That's when I realized it was lasting and real. Sad, too, the way it happened. For once those eyes weren't blinking. "Blinking fool" we used to call him when he did that. Amay, in the old days, blinked the way some people stammered. His eyebrows would furrow like inching caterpillars, and his eyelids would flicker up and down on his pockmarked face. You would think he was having difficulty following your conversation or was trying to digest the worldview before him; fact is, he'd be listening intently, and he'd submit his opinion quietly and cautiously, invariably in your favor. He was that kind of friend, with that kind of heart, and that kind of capacity to convince you that the world owed you a living, it should honor you for being what you are. He did it with conviction and with pride, and sometimes he wore a frown if he thought you were wronged, and he'd follow up to make sure there *was* some improvement in your luck, some progress to keep you going and inspired. Oh, what a friend he was, Amay—not such long a time ago. Sad that he had to be buried thus: in his Arrow shirt, Louis Denton blazer, and Gucci trousers, he would soon be worm fodder.

Amay and I grew up together. He lived nearby, in a quiet lane, where we would play cricket, kabaddi, and games of childhood without worrying about cars running us over. During the holidays, I would be sent to his home, where his mother would plan out an itinerary for us—*play, eat, sleep, study,* followed by *play* if the *study* was fine. Toward evening, she'd serve us soup and switch on a record of old Hindi songs. The songs would lull us into silence. After a while we would get depressed, realizing that the sun had set, we were a day closer to starting school.

During schooldays, we would take the same bus to school every morning: the single-decker 48. Two half-tickets to Byculla, Nesbit Road: that's what the journey was worth, that's what our parents could afford, and, if we could get away ticket-less, as we did sometimes, we'd have money left over for a pyali, a forbidden snack, laden with spices, sold outside the school gates.

Our school was St. Paul's. It took up most of our time, keeping us at our study books, wrenching out our brains in relentless forty-five-minute periods. Equally it gave us a fine store of memories and bombarded us with morals we didn't think we needed at that point.

In the recess, we would run through the cloisters, the assembly halls, up the spiral staircases, which opened onto white chipped-stone terraces with fiery-red brick walls and shingled roofs. There, we'd pick at the locks on the birdcages. The birds—a brightly colored entourage—would flap their wings and fly to remote corners of their cages, from where they'd eye us warily. We'd struggle with the locks till the despair showed in our faces and our pudgy fingers bled with rust. Our whole intention was to free the birds, these beautiful creatures that did not get the attention they deserved. From time to time, we'd cast furtive glances over our shoulders to see whether anyone was approaching. We'd chosen the lunch hour for our escapades so that most of the teachers would be occupied with their lunches, and yet we feared the arrival of the Jesuit fathers, whom we faced daily in class and avoided otherwise in corridors, and who ruled us with tyrannical precision, installing the fear of God in us, which, bless them, was no fear at all, as we'd learn later. But for then it was plainly "Thou shall, thou shall, thou shall obey!" and there was no reason our colored friends should do the same. They had wings, and no classrooms to bind them. And they had us as friends whom they never really trusted. Maybe it was just as well they were confined. They wouldn't have known what to do with their freedom. They wouldn't have known how far to fly, to what altitudes to soar, when to stop and descend. Good thing, I think now, the locks didn't open. Good thing, we didn't manage to free the birds. We'd have clipped their wings before they started. We'd have killed them with our good intentions.

My early recollections of Amay are that he was shy, inward, unimpressive in conversation and in studies. No flights of brilliance or grades that would feature him on prize lists. He was content to follow me to different parts of school, to places like the Jesuit quarters, the gray stone building where the fathers stayed, dark, imposing, and out-of-bounds to us.

On one such occasion we came upon a teak door slightly ajar. From inside we heard a voice, "No, Father, not again," and then a polished voice replied, "Come now, take it like a man. You know it doesn't hurt after some time." There was silence, a cold silence, which gave us an instant sense of dread. We felt something would change if we stayed any longer in the place. We both ran at the same time, our feet drumming against the wooden floor, our hearts beating loudly, while behind us a voice shouted: "Who is there? Don't think I haven't seen you."

Thereafter, we made it a point to avoid the place. It was like we had stumbled onto some secret graveyard, awoken some evil spirit who'd await our return.

We began to visit the garden behind the chapel. There, joined by some friends, we played games of hitty-kitty, bending and gripping each other at the waist, while boys from the opposing team vaulted onto our backs, shouting: "Hitty-kitty, what's the time?" But soon the game was invaded by the bigger-built Anglo-Indian boys, who left us with injured backs, smarting ribs, and bruised egos. It was sensible to opt out.

Amay and I began to venture onto the railway tracks that ran parallel to the school grounds. There we busied ourselves pulling tadpoles out of stagnant-water ditches. We'd try to get them at the first swipe, keeping score and making a game of it. We'd dump our aquatic catch in plastic bags filled with water and tied on top with rubber bands. We'd carry the bags to class and hide them in our desks, while our teachers prattled on about life-forms and evolution. Invariably, our pets would die before we could get home, and this made us crave for something new, something clever and closer to adulthood.

We began to sneak out of the main gates during the recess. We'd gulp down our lunch and run to the Byculla court, where in narrow cells out in the open the prisoners would await their turns while their cases came up for hearing. The atmosphere was idyllic: lush green gardens, moss-laden ponds, white marble fountains, and small curving pathways that led to the courtroom. Along the way were the cells, packed with prisoners.

Staring at the prisoners from a distance, we would try and predict each one's crime. In this, we'd be guided by the ferocity of their features, their lack of hygiene, or simply the color of their complexions. We would label them as dacoits, murderers, gangsters, kidnappers, or thieves, depending on how they looked. If we would agree on a particular type, we would shake hands and laugh heartily.

The prisoners wouldn't be amused. They would snarl and curse us. We, in turn, would gibe them. "Feels nice to be free. Such a beautiful place, this garden! What a shame to be locked up."

After a while, the war got intense. The prisoners would press their unshaven faces against the bars and aim gobs of spit, which we'd sidestep. We would take old plastic bags (the ones in which we carried our lunches), fill these with water from the ponds and, running past the cells, would splash the prisoners. We would howl with delight to see them recoil, wet, filthy, and furious.

This revelry ended one afternoon with a grimfaced darban gripping us by our necks and leading us before the prisoners, saying he'd put us in with them if he ever found us on the premises again. He slammed our heads together three times, and the prisoners roared with delight. All this while we were gripped with terror because our captor had kept very little space between us and the prisoners, and we had seen the spitballs in the prisoners' mouths and the gleam in their eyes. We didn't want it to end like this, them getting us as sitting ducks.

Our fun cut short, we looked for other avenues, an alternate sport in school itself. Amay decided on soccer, and I on table-tennis, and we occupied ourselves learning the games.

I realized soon enough that I would never make the school team in table-tennis. I had my limitations; I could spin and parry and hold out but I just couldn't drive myself to triumph against the more formidable players. For Amay, soccer became an obsession, a manifestation of his deeper instincts, a transformation from shy and self-effacing to spirited and unvanquished. On the soccer field, it did not matter who he faced, how big and strong his opponents were. He'd simply cut loose and fly: a firefly of a boy with sparks in his eyes. The ball would appear hypnotized by his feet, the wind would drop all resistance, and he'd refuse to slow until he had reached his goal, until he had got through the chain of defense, had outwitted everyone else, seen them stamp their feet in disgust and raise their hands to their heads in a show of damp resignation.

He ran best in the rain, when the weather was against him, the mud slippery, the wind a sheet of water in his eyes. He ran even when the big boys converged, when they stuck their feet out, elbowed him in the ribs, and fisted him with the full fury of incensed youth. Then he would pull the ultimate dodge. He would glide through the defenders, smoothly, fluidly, with a smile. It was like the goal was waiting to receive him. And he would waltz into its white welcoming space, the end beyond the end, where there was nothing left for the opponents to do but to accept defeat. Later in life he'd run again, and he'd see no impediments in his way. Not friendship, nor roots, nor the sweet whispers of childhood.

Amay and I go back together a long time, as long as the Hindi film *Yaadon Ki Baraat.* I remember the movie: it began with a murder, which is how all things should begin, not end; all stories of life, that is, where you pay to be amused and come out knowing you've got your money's worth. I remember Amay watching, blinking, when the villain, Shakaal, played by the actor Ajit, emptied his bullets into the parents of three young boys who would be separated later. The boys would grow into an angry Dharmendra, thirsting for revenge, a youthful Vijay Arora, yearning for romance, and a swashbuckling Tariq, strum-happy on his guitar, ready to break into feisty versions of filmy rock. They were to unite sometime in life, and life was to unite over them, to make sense and fall into place. And because we were so taken up by the movie, we began to believe in this make-believe world, we began to look for hints in our own lives that would give us entry into a similarly charmed destiny, and though we didn't quite hope for our parents to fall to some villain's bullets, we did fancy ourselves denied and deprived, saviors and superheroes with the potential to come through in a villainous world.

I remember Amay blinking, his mouth open, when Dharmendra jumped from a bridge onto a train and rode it legs astride, fists clenched. For some reason, Dharmendra chose to travel on the roof of the train, and in his mind so did Amay. I remember gripping Amay by the hand as we took the bridge on our way to Queen Mary's school. There, we'd lurk at the school gate and gaze upon girls in short skirts, girls with sweet round faces, soft brown hair, and legs flushed pink at the knees. By now it seemed the villains were having a good time, and we, we had taken to morning shows at theatres like Ganga Jamuna, Diana, Minerva, and Maratha Mandir, which we'd frequent by cutting school, pocketing our ties, and obliterating our underage identities. We had to do that because we were there for the skin—Padma Khanna, Bindu, Helen, and other dancers wriggling their butts and breasts and cozying up to the villains so intimately that we had to admit there was something wonderful happening between our legs. It was like there was another life brewing inside us, a force, warm, sweet, and mystifying. By now we'd lost interest in the birds in school. We were interested in our own freedom, seeing how far we could fly over uncharted territories. We would look for places we could smoke a cigarette—a Rothmans, because it was light on our lungs. The cigarette would take forever to light and we'd pull at it cautiously. After a few bouts of coughing and choking, we learned to get it right. We learned to blow smoke rings and to shoot a stream of smoke through them. We felt we had arrived; we felt invincible. The defining trait of masterful heroes and villains was ours to enjoy. We felt like men at last.

Nothing made an impression like *Yaadon ki Baraat*, nothing then and nothing now, and each time a train thundered under a bridge, Amay would shut his eyes and ponder dreamily, and I would have to reach out and hold him. Later I discovered he was counting carriages by the clattering sound they made. Just by listening he could tell which carriages had people in them, which had cargo, and which train was in a greater hurry to reach its destination.

This way, and through many years of friendship, I held on to Amay in the way one holds on to a pair of jeans that fit snugly or on to a piece of music one has grown up with. Ours was a compatible friendship. I spoke; he listened. I advised; he fell in line. And it went on thus for many years. Through school, college, professional life, married life, we shared problems, shared confidences, and came closer. We had a great friendship going and we collected memories like they were photographs, like they were coming free. In teenage years, we chuckled over the acerbic wits of John Lennon, Jim Morrison, and Keith Moon, and later, in our twenties, over Jack Nicholson in *The Shining*, limping after wife and kids, axe in hand. We found the irony in Nicholson's repartees funny and cathartic, a brusque foil to all of life's mediocrities. We thought him to be the original voice of dissent, the master blaster who held his own even in Hollywood. The Joker in *Batman* embodied our vision of life and we would conclude most of our conversations with "well, well, what a life."

Amay took to observing Nicholson carefully and cultivated the famous Nicholson sneer. He thought this would give him a sexual advantage. Like Nicholson, he'd draw the women, do it five times a night—God knows where he heard that from? He was impressed that

Nicholson helped himself to apple pie in between sex, and the man of appetites became his hero and his superhero, the big daddy of his imagination, and he promised himself that like Nicholson he would have all the women, all the adulation, and all the apple pies he could dream of. He didn't need Hollywood for that. But he would need to get to the U.S. at some point.

After college, Amay joined the army, in the footsteps of his father, Brigadier Suri. He was sent for training to the military academy in Dehra Dun, where he excelled. On finishing, he was posted to a regiment in Bombay, and soon after, he left with the Indian peacekeeping force to Sri Lanka. Before leaving for Sri Lanka, on the behest of his father, Amay married a tall, fair Punjabi girl with light eyes, waist-length hair, and the manners of a traditional Indian housewife. I remember being surprised at his choice. For one, the girl appeared meek and subservient. For another, she had come through the arranged marriage circuit, which gave them little time to know each other. She'd dress in full-length clothes, wear vermilion in her hair, speak in dulcet tones, lower her eyes when speaking to elders, and stand in attendance, serving us during mealtimes. I was surprised to find Amay comfortable with this arrangement.

Amay's wife stayed with his parents in Bombay for two years and left him while he was in Sri Lanka, shooting Tamil Tigers. She said it was a dysfunctional marriage; it had ceased working for her. She refused to provide a reason; refused to entertain Amay's pleas or his apologies, distraught and groundless as they were. The way she left him was Machiavellian; it suggested premeditation and craft. She returned to her parents' home in Amritsar, saying she found the chaos of Bombay too disturbing; she needed her roots to endure a long-distance marriage. She took with her the television, the music system, the kitchen appliances, the cut-glass, and the exquisite Noritake crockery that Amay had bought from Sri Lanka. She said it would remind her of Amay, the world he had built for her. Amay's parents, the simple-minded folk that they were, had encouraged the decision. Once settled into her parents' home, once all the items were laid out in various corners of the house, she broke the news: she wanted out of the marriage; she didn't want to discuss it or to talk it over; she had done all that and concluded that it *was* over. She said it was lucky for Amay that she wasn't claiming a hefty alimony. But there had to be a one-time settlement, a release fee, so to say. She smiled when she said that, just outside the divorce court in Amritsar, looking Amay straight in the eye. A month after the divorce, she married a cousin of hers, and from the settlement Amay had made she opened a dhaba for her new husband.

Shattered and confused, Amay left the army and returned to Bombay, to his parent's home, in the lane next to my house. There he tried to pick up the fragments of his life, to understand them piecemeal. During this time, his blinking increased. I'd find it impossible to hold his attention for more than a few seconds. He'd drift in the middle of a conversation, and from some planet faraway he'd look at the world with disbelief and pain. I tried to introduce him to girls who I thought would bring him out of his stupor, girls with the kind of looks he admired, but invariably he'd be too formal, too awkward and fumbling, and the evening would end before it had started. One day he sighed and said, "It's not going to work, Gussy. It's not going to heal this way. I must recover my self-esteem, which is at an all-time low. I need to qualify myself better, to understand this complex world of ours. I need to learn once again—how to survive."

A week later, Amay applied to a post-graduate program in human resource development and buried himself in his books to prepare for the entrance. He got through the examination and enrolled in the program. He moved into the college hostel, to avoid answering people in his neighborhood why he'd quit the army. He returned to academics, when most of his friends, far progressed in their careers, were looking at lifestyle options like time-share holidays, low-interest car loans, and investments in real estate. To him it seemed as though life was just beginning; he had begun to treat a fresh wound; the scars and the memories would take longer to heal.

Two years later, Amay graduated and joined a large Indian software company that overworked its people and paid so poorly that its employees were always leaving. It was Amay's job to find out why they were leaving. He'd meet them for drinks in a bar or a restaurant, and hearing their complaints, would proceed to assure them, off the record, that they were doing the right thing. He'd go back to his bosses and report that the employees were not suited to their work culture; they were short-term players, incapable of loyalty. It was one of those players who recommended Amay's name for the post of a human resource manager with a multinational IT company in Delhi. With his self-assured ways, his military bearing, and his experience of the software industry's manpower requirements, Amay bagged the job. With it, came a salary three times the amount he was making. He moved from Bombay to Delhi, set up home in the capital city, a home he rarely saw, as he worked long hours into the night and most weekends too. This impressed his bosses, who singled him out for out-of-turn promotions and fabulous raises.

In Delhi, Amay met Sharda, a girl much younger than him. She worked for an insurance company selling employee benefit plans, and although she was squint-eyed and plump-faced, she spoke her way into Amay's heart. Amay married her in Bombay, over a quiet ceremony, and he gave a small reception at a South Bombay club. Two days later they returned to Delhi, and a month later he wrote in, saying, "Sharda has been lucky for me. I have been appointed head of staffing for five countries: India, China, Malaysia, Singapore, and Thailand."

From his e-mails, I gathered that Amay's job was to identify and export IT talent from India. The talent came from India because it was easier to sell the big global dream to candidates from a developing country, where the taxes and cost of living made saving difficult. Amay used this angle to convince candidates to leave India and to chart their careers overseas. He wrote to me: "Really, Gussy, you should see how advanced these foreign countries are. It makes you ashamed of the rot in our country: the slums, the pollution, the indiscipline which is never going to change. Take my word for it."

In a sense, I agreed with Amay. After years of feeling hurt and angry about the bribery, the corruption, and the inefficiency that had become part of our daily lives, I had found my own way of exorcising my feelings. I was writing about the ills that afflicted my country, the rot that had seeped into its system. The more I wrote, the more I discovered. My country kept throwing pop-ups of history, of diversity, forsaken truths of spirituality. It threw up all the stuff that could only come from a five-thousand-year old culture, a land that had accumulated the good, the bad, and the ugly, from hundreds of dynasties, hundreds of kings, spiritual leaders, and poets.

Amay's death occurred in Delhi.

I was invited. Why else would I go?

I hadn't seen him since six years. He was busy traveling, meeting managers in five countries. On one of his trips, he stopped in Bombay, and that's when he invited us, me and my wife, Fiona, to Delhi. "The house is huge. The kids have grown, and hey, you guys have to check out my new Honda Accord," he said.

"Sure I won't have to push it?" I asked, harking back to college when we would struggle with his father's 1962-model scooter. It would stop on the way back from a night show, each time on Marine Drive, opposite the ladies' hostel, and the girls would crowd their balconies to see our attempts at kick-starting it. The scooter would rev and smoke after a few kicks, but as soon as we'd get on, it would whimper and seize on us, and I would be terribly nervous because we would be stoned on hashish, bought at one rupee per goli, off the streets of Colaba.

Hashish, I admit, wasn't frowned upon then. It was accepted as a form of street life. It had its own identity, its own aura, was thought of as sustenance for the mind, as ambrosia of the Gods.

In the seventies, in Bombay, almost every street had its own hash dealer, its chacha jaan, uncle of life. At dens, you'd find people from all classes of society, and each person had a story to tell, and each one wanted to listen to the other, for *that* was the beauty of pure hashish: it made you warm and expansive; it made you respectful and attentive; it made you realize that someone else had a story worth the telling and worth the listening; and it spoke of a time when lungs were deep, not pockets, and hearts were big and open, and minds eager and receiving, and the peace of brotherhood prevailed and flowed into all. Maybe that's why we smoked outdoors, in the open, different hands clasping the same chillum, different lips spread over the mouth of the same chillum, without fretting about things like communicable diseases. But there *was* anxiety of a different kind. We were kids after all, fresh-faced teenagers, and we didn't know how the cops would react to us smoking. Would they let us off with a warning, or would they call our parents, or simply throw us in jail for a night, bedding of straw, no pillow, no fan, lights out after ten, and mosquitoes feeding off us, in which case we'd emerge hardened, like Amitabh Bachchan in one of those seventies movies.

For our night smokes, we'd retire to the Gateway of India, where we'd gaze at the sailboats swaying and the ship lights twinkling, and we'd see our lives like that, adrift and coruscating. We'd break into a Neil Young song "As long as we can sail away," and passersby would think us mad and shake their heads, while we would think ourselves to be "so clever and casteless and free," which was a John Lennon line that seemed to have stuck.

All this hallucination would end with Amay looking up at the Hotel Taj Mahal, its rooms with long French windows and quiet, bleating air-conditioners. Then he would exclaim, "Say, Gussy. How much do you think a room here would cost?"

I would conjecture and exaggerate the amount. And he would sniff and say wistfully, "Shit, Gussy, such money should be ours. Should be, no, at some point?" And I could not tell whether he was being rhetorical or matter of fact, or decisively ambitious and over-the-top. He would continue to look up at the windows, higher and higher, and blink. And on the way down, his jaw would tighten, his lips would pucker, his eyes would twist into a scowl. There would be no blinking then, just a dark, stony silence. I didn't realize then that Amay was setting goals. He was plotting a course over unfathomed waters, seeing horizons unseen by me. I didn't realize how far he planned to fly. And what he'd forget once he got there.

It was a cool December morning when we landed in Delhi. It was not as cold as expected. The train chugged in at 11:30 A.M. Amay was there to receive us. He pushed and broke through the bustle: coolies staggering under heavy luggage, hearty reunions in progress, vendors selling their wares in shrill voices, touts canvassing for taxis and hotels, adhering themselves to likely customers.

Holding on to Amay's one hand was Sohail, his elder son, a sweet smiling boy of six, and on the other, Rakesh, his younger son, an angel-faced devil at four. We patted their heads. "How you've grown," "What big boys you've become," and "We hear you play soccer now," were some of the things we said to them. They smiled shyly, then warmly.

On the drive back, Amay was exuberant. "You have gained weight, Gussy. Is it due to the wife's cooking?" he said, looking at Fiona in the mirror. Without waiting for an answer, he stroked the wheel of his car and asked, "How do you like my new baby?"

"A beaut! A dream!" I exclaimed, trying to sound impressed. I was hopeless with cars. Didn't own one, nor did I plan to.

"After a certain stage, a big car is important," he said. "Maruti feels like a dabba now. I sat in one the other day and felt claustrophobic. You won't believe the kind of installments I am paying for this. Fifty K a month! It eats into my petrol allowance like crazy, but it is worth it, I tell you."

Sharda was at the door when we pulled in. She had put on a few kilos since their wedding, which made her look shorter. I noticed she had warm, intelligent eyes which squinted when she thought hard. She also had a tendency to laugh a lot, sometimes without reason. She did this when she saw us, immediately after the first hellos.

They stayed in a nice part of town, lush, green, and quiet, a relief after Bombay and its chaos. On our way in, Amay mentioned that all of Delhi was like this—the *residential* part separate from the *commercial*, unlike Bombay where lines of occupancy were blurred.

We parked in the living room. In a corner stood a Christmas tree twinkling with decorations; at its base were a pool of presents. The wrapping paper on the gifts fluttered noisily under the fan. It threatened to rupture.

"Don't worry, Gussy, some of the gifts *are* for you," said Amay, smiling.

"Yes, the kids insisted," said Sharda. "'Daddy, what about your friends?' they asked, when we set it up. 'Won't they be here for Christmas?'"

"No, really?" exclaimed my wife, Fiona.

"Yes," said Sharda proudly. "They even chose the gifts themselves. No prompting, all on their own. It's the school that makes them this way, teaches them thoughtfulness, amongst other values. The tuition is expensive, but worth it, as you can see."

With that she launched into a tirade against Bombay schools, the whole farce of admissions, donations, and compulsory tuitions, which made education an ordeal for the children and a burden to the parents. We clicked our tongues and agreed. They were lucky to be out of it—out of Bombay, that is. Delhi, it appeared, was much better.

"In every way!" she said. "Such a better quality of life it offers—and all this space." She looked around and did a 180-degree squint. "I don't think I can ever return to Bombay," she said, crumpling her nose disdainfully.

She was right. The house was huge. A bamboo finish gave it the impression of being light and uncluttered. Everything seemed to have fitted into corners, neatly, precisely. The look was warm, homely, and practical, everything available at hand.

In the living room, a computer, printer, and scanner stood in one corner, a tall bookshelf in the other. Along the wall was a bar—with acquisitions from foreign travels displayed prominently. Below the bar was a place for some showpieces: figurines, stirrers, a beer mug with a droll face, and a bronze Buddha, his arms raised in glee.

Amay made the drinks. He had a talent for it. In college days we had planned a trip to the U.S., where we thought we could fund ourselves on the basis of his talent. The trip remained a plan, a dream. Now of course Amay made several trips to the U.S. His company paid for them.

We picked our drinks off the tray: a Bloody Mary for me, a Screwdriver for my wife. Then we relaxed as one would in the company of friends to whom one had entrusted their holiday. It was a warm, flushed feeling and our hearts opened up; we chatted genially. In between, the kids would interrupt our conversation. They'd show us a game or a painting, and the younger one would follow the older one in his actions, more insistent, lest he be perceived as lacking. We laughed at their enthusiasm, and Sharda would wait for them to leave before relating something funny done in school, and together we'd laugh and feel the bonhomie that comes from knowing you've grown up, that your happiness and amusement depends not on rock stars, film stars, or books, but on a younger, more innocent generation.

Amay said he was navigating his career. That was the word he used. The goal was to get overseas. Everything else was perfunctory.

Sharda said, "It all depends on his American boss. We are pretty close to her. When she visits, I take her shopping. I buy her artifacts, bangles, carpets, clothes. I cook up Indian meals, which she loves. These things *are* important. They help." She glowed with achievement. It appeared she was working as hard as Amay. They both had the same drive.

Fiona rose and excused herself. She said she wanted to freshen up.

After a while, not wishing to appear slack in the hygiene department, I too excused myself and followed her. Ours was the last room along the corridor. I found her seated on the bed. She looked distraught as she said, "There is a maid in our bathroom and she is having a bath."

"A maid . . . you don't say?" I asked, surprised. "Maybe she is cleaning it for us."

"No," said Fiona. "Listen." Sure enough there was the sound of a shower and water splashing.

"What is she doing there?" I asked.

"Precisely what you hear," Fiona said. "She is having a bath. She saw me, stepped in, and shut the door to my face, liked she owned the place, like I was an intruder."

"That's it?" I asked.

"That's it," she said.

"Is there someone in our bathroom?" I inquired of Sharda, on our return to the living room.

"Oh, that's Nanda, our maid," she said brightly, pointing to our refilled glasses. Amay was at the bar fixing their drinks.

"You don't have to worry about her," Sharda said. "She is such an angel with the boys that we like to treat her well. She will be sharing the bathroom with you. She will be accessing it from the other side, so it won't disturb you. There *is* a toilet in the back porch, but it gets so cold at night that we don't like to send her out. Good maids are hard to come by, and they charge the earth. You won't believe what I am paying her."

We didn't ask; we just nodded, feeling slightly ashamed. We prided ourselves on being well-adjusted, fully-integrated Indians. So why were we getting snotty about a maid sharing our bathroom?

Three cocktails later we were introduced to Nanda. She was a thin, bony girl in her twenties. Her face was long and narrow. Her eyes were large and black; they appeared to dominate her face. Her nose was sharp and slender, and her lips were thin and compressed, with all the pertness of youth. When she entered the living room, her hair was wet and loose, all the way down to her waist, her head was arched to one side, and she was drying her hair with a towel.

"Nanda, these are our friends from Bombay," said Sharda. "They are in your hands now. You will take care of them, no?" The broken English was a deliberate attempt to involve her.

"Ji, didi, yes," said Nanda. Her head bent, she scrubbed away with the towel. "Should I serve lunch now or later?" she asked. "Now" was decided.

Thinking we would now get a chance to freshen up, we retired to our time-share bathroom. It was wet and stained with chappal marks. There were lumps of hair everywhere—in the basin, on the floor, in the receptacle of the toilet seat. The toilet paper was damp and soiled, and in the air a familiar smell lingered, a smell that was sharp, strong, and repelling.

"Smells like . . ." I said, sniffing in mid air.

"Lycol!" declared Fiona. She rushed for my aftershave and emptied out a third of it on the lice-killing molecules.

Lunch was served, a simple fare—three dishes. We ate quietly, stopping, once in a while, to refill our plates. The maid stood in attendance, and after a while Sharda announced, "Nanda is terrific with vegetarian fare. If you are lucky you will taste most of her specialties."

Hearing her name, Nanda came up and dropped creamy pieces of palak paneer onto our plates. She also splattered some dal and some aloo gobi, potatoes and cauliflower in a thick brown gravy. Her hair hovered above my plate, and I got a strong smell of Lycol. I flattened the palak paneer with my fork, listening for the discerning crunch of insects.

"Hey, Gussy," Amay said, his face fresh with revelation. "We are planning to turn you onto some serious vegan food. I hope you guys are okay with that?"

"Hey, treat us like family. No ceremonies, okay?" I said, but in my heart some confusion rose. I wondered whether I had heard right about Delhi being the home of tender meats, the food capital of India.

Gently, I took my chances. "We mustn't burden Nanda all the time. Let's eat out . . . try some Afghani, Kashmiri, Punjabi food . . . the asli dhaba stuff, you know?"

"Oh, those kind of places we gave up some time ago," Sharda said. "Now we go only to the five stars, like when Amay's foreign bosses come. We go on company expense, of course."

"We have some bravo meals this way," Amay said. "I call the hotel in advance and ask about their specialties. Then we pretend we are regulars there, which impresses the foreigners into thinking we are gourmet eaters."

The topic changed. Sharda spoke about light impact aerobics, which she had just discovered. Amay spoke about river rafting. The water from the rapids was cool, clear, and invigorating.

"You should try it sometime," Amay said to me.

"I don't know," I replied. "A friend of ours died doing that last year. He went down with a heart attack, and he was only thirty-two."

"A freak case," Amay said. "Shouldn't try it, if your heart's not in it."

"This summer we are doing Europe," Sharda said. "Amay's American boss has promised to coincide it with some official work, so we can save on travel expenses."

"Sounds great," I said.

"The advantage of working for a multinational!" declared Amay. "If they like you, they favor you, and they love yours truly, totally." He knocked back his drink and took a bow.

"But not as much as they like your wife," Sharda said, laughing. She laughed so heartily that her whole body shook and some of her drink spilled. We laughed too, although our laughter was infinitely less hearty.

Sharda said, "Amay's American boss wants to come down and stay with us. She loves the boys. She wants to adopt them."

"Gladly," Amay said, "give both of them away." Then pensively he added, "We had better get the house painted and the guest room done up before she comes."

When lunch was over, Sharda announced gulab jamuns for dessert. Nanda brought them in, steaming hot, and served them with scoops of vanilla ice cream. We ate silently, savoring the ambivalence of hot and cold flavors.

Defeated by the dessert, we slumped in our chairs and chatted some more. Then Amay suggested we all get some sleep. The children had been up early, playing soccer in the park.

As we were about to retire, there was a knock on the door. It was Amay.

"Hey, Gussy," he said. "I just wanted to remind you to keep the bathroom door on your side locked. So the maid can get in from the other side. She can use it when she wants to."

I nodded, fighting back a flush of annoyance. What was this Nanda obsession? What would happen when the American boss visited? Would she be expected to share the bathroom as well? It would be interesting to raise this as a matter of rhetoric.

Amused by the thought, I drifted off to sleep and slept a deep, dreamless sleep.

It was six when I awoke. The room was cool and dark. The curtains were drawn. Fiona was sitting on the bed, dressed in winter wear. In Bombay—with no winters to speak of—I didn't get a chance to see her this way and I thought she looked nice and comely.

Dressed, I got myself some tea from the kitchen. Then I ventured into the living room, where I gazed at the books on the shelves. I was surprised to find many of the titles were from my collection. There were books lent over the years and not returned, and for a while I became burdened with this. I felt a sense of loss, which swept through me like a wave of anger.

I moved out onto the lawn, where Amay and family waited.

The evening had brought with it a pleasant breeze. The sky was dull, gray, and empty, like a giant auditorium with excess space. I'd never known this feeling in Bombay, this feeling of overwhelming space, this sense that I could be ignored, or overlooked, or forgotten.

"There *is* a nip but no winter yet," Amay said, as he drove us around. The city stretched before us like a python, and the road dipped and loomed up suddenly to reveal a cast of winter gray.

After Bombay's perennial summer, it was nice to wear a cardigan, I thought. Winters, I realized, were essential to writers. You could look like Sean Connery in *Finding Forrester*, or thickly clad and bearded, you could stir firewood and other memorabilia in a log cabin up in the hills. "There are some nice spots around here," Sharda had said earlier. "You should visit Kasauli, where many writers live. They live in self-imposed isolation. And their fans hang around in the bazaar or at the coffee shop, waiting to catch a glimpse of them. I wonder why these writer-fellows get so much attention. What makes them so special?" She had laughed, and we'd joined in, too, a holiday well-begun, a camaraderie of hearts raring to unwind, to expand, and wits dying to sparkle.

I thought her suggestion about going to Kasauli and bumping into some writer was nice. Who knows, I might even get invited for a drink and a meal, an evening of wine and literature. Oh, what good fortune that would be!

I lost myself in thoughts of meeting my kind of people, those with gentle literary manners and pleasant elevated thought. I plunged deeper into my daydreams, until I heard Amay say, "These parks are the lungs of the city. They were Sanjay Gandhi's brainchild, you know?"

Sanjay Gandhi? Indira Gandhi's younger son, long dead now! I tried to imagine him transplanting green hairy lungs with his brown hairy hands, while his men were busy sterilizing young men in villages. Slit, slit, they would go, the nasbandi experts, tearing at potential roots, and the victims—broken-hearted men with lifeless cocks—would slink away, shamed by their inability to produce. Seed, but no crop; no crop, always hunger, paranoia, and somewhere shame, searing, unbearable shame. What had the country gone through during the emergency? I wondered. What was it that I did not know because of my tender years and my conviction that only birds lived in cages?

Don't educate, amputate, has always been the Indian way, I think, as Amay takes a turn. That's how the country was run during the emergency. That's how tribals were being displaced from their roots, even today, sixty years after independence, to make way for large dams with promises of water, power, and prosperity diverted to eager, waiting corporates. And the real sons of the soil—the tribals—would take their ambitions elsewhere: to cities and slums, where they would usurp places not their own, and they would feel fine about it because *that* is what someone had done to them, taken away their fields, their huts, their history—all in the name of progress.

I told Amay this when he asked me what my worldview was, the issues that weighed on me as a writer. We were back from our drive and parked on his lawn now, settled in deck chairs, which, to my mind, was a specious way to discuss the country's future. Lights twinkled in bungalows. Curtains were drawn. Shaded by trees, the neighborhood was silent.

"So what are you saying?" Amay asked, leaning over a coal fire he had just begun. The nip had arrived and the sky was florid with stars. "There should be no progress, no development; the villages should remain as they are—untouched and steeped in ignorance?"

"That's not the point," I said. "There are fairer ways to approach development. It cannot be city-centric, that's for sure. It has to respect the tiller and his way if living. We can't displace him to feed our own ends. We have to respect his roots, his privacy, his concept of existence."

"Which is what?" Amay asked. Using a poker, he lifted some coals and placed them near the ones burning. He stood the poker against the side of the oven and rubbed his palms.

"Which is a cashless society, a society that knows no corruption, no greed, only inter-dependence and contentment. A society that gets it food from the river, its shelter from the forest, its sustenance from the land it works on."

"So you are saying, let them stay that way. Let them be in their original primitive form. But isn't that selfish? Isn't that a denial of evolution, a denial of civilization? Aren't you denying them a chance to progress?"

I took in a deep breath. I had been down this road before. I knew almost every nook and corner, every turn and curve, and could see the bumps a mile away.

"So what is civilization?" I asked, reaching for the poker and prodding some coals that were not yet aflame. "In your words, how would you define it?"

Amay thought for a while, then spoke slowly. "Progress, development, needs processing, wish fulfillment, the ability to do more, to rise beyond oneself, the ability to discover, to understand, to achieve, conquer, and be masters of the universe." His face was flushed. I could picture him in boardrooms, making a pitch to his American bosses, and at management campuses, selling the big global dream to candidates. I looked at the women. Sharda was silent. Fiona looked anxious.

"No, specifics!" I insisted. "Give me specifics, in working terms."

"I don't follow you, Gussy. Civilization is civilization. What kind of definition are you looking for?" He looked confused now. A scowl had appeared on his face, the kind a man wears when he suspects he might lose ground in the presence of the fairer sex.

I smiled. "Just the kind you see around, Amay: congested slums, choked gutters, water shortages, pollution, population increase, inability to cope, inability to absorb; hence, growing crime, growing greed, land grabbing, encroachments, a buck here, a buck there, no end in sight, a cesspool underneath, a storm overhead, and all of us in the thick of it, with our blinkers on."

"But that is terribly fatalistic," Sharda said. She sounded agitated, left out on her own turf.

"But you will agree that these *are* the problems of evolving cities?" I said, ignoring Sharda and looking Amay straight in the eye. He was blinking now. Fiona, I realized, was trying hard to catch my eye. I took care to avoid hers.

"Yes, yes, but that doesn't take away from the importance of cities, and they *are* trying to find solutions, I am sure . . ." His voice tapered off.

A cold wind appeared and scattered some sparks, which landed on our clothes. We brushed at them furiously and they glowed and died out. We looked to see no malicious specks lingered.

"You see the nexus?" I said. Rural population pushed towards urban, urban boils over and claims some rural land next to urban limits, and urban accommodates the spillover at urban rates. That's your civilization—designed to favor the few at the expense of many—and you, you are the pawn, not realizing that you are being moved around, shunted or shafted in the name of progress."

"That's warped and shortsighted," Amay said. "Now you are saying that cities shouldn't expand. That there is a conspiracy at work, a collaboration of forces, a planned destruction—crazy!"

"No, it is you who are crazy for not seeing and not admitting," I said robustly. I was enjoying myself, for if he could advocate big cars, expensive salaries, maids, drivers, overseas travel, an overseas posting, surely I could speak up for a few who I thought should inherit the earth.

The night had turned cold. I preferred to stand or walk around. My mind felt sharp; it could negotiate and receive the cold. The fire too was well lit. Behind me, the French windows showed our reflections—murky in the light of the oven.

Rubbing my palms, breathing into them, I said, "Tell me, Amay, why do you want to go overseas? Why do you want to reject development in your own country?"

"Why? To give my family a better life! To achieve what I want. To realize my full potential. And to test myself in international waters."

"Yes, but why overseas? Is something pushing you away? Is it the rot? Is it the crowding? Don't you think you are running away? Fleeing from your own intolerance? Before the city dies you will be gone, but when the village dies—that's okay, because anything is okay for the villagers. *That* you have decided, accepted already in your mind. And so you will skip, while your country evolves, while it goes through labor pains. You will abandon her, while she gripes and groans in the throes of civilization. And you won't wait to see her give birth to more like you, who will turn their backs because they can't bear to see the pangs of civilization. Yet progress must go on, even in your absence, because that's how markets are being created, segmented, and targeted. Targeted by whom? Your big multinational bosses—that's who! They who feed off your market intelligence and who want to know how the average Indian thinks.

What does he dream? What does he desire? Tell us, Amay; tell us all. Here! We will give you a fancy car, and a fancy house, and a big, fat expense account, so you can eat in fancy restaurants, and you can convince us that you are like us, the same tastes, when in truth you are not. But tell us all, Amay, tell us all. We want a share of the Indian mind. No, we are not looking at market share right now, only mind share, mind you. You've got the mind, you've got the market. And you get the picture, don't you, Amay? The big picture . . . before you . . . in 70 mm contrast, with the world as your oyster?"

"Stop it, please," Sharda cried. She was pale; her lips were trembling.

The color had drained from Amay's face. He said, "You are crazy, Gussy. I should never have invited you, never."

"Too bad," I said. "We are here now and you are stuck with us." And in my sweetest voice I added, "Well, well, what a life."

Fiona lay in bed, trying to sleep. Her back was to me, her legs were drawn in, her fists were clenched, and between us was a mountain of blankets. I was sitting up in bed, trying to read, when Sharda knocked at the door and said there was a bowl of pasta in the microwave; we could have it for dinner or keep it in the fridge. "Thanks," I said, buoyantly. She moved away without saying good night. That suited me.

We were in no mood to eat. Fiona, I realized, was terribly upset. She said I had acted in bad taste. I had gone too far, indulged in cerebral homicide, which showed a lack of refinement in me. I didn't care to analyze what she said, and I certainly didn't want to take it to heart. Fact is, I had enjoyed myself greatly. It was the kind of enjoyment that comes out of catharsis, out of keeping quiet too long. I had come to the conclusion that Amay and Sharda were far removed from my sphere of understanding. They were trapped in a cycle of wants and vanities. They were in a giant store where they had seen too much, too soon, and they wanted all of it at the same time. If it came free, so much the better, and if it didn't, they'd get it anyway. And they'd make sure that people knew how much they spent on their car, their kids, their kids' education, their maid, their holidays, and their home. All this was important, for it fed an image that had come to stay. I could see where they were going with the image. It would grow in their minds, craving and clamoring that all things in life must come their way. Then, later, if they were in the U.S., if they had their way with the American boss, that is, someone would suggest a shrink, someone patient, not a clock-watcher, who would help them get in touch with themselves. And if they were in India, which I doubted very much, they'd try their hand at reiki, pranik healing, or meditation, which would make them feel calm, erudite, and superior.

Twice that night the maid went into the bathroom and made a racket of herself. She thought it cool to drag a bucket, to open the tap, to let it roar into the bucket, and empty the bucket into the cistern. I waited for the sound of the flush. It was as if she had decided not to use it. A nightmare played up the smell, the chappal marks, and the dirty hands on the hand-towel. I tossed and turned, eyes shut, but mind wide open.

It was 2:00 A.M. by the time I slept. I could do so only with the weight of a pillow over my head. During the night, I dreamt I was out in the wilderness, a hilly part of India, dark and resonant with footsteps. I was part of an army of feet treading softly. No one knew where we were headed. No one asked. We would walk in silence, plodding the slopes, navigating the descents. When we were up on the hills we would spot the river, Ma Narmada, as she was called. We would stop and look at her, floating like a mystic maiden. She would glide, and with the flick of a wrist and a spin of her waist would celebrate her freedom. We would walk again, a sense of unease pecking at our hearts, for we knew that her freedom was short-lived. In better days, she—the mother of all rivers—would have attracted princes and poets to her banks, today she had only writers and artists grieving for her life, pleading to the world: damn her not, no dam her not, for she is a lady.

My eyes opened. Even with the windows shut, I felt cold; I found it difficult to breathe. I felt I was in a solitary confinement cell where I had no one to depend on but myself. I'd been brought here by some conspiracy of forces, a strange karmic plot intending to deliver a life-staggering blow. I yearned for Bombay and its warm, insipid winter. I hated the thought that I would have to spend Christmas in this strange, cold city, with friends who had become strangers. Tormented by this thought, I pulled the blanket over my face and slept under its thorny bristles.

It was 8:30 A.M. by the time we awoke. We would have slept on, but for some intermittant banging at our door.

It was the boys playing soccer, our door their goalpost. They smiled sweetly and said, "Uncle, Daddy didn't play today. He went to office early. You will play with us, please?"

Nanda came out of the kitchen. She smiled and said, "I told them not to make noise, but they wouldn't listen. They get bored, no, in holidays." She added, "Sahib, Memsahib, both gone for work." I nodded and shut the door.

While I was having my tea Sharda called. "Sorry," she said, "but we had to get to work. Tomorrow being Christmas, I had to send out some urgent e-mails, and Amay too has to get a few things done.

"About last night . . ." I started.

"No, please," she said. "It's best forgotten. If you must, speak it over with Amay." She paused, then added, "I thought you could do some sight seeing today. So I've told Nanda to pack you some lunch, and Shyam Singh, our driver, will take you around."

"You ought to be ashamed," Fiona said, when I told her the plan. "And you were planning to return to Bombay. I don't know what gets into you, but you take things so seriously. Always ready to pick cudgels. If you have a theory, why not keep it to yourself? Write about it, vent it out, but why get into a quarrel, that too when you are a guest."

I realized she hadn't slept too well. I felt bad for her. Maybe she was right. I should try to normalize things, perhaps even apologize. I was glad we were out for the day. Some diversion might defuse the strain. It would also give me time to think things over.

Equipped with a hamper—chicken rolls, fruit, and two bottles of Bisleri—we set out on a tour of Delhi. Amay's driver, Shyam Singh, drove too fast for my liking; he would cut lanes, overtake, and challenge other drivers to race. But he slowed each time he passed a dignitary.

"There are over a thousand monuments in and around Delhi," I read from the guidebook, which I had picked up at Bombay Central station. It was a crummy-looking book printed on cheap paper. "Many of them are located in areas like South Extension, Green Park, and Hauz Khas, and reflect a sense of history long forgotten, yet which can be unearthed by those willing to exercise patience. Sadly, many of these monuments have fallen into disarray. They are beyond recognition, incapable of bearing testimony to the glorious era from which they hail." I stopped. I thought of Amay and our childhood years, and of the gap that had crept in sharply and decisively. Here was a monument as much in disarray. One night's storm had shown up the differences, the cracks that had crept in unnoticed.

Shyam Singh spoke. What would we like to see first: Humayun's tomb, India Gate, the Qutub Minar, or the Red Fort? We decided on the Red Fort. It was where the tricolor was raised when we got our independence, and every year thereafter, on Republic Day and Independence Day.

Shyam Singh maneuvered through the narrow lanes, slowing for cows, goats, and handcarts. Soon we found ourselves at the gates of the fort, where we were told that the English-speaking guide was on tour;

we'd have to wait for him to return. At the side, some foreigners waited, too. They wore Bermudas and T-shirts and had expensive-looking cameras draped around their necks. Fiona and I decided to take a walk. Shyam Singh parked the car and went for a chai.

We took pictures of the bright, busy street. A girl and a boy offered to pose for us, doing stunts on bamboos. We took pictures of them and treated them to sherbet and vada pav.

We sat on a parapet outside the fort, absorbing the street life, when a dark, scruffy vagabond approached us. He was around forty-five years of age, with thick, matted hair, a wisp of a beard, and wide, earnest eyes. In one hand, he held a staff, with which he propelled himself. He had one leg missing, the right one, and had a cape, a grayish-black blanket, wrapped around his shoulders.

"Hello, sir, madam," he said, bowing. "Allow me to introduce myself. I am Ehsaan Ali, keeper of the fort, direct descendant of Emperor Shah Jahan. With your permission, I will tell you the story of how this great fort came to be built." He banged his staff three times, winked at me, and stood at attention, as if awaiting our permission.

At least he wasn't drunk or begging, I thought. He was living off his wits, and so deserved to be heard. Fiona thought otherwise. She would have led me away, but I was sold on his audacity. "Go on, speak," I said, "but what will you charge? Settle it now. I don't want any hassle later!"

"Charge? Why you talk about charging, sir? Who can put a charge on history? Not you, not me," he said solemnly.

Fiona gesticulated, a screwdriver motion at the temples, to suggest he was crazy. But I was mesmerized. I wanted to see whether he was a conman or plain crazy.

"The only man who can decide the charge, sir, is Shah Jahan, your and my great grandfather, and he is dead, sir, so we won't insult his memory. You pay me what you like . . . what you think it is worth, and if you don't pay me, that is also okay. Because what value on history, sir? What value—when it is no more?"

I nodded, and Ehsaan Ali slid to the ground and sat at our feet, placing his staff beside him. He cleared his throat and began his tale.

"For eleven years the great Shah Jahan ruled his kingdom from the city of Agra, until one day he began to feel restless. His palace could hold him no longer, his fountains and gardens lost their meaning, his queens found him absent and distracted, and his Generals began to whisper that there were matters on his mind far removed from matters of the state. Being a wise man, Shah Jahan himself was quick to realize

222

his altered state, and calmly he went about understanding its cause and getting to the root of the problem.

"Through his musings, he found that he was tired of Agra. The climate bothered him, the streets were too narrow for the grand processions he led, and the builder in him dreamt of a new citadel, something that would show the world that he could be as great a builder as his grandfather, Akbar, who'd built the city of Fatehpur Sikri.

"The Emperor decided on a change. He wrote in his diary: 'Delhi has historically been the capital of India, and so it shall be once again. The new capital shall hereafter be the seat of the Mogul Empire. It shall reflect its glory as the sun reflects the power and the brilliance of God. And there shall be a mighty fort, which shall be open to friends and unassailable to foes.'

"Soon after, he dispatched his Mir-i-Imarat, his superintendent of buildings, to select a site for the new fort. It had to be a place that would be rich in scenery and able support the structure.

"After surveying the city, the superintendent chose the area around Talkatora and Raisina Hill, and he returned and reported it to the Emperor, who, for a second opinion, sent Ustad Hamid and Ustad Hira, two of his most skilled and trusted masons.

"The masons inspected the site and found it unworthy. The soil was full of minerals. It had high quantities of saltpeter, which, in the long run, would damage the buildings. Instead, they found a place on the right bank of the Yamuna where the soil was free of minerals and where the landscape presented an outstanding view. They conveyed this to the Emperor, who was pleased with their foresight. The Mir-i-Imarat too agreed with them."

Ehsaan Ali paused. He stretched his neck out like a giraffe, and swirling the skin on his throat with two fingers, emitted a low gargling sound. Fiona began to look worried, but I thought this terribly funny, especially when he opened his mouth and let out a loud protracted burp.

He continued, "You can imagine, friends, what happens when a great Emperor like Shah Jahan sets his mind on building a vast and impregnable fort. Labor was imported from all over. Stones were carried in all the way from Agra. All incoming roads were blocked for days, for months, and even the English factories could not move their produce to the coast. They suffered great losses in silence. But what could they say—when the great Emperor had made up his mind?

"The construction began in 1638 and Ustad Hamid and Ustad Hira were placed in charge. This was over experienced officials like Izzat

Khan, Alah Vardi Khan, and Makramat Khan, for such was the faith the Emperor had in them. But no sooner had the foundation been laid than both of them disappeared. Not a word or a whisper to say where they were going, how long they'd be away, and when they'd return—not even to their families.

"The Emperor was furious. He blamed himself for trusting them, and thought perhaps they'd discovered that the selection of the site was indeed faulty and they'd run away to save their skins. He decided to issue a fatwa on them, and was about to order his troops to hunt and kill them when they turned up smiling. They appeared before him and explained the reason for their absence. They said they had wanted the foundation to remain exposed to the elements for a certain period of time. Only then would the soil get seasoned enough to support the building. But, had they been around, there would have been pressure from the palace to complete the work. Hence, they had thought up this plan.

"So pleased was the Emperor when he heard this that he forgave them and made up his mind to reward them generously once the fort was built.

"Gradually the fort came up—first the battlements, sixty feet in height and two miles long. Then the royal apartments, and at their entrance the Nakkar Khana, the chamber of music from where ensued the sweetest of melodies, depending on the time of the day and the season.

"Then came the Diwan-i-Am, the grand hall of public audience, with columns of silver, pillars of gold, and ceilings of gilded stucco."

At this point Ehsaan Ali's face assumed a challenging look. Dropping his voice, he asked, "Surely, sir, madam, you have heard of the famous Peacock throne, which took seven years to complete, and whose design, it is said, was ordained by the Gods?"

We nodded. Fiona, I noticed was rapt now, almost reverential.

"Ah, this throne was seated in the Diwan-i-Khas, where the Emperor entertained his special guests. It was shaped in the form of two dancing peacocks, and each peacock's eyes glittered with actual diamonds, and between their tails was a parakeet of pure emerald. The legs of the throne were studded, too, with diamonds and emeralds, and above it was a gold-laced canopy, and below it a platform of pure marble.

"For ten years the laborers toiled, carrying stones and precious stones from all over India. It took seven years to build the wall of the fort, which was seven miles in circumference and had thirteen gates and sixteen side gates and back entrances.

"On a bright April morning in 1648, the Emperor entered his newly

224

built fort. He came in a grand procession, the kind never seen or imagined before. Eight thousand horses, one thousand elephants, macebearers, midgets, clowns, jugglers, acrobats, musicians, and foot soldiers in front, and the cavalry behind, and men carrying symbols of power—a fish head, or a horse's head, or a tiger's head, on a stick. And actual tigers, too, in cages, fierce and pacing, rolled along on carts, and kept in place with clubs of fire. And there were servants in front, to sprinkle perfumed water on the roads, and gong bearers and rocket bearers going mad, and dancing girls and dancing bears to add to the excitement. And then the Emperor, on the largest elephant, the tusker they called Meghdambar. And behind him sat his eldest born, his beloved son Dara Shikoh, who, from time to time, dug into a chest and tossed gold coins like they were peanuts. And a new coin was minted that day and the new fort was named Qila-e-Mualla, the auspicious fort, and the city was called Shahjahanabad, after its visionary ruler. So you see, my friends, this great marvel where you now stand owes its strength to two great masters, Ustad Hamid and Ustad Hira, and its grandeur to the great Emperor, who saw what it was like to build for the future."

Our friend fell silent. His lips began to quiver. He wrapped his blanket tightly around himself. I began to agree with Fiona that he was a little touched. But what a wonderful tale it was, and said with what conviction and knowledge.

I extracted a hundred-rupee note from my wallet and asked Ehsaan Ali why he wasn't a guide, why he was so poorly off, but he just said "Bah! Naseeb! Destiny!" and drawing himself up, hobbled off without taking any money. He went and stood at a tea stall down the lane; he stood, sipping chai, rubbing his nose with his blanket, staring at us intently.

Feeling awkward and a bit saddened, we decided to get away from his gaze. We decided to go inside, where we found the English-speaking guide had arrived. The foreigners had engaged him, and he had begun his talk.

"Ah," he said. "A four-hundred-year-old fort you are looking at now. Not a fort, but a township, so vast and beautiful in design. Built by the great Shah Jahan, who was imprisoned by his son, the dreaded Aurangzeb."

The guide was a thin weasel-faced man. He had large, protruding teeth, which made him appear artificial when he smiled. He spoke in a theatrical, singsong way, very different from our vagabond-scholar who'd spoken so earnestly. We joined the group, hoping it wasn't one of those exclusive hotel cliques, but the foreigners smiled at us a lazy holiday smile, so we assumed it was okay with them. The guide droned on, his attention fixed on the foreigners.

"Heights of glory, depths of tragedy, what has this fort not seen? And pomp and progress, and death and betrayal, all in the same place. It was here that the great Emperor spread the fame of the Mogul empire, here that he was captured and unseated by his son, Aurangzeb, and here that he saw the death of his son, Dara Shikoh, at the hands of the treacherous Aurangzeb." The foreigners listened. Some took notes, others, pictures.

The guide's style was more melodramatic than factual, and in this manner he took us through the fort—its arcades and bazaars, its halls and apartments, its courtyards and gardens, its gates and pavilions, and at each stage he would put up a performance for the benefit of the foreigners.

At the Nakkar Khana he stopped suddenly, tugged at his ear, and said, "Ah, can you hear the flutes, the harmonicas, the drums of harmony? For this is the place where Shah Jahan welcomed his guests with sweet music." He broke into a ghazal, one hand to his ear, the other hand stretched out rapturously. I thought this to be flippant, but the foreigners found it delightful. They smiled and cheered him on. Seeing the contrast between Ehsaan Ali and him, between a genuine custodian of history and a performing artist, I thought of Amay and our welcome, which was not about us or our comfort, but about *his* growth, *his* acquisitions, which had served to caution me that we were slowly but surely getting out of sync.

We stopped at the Diwan-i-Am, and there our guide pulled in his chest, and in a deep voice said, "Ah, this was the place from where the Emperor ruled. From here he granted favors, conferred titles, and imposed sentences of death or exile." And I thought: Amay wasn't an Emperor either. He could have been, but he wasn't. He just didn't have the heart for it, or the vision.

And then we came to the Diwan-i-Khas, the hall of special audience, where in a hushed voice the guide told us that it was here that the Emperor sought to impress his foreign visitors. And then I thought: Surely the house would be painted. Amay's house would be painted and done up in chic, ethnic upholstery for the benefit of his American boss. I could hear Sharda say, "We can take these with us when we move." And I was sure also that there would be an imperial spread: spiced meats, biryanis, curries, kebabs, and roasts, a banquet fit for a King, laid out daily.

226

And, then, whichever rooms we saw, I found them bare and stripped of history, a reduction of what they once stood for, convenient for an afternoon of sight seeing but forgettable in the hub and throes of daily life. Now there were no signs that life had once existed, that the flesh and blood of a dynasty had thundered through these walls, and that weighty decisions were taken that had impacted not just the inhabitants of the fort but the entire population of the kingdom.

Eventually we came to the Hammams, the royal baths, which were still impressive and somewhat intact, well, because they were well maintained, and not left to servants to soil and misuse.

Everywhere the foreigners took pictures. They shot the columns, the pillars, the latticed windows, the minarets, and the pavilions, which had once sparkled with streams of running water lit from below. They cornered the guide and asked for more details, which he didn't have, but lied about all the same.

When the tour was over, we found ourselves back where we started. The guide went around with his head lowered, his hands outstretched—a slave anxious to collect baksheesh from his King. He stood that way and raised his head only when he was sure the right amount had been deposited. The foreigners were generous. They left five-hundred-rupee notes in his hand.

Any moment he would approach us. I realized I had to think fast. I had to decide how much to give, what the experience was worth. Where you preside does not make you a poet, as where you live does not make you an Indian, I thought. And how low you bow, and for what, is what you are and what you shall remain.

Convinced thus that that I was dealing with a beggar, I drew out my wallet and pulled out a fifty-rupee note. He came up. I squeezed the note into his palm. He waited. I fished deep into our hamper and came up with a banana and an orange. "This shall prevent cancer, and this the common cold," I said to him, in the kind of voice he'd use for the benefit of the foreigners. I squeezed the fruits into his hands. And then I bowed, and stayed bowed, and he scowled and went away nodding.

As he walked away, Fiona said, "That was mean, desperately mean." But I wasn't listening. I was busy relishing the scowl on his face. It was the same scowl I had seen on Amay's face as he had contemplated the Taj windows. It would be the same scowl I'd see later when I'd ask Amay what he would do were he to miss the foreign posting. Should his American boss get transferred, or should she leave the company, or get dengue and drop dead on her visit to India.

We returned to the car. On checking with Fiona, I found that she was as hungry as I was. We opened the hamper and brought out the chicken rolls. The chicken was tough and stringy, not properly de-frosted; the bread was stale. Winter hunger plucked at my belly. I felt restless and dissatisfied. On impulse, I leaned across and said to the driver, "Shyam Singh, where does your sahib eat when his foreigner-guests come? Please take us there."

And while Fiona protested, while she pleaded, saying we don't need to prove anything to anyone, I picked up the tourist book and read: "A must-see, the Qutub Minar, the highest stone tower in India, a pedestal of a monument built to celebrate the rise of the Slave Kings; in recent years, a suicide point."

Why, I thought, shutting the book. That was just what had hap-pened to Amay. It had taken him a while to get to the top, to his ex-quisitely padded ivory tower, from where he thought he could see the world. Then, without warning he slipped, taking our history with him.

I looked at the chicken rolls in my hand and wondered if Ehsaan Ali could use them. But, no, he deserved better treatment than that. He de-served better, simply for cherishing a period of history, for taking pride in it, for recollecting it warmly, vividly, and so precisely. In this day and age of crowding self-interest, of fast fading memories, I had to admire this keeper of history. I had to admire him for preserving so passionately what others like us might willfully forget.

Steve Yates

Report on Performance Art in One Province of the Empire Especially in Regard to Three Exhibitions Involving Swine

I am citizen Dennis Cyril Gebhardt. For Raytheon Co. (NYSE: RTN) in West Point, Mississippi, I supervise the engineering team that designs components which guide Cruise and Patriot missiles to their targets via a system of gyroscopes, accelerometers, temperature, infrared, and ultraviolet sensors, resistors, capacitors, and magnets that allow the missiles to position themselves globally within a theater of operation from threshold / launch to target. I cannot tell you more even though statistical evidence and much personal experience with previous reports assure me no one will read this.

However, neither my capacity at Raytheon nor a lack of serious readers is the problem of this report.

The Problem of This Report

My son, Dennis, whose name I did not choose, whose name his mother chose because it was she who filled out the Certificate of Live Birth, my son whose classification by the estimation of the New Age Study Group his mother belongs to is now an Indigo Child, a non-traditional learner with a warrior spirit. This means from my observation that Dennis cannot or will not sit still while well-meaning teachers try to educate him, and so he is failing and, though sixteen, will remain a freshman in high school until he chooses to pay attention and matriculate or until the school system expels him and he is forced to join the Imperial Army and fight in Arabia.

It is because of him that I am known as Cy Gebhardt to all my associates and family—I could not brook the confusion and knew immediately on learning of my wife's betrayal of an expressed agreement to name him otherwise that I could not bear him to be called Junior and live in this province with its often undeserved stigma. It is because of him that I am not at work keeping one team member from designing foolish and wasteful measures such as the baffle she proposed that would cause a Cruise missile to throb and fart like the old German buzz bombs, when Cruise missiles, which travel at sub-sonic speeds and often at very low altitudes, are already terrifying and demoralizing in the extreme based on ample field evidence obtained from many individuals in failed states subjected to Cruise missile attack. It is because of him, Dennis Junior, that I am now driving to the West Point police station where, I have been officially informed, a surprise awaits me. That, Dennis Junior, is in sum the problem of this report.

I am not any too pleased to be met at the police station by three officers all of whom appear to be hard-edged. (This description of the officers and any descriptions that stretch beyond the pale of what is observable or what can be repeated in the laboratory I credit to my wife who is a diagnosed synesthete, one for whom the delineations of the five senses are blurred such that she describes tasting shapes and smelling colors and has undergone years of Jungian therapy, which is indeed available in West Point, Mississippi, a town of 13,500 at the apex of the Golden Triangle being Starkville, Columbus, and West Point, Clay County seat and fastest growing city in this province of the empire.) The officers claim to have video to show me, so at least there will be no question of innocence or guilt. I ask to see my son but I am told, Not just yet. I doubt, when dealing with any detainee under the age of eighteen, whether it is permissible to deny a parent or guardian audience when it is requested by either minor or parent, but I go along with this directive. I am not from Mississippi but from Manhattan, Kansas, by birth and education, and have learned by experience and observation there are many occasions, be they official, formal, or casual, in this province of the empire that are best tolerated and monitored rather than immediately disrupted, suppressed, and set to order. "It will all work out in the end." I have my wife, a native of this province to thank for this useful advice regarding many local processes, at least useful as of the writing of this report.

It is through a doorway labeled PROCESSING, which I am led and after passage of which there commences no process I can detect, and for this I am thankful. The three officers and I are waiting in a low-ceilinged, tan linoleum-floored room with cinderblock walls. Despite some of the highest humidity in the nation and heaving strata of unstable soils which cause fault lines in floors and so warp door jambs that the doors will never close, I am impressed that someone has mopped and waxed this linoleum and even shined the four ominous steel bars fastened to the floor so that this processing portion of our constabulary fairly sparkles. It is in moments such as these, admiring cleanliness and sanity where none should statistically be, that I gravely consider the advisability of tax reform. In Mississippi, the most regressive tax system in North America insures that no more than thirty percent of citizenry in this province achieve a high school diploma and of those unfortunate seventy percent left behind, seventy-five percent of those will be incarcerated. A people forced to make do have become formidable at it. Do not obstruct excellence, as my direct supervisor often warns, and in the presence of these well-groomed and fit officers I adhere to this advice by remaining silent.

The locking mechanism to a door buzzes loudly and the officers usher me into a smaller chamber, not as tidy, and furnished with a much divotted and scarred wooden table, several chairs, and a television attached to a video-cassette recorder. I test three chairs for soundness before settling in one.

"Do you have any idea what we are about to show you, Mr. Gebhardt?"

"You said it was to remain a surprise."

Blinking, wrinkling their foreheads, they seat themselves and with a remote, one officer snaps on the television and directs the VCR to play. The scene is grainy and cramped, rendered in black and white. It is a hotel reception desk, well lighted, and behind it a clerk is focused forward on something outside the picture's frame. The time signature reads 2:52:04 A.M., August 2, 2006.

"This is the lobby of the Holiday Inn Express," the officer with the remote says. "Do you recognize it?"

It is disconcerting that I am not handed the remote when it is my time to respond. "I have not had the opportunity to do business there."

"Well, your son has."

On cue, a large figure moves sluggishly into the picture. Though the face is covered by a ski mask I do not recognize, the subject in the video has Dennis Junior's frame and is wearing a T-shirt and baggy shorts I do recognize. Judging from the time signature the video's speed has been greatly reduced. Dennis Junior, I'm certain of it by the bulging construction of his left soleus and the blond hair poking under the ski mask, is struggling with a weighty bundle. It is this moving bundle that the clerk seems most focused upon. Time advances and Dennis Junior exclaims something. Waving his hands and shaking his head vigorously, the Indonesian clerk, I am assuming from his slight build and facial structure though he may be Philippine or Thai, indicates he wants nothing to do with what Dennis Junior has brought. Dennis Junior, a brutish boy who disgusts football coaches in middle school and now senior high school because, while his physique and energy are ideal, his participation in the sport was violent and without discipline and he resisted all regimentation, meets the clerk's refusal with his usual if artificially delayed exuberance. In slow motion he heaves the bundle at the clerk as if shot putting. Once airborne and tumbling, hooves and trotters are evident and it becomes clear Dennis has heaved a hefty pig at the hotel worker, who is gradually, almost gracefully cringing while covering his head. I estimate this pig to be at least fifty pounds and feel I recognize it as one of three long missing from my wife's herd. Striking the counter on its back with its feet in the air, the pig and its trajectory give us a long look at its very aggravated face, albeit with mouth wide open and features upside down. At this the officer with the remote freezes the frame. Suspended, Dennis Junior is fully extended in what appears an exemplary follow through to hurling an object of this weight and volatility. The clerk is about to exit from the frame if one were to project his telemetry, and the pig is laid out before us. Clearly these officers have repeatedly watched this video presentation and knew precisely when to stop the extraordinary action.

"Recognize anybody?"

"That pig is organically grown."

"Meaning what, Mr. Gebhardt?"

"Meaning that it slops in mud bought at tremendous cost by the bag from a Columbus nursery."

The three officers glance at one another. "So you know the pig?" asks one. They do not even hand one another the remote to insure that all conversations follow in orderly fashion, so I am checked in my impulse to think that these Imperial Guardsmen might behave like a family unit.

"I knew the pig. It has been missing."

"Since August the second?"

"To the best of my knowledge."

The officer with the remote releases the frame. Bouncing off the counter and twisting to right itself while once more in flight, the pig which I believe my wife named Jasper and which was on the whole a solid but unremarkable barnyard animal proves otherwise by demolishing a fax machine and credit card reader well behind the counter, then dropping from view. However, it is soon evident that the pig is ambulatory. The clerk, in slow motion, is waltzing about behind the counter but it is not clear if he is attempting to get Jasper under control or if the clerk is being pursued. The clerk is making the most of a small space, and he is, it turns out, a very dexterous individual with an impressive vertical leap. After careening around he gives a shout and he has clambered over the counter and landed safely in the lobby where Dennis Junior has exited in the direction he entered soon followed by the much animated clerk. Skittering on the tile, Jasper the pig rounds a corner and comes racing from behind the counter. The pig does several wild circuits of the lobby, sometimes out of the frame but its progress can be followed by the upending of a water cooler, a toppling chair, some snack foods and potpourri ricocheting, and assorted other chaos. Jasper stops abruptly in the midst of the lobby and stands in a desultory manner for quite a long time. Then he trots off to near where the pretzels had last been flying.

The officer stops the video. "That has to be the goddamnedest thing I have ever seen done in a public place."

I reflect on the blessing of his limited experience and how his isolation from upheaval and social deviation are hallmarks of what attracted me to try to raise a family in a place as appealingly pacific as West Point. And I am just about to share this moment of civic pride with him (citizens of this province greatly enjoy hearing an outsider praise any aspect of local life) when he interrupts my train of thought to say, "We have more."

This time the surveillance camera has captured a much clearer picture than was offered from the Holiday Inn Express. The picture shows a fast food establishment and a heavyset black woman asleep or nearly asleep with an elbow on the counter and her ample face propped in her hand. Jutting behind her, her tremendous bottom gives me pause. If we

are about to witness another pig being hurled by the problem of this report, then her escape may well be impeded. Judging from the time signature, very early of a morning on September 1, I am recalling another
of my wife's organically raised pigs going missing, and so I am less surprised when the black woman rises from her torpor and begins pointing
and angrily talking, and Dennis Junior, again with this unprecedented
ski mask, steps into the picture holding a smaller and seemingly more
motile pig.

This particular surveillance camera, I am almost certain, is manufactured by Vicon Industries, an overlooked leader in the field. Noting
the deterioration and now wholesale abandonment of the noble notion
of public education, I feel certain, and earlier cited statistics and the peculiar case of unreachable Indigo Children such as Dennis Junior here
bear this out, we will soon be building prisons at a rate that will humble
all the world, and so I have gathered in an Individual Retirement Account, a substantial portfolio of security industry stocks. It is not too
great a deviation from the problem of this report, who is clearly showing himself to be prison material, that I mention several ticker symbols
to watch—NSSC, CKP, HBE, TASR, and MAGS, which is Magal Security, the Israelis, an unrivaled nation of fence and prison builders! The
clarity and composition and the slightly annoying way it cups perspective on the periphery of the picture leave no mistake: 1) This is a Vicon
Industries camera, NASDAQ symbol VII; and 2) This is Dennis Gebhardt II, the problem of this report holding one of his synesthetic, earth
spirit mother's organically raised pigs, around forty pounds. Its name was
Pearl and it was a very perceptive and adaptable creature in that I was
able to train it to approximate counting by tapping its left front hoof in
answer to math problems resulting in numbers one through five. The reward, always in my left pants pocket where I would flash the number of
fingers corresponding to the taps required, was a little cube of dry dog
food, not organic and in violation of my wife's farming practices. But the
ends justify the means. Do not obstruct excellence. When I turned my
side to the viewer none could detect our deception, and that pig and I
were featured on the *Early Agricultural Report* and together were driven
to the Starkville television studios in a shining white Ford hybrid SUV
owned by the Mississippi Agricultural Cooperative Extension Services
and were interviewed at 4:30 in the morning by no less than commentator Bubba Hubbard and host Randy Iberia. Later when Pearl and I had
finished our demonstration and the *Ag Report* surely had more pressing
news to relate Mr. Hubbard chose to wax lyrical, for which he is paid,

and declared Pearl the pig and, I assume, her conditioning to be a miracle along the order of one in which a pig and a spider cooperated in a study I have not seen but which anchor Randy Iberia affirmed, though I remain unsure whether Mr. Iberia's affirmation applied to the miracle of Pearl's conditioning or the earlier pig / spider test case, Mr. Iberia being the more taciturn of these two excellent newscasters. With this much profile accrued to this animal, I know for certain the jig is up. I raise my hand before the problem of this report can hurl the lost creature. Mercifully the officer halts the tape.

"Officers, there is no denying it any longer. That pig has been on television."

The officers turn to one another with slack faces and I sense ahead one of those moments when I am at a loss to understand why valuable information I convey is regularly treated with contempt, astonishment, acrimony, all manner of emotion, but never the least hint of decision and action, and that is all I have ever desired of my fellow citizens in the Golden Triangle.

"Gebhardt, we know you're mighty smart and make them missiles that bust up SCUDs and pound caves full of evildoers." He pauses and something tells me not to correct him but to let his discourse stand for now. "Why are you making light of a situation that involved more manpower and overtime hours than any in the history of the West Point police department. Not to mention live animal authorities?"

When I give no reaction he goes on. "We can damn well see the pig is on TV."

"I did not mean closed circuit television. This pig has been broadcast statewide on the *Early Agricultural Report* with host Randy Iberia and commentator Bubba Hubbard."

Their faces clench and twitch and elongate and these motions mean no more to me than the stirrings of leaves in the utmost branches of a mulberry tree.

"So once again you recognize the pig?"

"Without question, it is Pearl."

"Well, what of the fellow about to hurl Pearl?"

"You have told me you have the problem in custody. We know where he is located. We do not know where Pearl has gone after being so rudely cast across a counter. Nor where Jasper has got to after his capers at the Holiday Inn Express."

The officers begin to give off a kind of heat and the air is as thick as the lime water trembling around hot copper when it is coiled and doused, coiled and doused. These men in their brown shirts and gray pants may profess to being faithful servants of the empire, but I am beginning to hypothesize something else, or as my wife would claim, with no discernible data to move others to such a conclusion, I am hearing / tasting / seeing a bitter threat to the pigs, to my supernaturally perceptive wife, to the problem of this report, and to the futures of all these in tandem.

"So you admit that is your son, Dennis Junior, with Pearl the pig on this tape?"

"Without hesitation."

All three officers produce notepads advertising Service Printers of West High Street across the top of each sheet, which indicates that these notepads were very likely provided them for free, no tax dollars involved here. Excellence unobstructed!

"And did you aid your son in getting the pigs?"

A very imprecise question, exactly the sort of trap conceived by those who hate Sir Karl Popper and evidence and conclusions that can be proven and repeated and predicted. If my wife were here to smell / poke / bite these brown shirts I am considering that she might perceive in these three Imperial Guardsmen the cold, scaly aura of those locked in the clutches of the snake spirit.

"Define *get* or describe *getting*."

Once more the officers' faces widen.

The one who had manned the remote earlier seems still to be in charge. "Is there something wrong with you, Mr. Gebhardt, that you can't see how serious this is?"

"That is a problem beyond the scope of this discussion, but most certainly I have often been asked to address situations the seriousness of which I have failed to perceive." Since I never speak with any vigor and with a slight lisp it is beginning to dawn on these three dull snake spirits that I am and have been from birth set apart, high-functioning, any and all the labels they may or may not yet know under the rubric of autism. I stepped in this office of law enforcement wearing checked slacks, Redwing work boots, and a peach colored button-down shirt, my daily, undeviating, self-ordained uniform, and these charged with vigilance and preservation of domestic tranquility did not perceive, as the problem of this report has so often stated, "Dad, you are one fucking weird dude."

After explaining how serious this is and how if I am not more cooperative they will become convinced that I have aided in these escapades—What assistance could I possibly have given having never conceived of such procedures with swine?—the snake spirits bring up a third incident. Then they grow belligerent once more when I do not express surprise. "There is," I say, to stop their exclamations and obscenities, "a third pig missing. It stands to reason a third incident is a strong likelihood."

"Once again, it's the pigs," an officer without the remote comments.

Even though I am in full agreement with the soundness of this observation, I choose to remain silent.

The officer with the remote plunges the video forward at extremely high speed. The problem of this report launches Pearl across the counter at a super-sonic velocity. Whereon the black woman sets upon the Counting Pig of Clay County in frantic, jerky stampings and concludes the altercation with several violent swings of a mop wielded over her head with both hands like some medieval ax. So ends the saga of Pearl.

"Return to the frames just before the pig was thrown."

"You want to gloat?" The remote is not in the querying officer's hands—there is no order here though this is an office of law enforcement.

"I am not in favor of what has happened to either of these two pigs."

With some grumbling and cursing, they comply: The black woman brandishes the mop in an amazing manner then dances eerily; Pearl reappears and flies into Dennis Junior's arms, and Dennis Junior hugs Pearl tightly and walks backwards two steps. I raise my hand. "Forward at reduced speed."

Clearly Dennis Junior's lips are moving, but what he says to the black woman differs from what he said to the Indonesian clerk at the Holiday Inn Express. Very soon I am sure a security firm such as IEIB or DETC (no longer publicly traded after a German holding company bought it outright for cash!) will create an affordable security camera that collects audio as well as visual. But until then I can only stare and guess at what the problem of this report could possibly be communicating before flinging a pig at some stricken, but not entirely defenseless (as the black woman proves once more by pummeling Pearl) citizen of the empire.

What could Pearl have thought of all this? Dennis Junior did not care for her counting tricks, but certainly he won her trust and the trust of all pigs in his mother's sty. He frequently lifted and carried them about. Now I see his diabolism brought to full expression. He acclimated these pigs to being so handled while his mother proclaimed his hoisting of her pigs and parading around with them in his arms to be evidence that Dennis Junior was the reincarnation of the ancient Greek athlete who trained himself by lifting a bull calf every day and walking the farm-yard with this bull on his shoulders as it grew and grew until said athlete could carry the full grown bull into a stadium of astonished and wildly cheering Greeks for whatever good such an act would do in the ancient world. I find myself seeing / swallowing / pulsating the color red, which smells like sulfur, my wife claims. How many fox traps I have set and checked early of a morning sure we were losing uneconomically raised swine to fox or feral dogs and here it was the problem of this report win-ning the trust of pigs only to heave them over retail counters and to who knows what fate all this time.

"You done?" asks one of the Imperial Guardsmen.

I do not ask for a definition of *done* sure that I have only begun.

The video shows blue. Then a black-and-white view this time from a ceiling-mounted camera flickers. The signature is this morning at 5:32 A.M. above the staffed but as yet customer-less checkout counters at Hudson's Super Salvage.

"In what fast food establishment did Pearl perish?"

"The Hardee's on Richelieu."

Three H's. The problem of this report was banned from the local 4H at age eleven. I do not yield the pattern to these snake spirits. From evidence already presented it is clear they will scoff, but I could tell them that if the problem of this report is loosed once more upon West Point, Mississippi, and provided he can obtain a fourth pig, he will un-doubtedly attempt to strike the fourth H of the empire in this town—The Huddle House Restaurant. Holiday Inn Express, Hardee's, Hudson's Super Salvage, Huddle House, all national or supranational chains owned by no one in this province and out of which our money pours to miasmic nether reaches of corporate America accessible only via the middling opportunity of stock exchanges in distant urbanities and the ownership of paltry shares therein. I am nearer an understanding of the problem of this report than I believe I ever have been in sixteen years of mystifying association with him.

Though logic has prepared me for it, I am still stunned when Den-nis Gebhardt II arrives on camera listing beneath the weight—nearly seventy pounds—of Sumo, so named by my wife for his insatiable ap-petite and tremendous capacity for weight gain. Once more, Dennis Ju-nior makes a statement. I raise my hand.

The tape is stopped. "In each of these segments, the assailant speaks before expressing a pig, and in each, something different is said by him. What?"

The officers slither around in their free notepads.

"At the Holiday Inn Express, he said, 'Happy Birthday.'"

"Attacking Hardee's he said, 'Haven't you heard? It's Ramadan.'"

"And at Hudson's Super Salvage, he said, 'Here's to the Empire of Shit.'"

What is thy name? Thy name is legion. For those that have ear, let them hear. All those pigs lost for nothing better than a man to be at peace with his H's.

"You will now let me see my son."

The officer with the remote narrows his eyes and lowers his head. "Not before you watch this."

The tape he releases. The words are proclaimed. The third and final pig, Sumo, is thrust at some petrified little blonde wearing a Mississippi University for Women sweatshirt. Behind her so much is in jeopardy it nearly stops the mind to consider it all: beef jerky, sugarless gum, tabloids, horoscopes bundled in tiny scrolls, shoe shine sponges, lint rollers, Santa hats with blinking diodes. Sumo strikes the black conveyor belt and bounces. The resultant tumult is stupendous.

This time, like Black angels of mercy, two gigantic African American security guards descend upon Dennis Gebhardt II. A struggle, but he is overcome.

"I fail to see the point in showing me anymore than the two incidents I have already endured."

The officer with the remote places it firmly on the battered table and, bowing his head, begins to stroke his eyebrows. "Mr. Gebhardt, we've been around Dennis Junior here since not too long after them security guards throttled him. What troubles us is, well, we don't think Junior is sharp enough to have done all this on his own."

"How sharp do you imagine one has to be to carry a pig anywhere when both the pig and the one doing the carrying are quite accustomed to one another?"

The officers exchange glances and all three sit forward on the edge of their chairs. "But choosing these three places and timing it so as hardly anybody is there. That's what we think is a little beyond Dennis Junior's ken."

"Have you explored your theory with his teachers or school administrators?"

"Hell, no."

"On what, then, do you base your hypothesis?"

"On the fact that your son is a raging idiot who can't even be made to play football right."

"You have charged him with this inability?"

"No. He's charged with disorderly conduct."

"That is just and accurate," I say, rising. "Now a third time, I ask you to let me see my son."

They rise. "But we think you assisted him."

"Based on what evidence?"

"Based on he's a raging idiot and you are not."

That red feeling I previously described has not abated and on hearing this it nearly overwhelms me. "I assure you that by the standards you have applied to my son you will find my idiocy by far superior in both its quantity and pervasiveness, and if I am not allowed to see my son very shortly, the raging quality of my idiocy may also soon be amply demonstrated."

The three officers excuse themselves and leave me standing / gulping / boiling. But they return after some minutes of what I assume must have been heated discussion for their faces are tight and flat. I am led once more into the processing room and we wait while another locking mechanism buzzes—I must ask before leaving what company has vended the West Point Police Department these menacing and voluble locks, then see if said company is publicly traded.

The officers divide and now only one leads me into a cramped cell block. If this meager set of bars is the extent of the gaol here in West Point, county seat and apex of the Golden Triangle, then the authorities are by no means prepared for the future which will be overrun with ill-educated and ineducable children (such as the problem of this report) and so I recommend that all No-New-Tax-Loving electors across the length and breadth of the province investigate closely the financial statements of ticker symbols CXW, CRN, and GGI, the three publicly traded companies that build and maintain private prisons. I assure you, citizens of the Golden Triangle and beyond, a private prison is coming to a location near you in short order. Had you only listened to me in 2003!

This cell block is in turmoil, much yelling and the foulest language I have heard since Kansas State's engineering school. Above all the caterwauling, I recognize, ringing out, primal screaming from the problem of this report, primal screaming being one of the many obnoxious stress-relieving exercises that my wife's Jungian therapist has taught Dennis

Junior, and, unfortunately, one of the few things Junior has retained from any instructor. It appears none of the more permanent detainees appreciate Dennis Junior's stress-relieving techniques any more than I do, and it is this screaming that likely has them all in a froth.

The escorting officer raises his voice to be heard, but even so I must ponder / fondle / suckle his every word phoneme by phoneme to comprehend above the riotous din. "We don't have the money for a juvenile wing. So we just throw them in the drunk tank till the parents come." He opens the drunk tank, which is just another cell but without a cot and toilet and in which a slimy drain is recessed into the concrete floor. The primal screaming continues. Against the bars is curled a bearded, pale man wearing a torn Mississippi State University T-shirt. His bloodshot eyes widen at the officer then at me. Dennis Junior screams again, and the bearded man shakes violently.

"This is torture," he says. "Please make this asshole shut up." His bloody nose may well be forensic evidence that the drunk has already attempted but failed to convince Dennis Junior to cease his resounding therapy.

Dennis Junior turns to him and says, "Join me, buddy. I swear it will do you a world of good." Then he screams once again.

The escorting officer curls his upper lip and asks, "Mr. Gebhardt, may I please mace your son to the ground?"

Definition of the Problem

Dennis Junior is a strapping teen built along the big-boned, beefy lines of his mother's people. Today he wears a black T-shirt proclaiming Alternating Current / Direct Current abbreviated as AC/DC but this is not a hopeful sign of a developing penchant for electrical engineering. His blond hair is matted down and one nostril bears a brad thick enough to have needed a crate stapler to fasten it. Were he a bull I would hook my fifth finger in the crook of this copper hoop and yank him to reason, but he is all too human and is, regardless of this incarceration, still my son and therefore legally entangled with me as the constables have already reminded. That red feeling still simmers and tells me to abandon him here among his compeers, serves him right, justice through boredom and filth, but out of mercy for these others, who in the sudden lull from Dennis Junior have not relented in their considerable criticism of him, I offer to bail him.

As we are led out of the cell block amid a withering fire of critiques from seasoned inmates, I take the opportunity to question directly the problem of this report. The escorting officer does not bear his free notepad and is likely still quite focused on his desire to apply pepper-spray to the problem, said anti-personnel aerosol manufactured, you should take note, by Mace Security International (NASDAQ: MACE), a company which despite a recent inexplicable diversion of capital resources into the purchase of car washes of all things still makes a mean and useful product—a noun which to my satisfaction the escorting officer used as a verb, a sure sign of successful branding.

"What did you mean, Dennis, by treating these pigs in such a manner?"

"Hasn't mother told you?"

Somehow I knew his synesthete mother, my wife, the keeper of organically raised swine, would play a decisive role in all this.

"I am a performance artist," Dennis Junior announces to a lobby full of uniformed officers, other plainclothed servants of the empire, and beleaguered citizenry come for redress of grievances or supplication to justice. "My three performances have been filmed and preserved for posterity in the annals of your empire, Dad. You make horrendous missiles, and now I have expressed my own into the heart of corporate America."

A round and grim looking female officer passes me a clipboard of paperwork and a pen. I interrupt her explanations. "To exorcise your own demons you have thrown swine over countertops and thought nothing of the future disposition of the pigs or the swineherd, your mother."

The escorting officer chimes in, "Not to mention the cops and animal control or the terrified gal from MUW and them other poor people."

Dennis Junior ignores all this as it is not to his mind properly focused on him, the artist. "Don't you want to know what I have entitled these three now famous performances?"

I stop reading the ream of officiata I am to sign to say: "*Happy Birthday; Haven't You Heard? It's Ramadan;* and lastly *Here's to the Empire.*" I leave out the obscenity.

Dennis Junior's jaw drops. "How the fuck do you do that? You can't even drive at night. How do you figure this shit out?"

"This is a public place and there are ladies present," the escorting officer warns Dennis Junior with a gesture at the unimpressed lumpkin still waiting on my signature.

Dennis Junior bears him no mind, but continues. "No noise after dark. No dancing. No music with pianos in it. No fluorescent lights. No hugging. And all day long you make the nasty little brains that tell death where to land in grubby shitholes like Afghanistan. You are the reason I am so fucked up."

This explication of the problem of this report may well lead to much revision. I have never of my own volition touched Dennis Junior save in violence to make him cease some activity I could no longer abide. His face is red and I wonder / yearn / despair that he might feel my own red rage against all this racket, might feel for just a moment the way I so often do. But I can no more read understanding in his facial expression than I could perceive love from some Deity beaming down from a partly cloudy sky.

"I have warned you once already, you turd," the officer bellows. At this there is a sudden clearing of space, and a pool of quiet forms around us. The round and grim female officer has quit her chair and is endeavoring to crouch, her goblin visage sinking behind the counter till just her eyeballs show. How I envy this officer a career in a place where mere tone of voice signals all colleagues that action must be taken! "Mr. Gebhardt, I am ashamed that you seem unwilling to bring this unruly teen to right. And here you are about to bail him out and set him back loose on West Point, Mississippi. What the hell kind of father are you?"

"Hey," says Dennis Junior, in a booming voice made magnificent by all his primal screaming. "Nobody disrespects my dad but me, you prick."

What bodily signal could Dennis have possibly read that leads him to lunge at the officer and thus spurs me forward both to suppress Dennis and to protect him? And the officer responds by taking two steps backwards. In a cowboy-style flash he prizes from his hips a can of pepperspray in each hand, and, joined by other equally responsive servants of the empire likewise armed, he fulfills his previously expressed desire and maces both the problem of this report and me to the floor.

Having never experienced a sensation quite as overpowering as this from a product produced by a company in which I hold significant stock, I am rapidly won over. But Dennis Junior bravely holds forth despite the hissing continuance of chemical and propellant to shout: "I am an Indigo Child. I am extremely bright, precocious, with an amazing memory and a strong desire to live instinctively. I am a sensitive, gifted soul with an evolved consciousness and have come here . . ." He gargles for a moment but does not surrender. ". . . Have come here to help change the vibrations of your lives." There is the pleuritic sound of an humungous evacuation of phlegm. "To create one land, one globe, and one species." His mother's claptrap never sounded more compelling.[1]

"Yeah, and to throw pigs," adds some official voice.

And with a last generous application of this remarkable suppressant both Gebhardts, Senior and Junior, are finished for the day.

Recommendations Toward a Solution to the Problem

First let me encourage all citizens of the empire, far beyond the province of the Golden Triangle from the wild savannahs of Los Angeles to the frozen tundra of Chicago to the steel and silica jungles of New York City, to subject themselves to a thorough macing professionally administered and to avail themselves of this service frequently. After a successful mac-ing experience one is filled for hours with an endorphin-enriched calm devoid of all distractions and thoughts save the very intense conviction that one's situation could not possibly be made any worse than it has al-ready become. Imagine the inevitable, ineradicable hypocrisies, inepti-tudes, and injustices of empire that could be borne with cheerful equanimity if all citizens were maced by public servants or by briefly and inexpensively retrained clinicians as often as is reasonably convenient.[2]

Night has fallen and silence prevails in our humming, hybrid SUV as my synesthete wife drives and the two very tranquil Dennises, Senior and Junior, ride buckled securely in the backseat. My only memory of a choking, tearful, but illuminating incarceration is the voice of the bearded drunk who greeted our return to the drunk tank with many in-flammatory declarations against the government until the opportunity to be maced was offered him (clearly West Point authorities have stocked their war chests well with this superb product) and the drunk ill-advisedly refused such an entitlement.

In the rear-view mirror, my wife's eyes stray from the blazing neon, fluorescent, and incandescent coruscation of lights convecting in a cor-ridor of all the H's, M's, K's, W's, and C's of the empire that now domi-nate the main drag of West Point. Her eyes glance at me, then at Dennis Junior, then at me again. "Two monsters," she says. "I have two monsters in my backseat."

When I speak I sound as if I have a colossal head cold. "I would like to ask the second monster what he believes has become of the three pigs." There is so much artificial light from national chain eateries and

big box retailers shining in this automobile we could be cruising the surface of the planet Mercury for all my swollen eyes reveal.

"Ayn Rand says, 'I will not run anyone's life—nor let anyone run
mine. Man is not a sacrificial animal on anyone's altar. I raise this god
over the earth and it is me,'" mumbles the problem of this report. "I am
a great performance artist, and when the story of my three exhibitions is
carried over the national wire services in news of the weird, I will be
more famous than your missiles flying over Baghdad, monster number
one."

The frequency of these proposed macings may have to be closely
monitored and revised upward, for I am distressed to find myself once
more in a red rage. "Pearl was killed with a mophead." I have my seat-
belt unbuckled and soon have Dennis Junior's belt unfastened and my
hand is on his door handle to open it and push him out, and I have the
door open and wind is whistling and I am pushing but he is resisting
with his chest thrust forward and he is keeping his arms stiff and his
hands fastened to the panic bar and seat cushion. My son has grown into
an immovable object, and I would have been better served to have
pushed him out of a moving vehicle once every day while he grew so as
to be ready to do so more effectively now, to the cheers of all my fellow
provincials.

"Mother," he says, very calmly, very plainly.

With a glance at us in the rearview mirror, she swerves hard to star-
board. The problem of this report and I tumble across the backseat and
smack into my closed door. My wife jumps the SUV over a median—we
are briefly airborne and in freefall—then the two Dennises are slammed
against the unyielding seatbacks of the front seats when we suddenly
halt in the white hot parking lot of the new Target store.

My wife has unbuckled herself and turned around. The car ignition
is in the off position, and it is then I recognize I have a raw feeling in
my throat because I have been screaming. I stop abruptly when she grabs
me by the hair and lifts; she has Dennis Junior by the hair as well. "We
are going home. Sit down both of you. Pay attention." We comply with
a military regimentation. "Buckle," she hollers.

At home, despite my expressed desire that this never happen while
the domicile is vacant, sandalwood incense is burning. "Sit," she orders.

We are recovered enough from the macing and near car wreck to
hesitate, Dennis and I, but she pinches us both. We sit Indian style with
our knees touching, as she will demand they be if they are not touching.

She lifts the television remote from the coffee table and settles herself similarly. With remote in hand, she is in charge; she has the floor.

"I have to live here. You may be some savant engineer and Boeing would love to have you out in Seattle, and you, Junior, may be ready for the Tenderloin District or Broadway, I don't know which." Her voice grates like charcoal crumbling in a filter. "But I am from West Point and have to live here with what you two do to our name."

After several deep, controlled breaths with her eyes closed, she points the remote at me. "Do you have anything to say?"

I take the remote and hold it a moment. These are the calm, egg shell white walls of our living room dappled with swimming candlelight, not the bars and frying acetylene of the fluorescent lights in Imperial prison. That is my wife and that is the problem of this report, my son. "I want to know," and it is very hard for me to force the sense of this to come up from the deep structure and into the wafting sandalwood atmosphere. "I want to know, how do you feel?" It is my wife I am addressing. "Feel about the way Dennis Junior has betrayed the pigs and you and me through his performance art?"

Past experience would dictate that Dennis Junior will now begin a long and angry defense of himself disregarding the remote and our family rules of order entirely. But instead he opens his hand. I give him the remote. Then in an uncanny imitation of the voice of my wife's Jungian therapist he says: "I want us all to pause and recognize a real breakthrough here in that Cy Gebhardt has just asked, for the first time in this therapist's presence, how another person *feels* about something." The impersonation is in fact so frighteningly close that with the candlelight casting shadows one could mistake the performance for a brief spirit possession.

His mother gently takes the remote. She is becoming emotional I note from the rate at which her shoulders rise and fall and a wetness glistening along the bottom rim of her eyelids. It is so quiet, outside the empire may be raining missiles down on all its enemies, Tomahawks cracking among the mud huts and unattainable mountain aeries, but in this living room I can hear a candle wick sputter.

"Cy, he has this talent, you see," my wife begins, "but I have no idea how to help him find direction." She is visibly upset.

I do something I never do; I start something it has ever been my neo-pagan, spiritualist wife's role to initiate, usually by threat of force; I call for something I detest. "Hands," I say, opening one hand to my wife and one to Junior.

They both sit with wide eyes and wide faces. But eventually they extend hands and we clasp, the three of us, knees touching while the fluorescent order and homogeny of the empire glows and churns like a false dawn outside our windows.

"One," my wife intones, beginning the chant. "One," Dennis Junior joins her on the third recitation. "One," I complete the triad on the sixth, cognizant of the way chanting this prime number makes the knee caps vibrate and the fingertips tingle. "One."

And we are one, a golden triangle. Is this an illusion, an opiate for the familial masses, a panacea, a white noise buffer against the rumbling of armor and oil tankers crushing outward from the heart of Dixie to the front lines of never-ending warfare?

"One." Maybe there is no empire can govern the monsters of havoc and the keeper of flying pigs. "One." We are a system at rest. No guidance is needed. "One." We will know exactly where we are.

Bibliography and Notes

1. His mother's claptrap can be found in a book called *Understanding Your Life Through Color* by Nancy Anne Tappe, another synesthete!

2. The writer of this report holds a sizeable stake in Mace Security International, Inc. (NASDAQ GM: MACE) and stands to benefit financially—in the extreme—if the self-defense product Mace™ is applied to all citizens of the empire in a frequent and systematic manner, as is proposed in this report. When this program comes to fruition, and you find yourself without ownership of a single share and with only the consolation that the empire cannot possibly make your situation any worse than it already is, I will not hesitate to make it worse by reminding: If you had only listened to me!

Margaret McMullan

What I Want to Know Is When Did Charlotte McIntosh Get to Be So Jealous?

We're out there standing in front of what used to be St. Paul's where her little Cee Cee is swinging on monkey bars FEMA and the Home Depot put up, while I'm looking at the brown creases in Charlotte's cleavage, swearing off ever sitting in the sun again. She starts in: *I got that invitation to some party celebrating your upcoming nuptials a few years back, but I guess you found out something about him, because there never was a marriage, was there?* She yells out for Cee Cee to be more careful, not to kick the little boy's eye out. Then she turns to me and says, *You just never know about a man, do you?*

I say something about not liking him anymore. I don't say anything about his drug habit or the dealing. Those don't even seem important now.

She tells me her mother has Parkinson's. Since the storm, she says, and she's the *primary caregiver* now, not her sister. That's what she says. She rolls around in that word *primary.* They lost both houses in the hurricane, but they're rebuilding on her mother's property, old property high up and elevated above sea level, even though we both know that being in the cut glass set didn't make a bit of difference in the end. I don't say we used to call the people living on Charlotte's side of town cake eaters, or that her mamma's old house needed a paint job way before the storm, or how I knew the columns in front were hollow and not

248

made of wood at all. She doesn't say what I know she's thinking—that bitch Katrina was good for one thing, washing away all the riffraff, like me.

A little dog licks her leg probably because Charlotte smells of the pink grapefruit soap the town is manufacturing now. Or is that the scent called Energy or Gulf Waters, the one that colored newscaster covering the aftermath went nuts over on that morning show? When Charlotte talks baby talk to the dog, the dog can hardly stand it and pees.

She says her husband always thought people were so uppity here, but it's different now, after the hurricane. She says, *Aren't you near Menge in that first house on Second?*

Red brick ranch, I say.

Doesn't the train bother you?

We think it's soothing. Where do I get *soothing?*

Charlotte looks to have put on twenty-five pounds of what everyone here calls the FEMA-fifteen, but even fat looks good on Charlotte McIntosh—what with her streaked hair, frosted pink lipstick and the blue, flowered dress and black slip-ons. Me, I have so many hours as a black jack dealer at the Grand, there's hardly time to eat.

She calls out to her Cee Cee again, sweet this time, telling her to play nice with the little boy.

He comes running. Charlotte watches me wipe Billy's nose with the hem of my cut-offs. *Well he's a cutey isn't he? Aren't you a cutey?* she says, picking up her dog. Billy turns his father's black eyes on Charlotte, then says *Come on Mamma, let's go,* and I love him more than ever for saying this. I tell him I'll buy him a Snow Cone. Later we'll go check out a movie from the double-wide that serves as the library where they keep the air at sixty-three degrees all summer.

Charlotte says we ought to get our kids together and play. She puts her dog down. *You all should stop by the house.*

I tie Billy's shoes.

Charlotte smiles, shakes her head, yanks on the little dog's chain, and says, *Seems like all our lives, the two of us have been trying to bust out of this place. We had our chance, you know, after the storm. Can you believe we both landed back here? Even you. You of all people.*

Justin Quarry

Heart Farm

The chimeras need feed. Their trough is empty except for pieces of orange rind strewn like busted taillights. They spit cud at its sides in protest. Their trough is an old fishing boat, Eddie's dead father's; the mushy lumps thud hollowly against the metal, inching the boat across the dewy grass at angles.

Eddie goes to the barn to prepare their feed. A lump, greenish, clips his arm from behind on the way. Per Dr. Wu's instructions, and the American Heart Association's recommendations, each serving of feed includes a measured blend of fruit (primarily citrus), legumes (beans, peas), vegetables (broccoli, zucchini), and whole grains (such as oats), tossed with cod liver oil. The chimeras also graze the field around Eddie's mother's house, munching grass and preferring weeds, as all other sheep. The feed Eddie makes is supplemental, for the chimeras' hearts, which are human.

In the barn is hidden a U-Haul that dominates the space and instills it with a warm metallic odor. Flabby sacks of oats slump under a long workbench. On top of the workbench, a commercial-size container of peanuts is overturned before stacks of the feed's other ingredients. Peanuts sprinkle the dirt floor. Once again Eddie surveys the barn to see how the chimeras might have gained entry. There are only the doors, which are kept latched, and a row of new freezers blocks the back one. This is not the first incident. It appears the chimeras are breaking into the barn, though Eddie suspects his mother Jan is responsible. Soon after he and the chimeras arrived two weeks ago, he caught Jan concocting them a snack, using incorrect proportions. Jan believes the chimeras get hungry in between feedings. In addition Jan thinks the chimeras may be humans trapped in sheeps' bodies. This is why she feels sorry for them, this was why she was making them a snack in the first place. Just when Eddie has her convinced that they're sheep trapped in sheeps' bodies— except for their hearts—she circles back to the one with the thumb on its forehead.

The thumb, not the hearts, is Jan's real hang-up.

The thumb is the government's hang-up, too.

Under Dr. Wu, Eddie works as a research assistant in a University of Nebraska lab that, for years, has developed human hearts in sheep so that one day livestock may act as organ donors. For a heart to grow, a subpopulation of adult human stem cells must be injected in the brain of a sheep fetus during a window halfway through gestation: before the fetus's immune system learns to detect foreign cells, so it can't reject them, but after the blueprint for its body forms, so it looks normal. The timing and site of each injection are the variables. These are being perfected. The current chimeras' hearts are between eighty-nine and ninety-two percent human.

Also there is the one with the thumb, whose heart is more like ninety-seven.

As soon as its head jutted out from its mother, thumb-first, Dr. Wu saw he had injected it too soon. Still the lab managed to hide it, studying it in secret for fifteen months. Then, three weeks ago, Dr. Wu got wind that the University was launching an investigation. Bioethics committees from the Department of Agriculture and the National Academy of Sciences would assist. Both had endorsed the cultivation of internal organs when Dr. Wu proposed the project, but anything visibly human they had advised against. Limbs and dicks, as one ethicist said, were yuck factors.

Dr. Wu decided Eddie should take the chimeras on vacation. He said he would send Eddie a text message when they could return, when he was assured of the project's future.

But that was three weeks and three states and five dead chimeras ago.

Now Eddie feels like a shepherd with a master's degree.

Eddie fills the wheelbarrow with its first heap of freshly mixed feed. He glides the load toward the door. In the corner next to the door lie three stray oranges. One of the oranges, as if stirred by observation, rolls several inches toward the wheel then rests again.

Outside, Eddie contemplates checking the chimeras' breath for a nut or citrus odor. The chimeras gather around the wheelbarrow before Eddie makes it to the boat, gorging and butting. Predominantly the chimeras are Katahdin sheep, a hornless breed with hair instead of wool, selected by Dr. Wu for these reasons. This way the chimeras don't need shearing, and the scientists don't need gear to guard against ramming. Also Katahdin sheep possess a natural resistance to internal parasites.

Sometimes Eddie thinks of things like love and devotion as internal parasites.

Abruptly he notices that one of the nine chimeras, the one with a thumb like a horn, is unaccounted for.

Then Jan comes into view walking toward the field, inching bigger and bigger as she closes the distance. The missing chimera grows behind her. Jan is one strange-ass specimen. These are the words she uses to describe herself after she mistakenly dials her own phone number, accidentally throws away cash, or searches for her keys only to find them having been in her hand the whole time. Eddie doesn't consider his mother that strange, though her hair is longer that that of any female he has seen past puberty. Jan is sixty-two. She wears a voluminous shirt that belonged to one of her three dead husbands; the shirt, unbuttoned, cocoons a white tank top and black leggings. Her body has been whittled thin by a belly-dancing class geared toward widows.

Recently, however, Jan has skipped several bellydancing classes to tend to a new hobby: aiding and abetting fugitive animals.

"This one"—she points to the chimera following her—"this once came to the door crying. *Crying*, Eddie. It *knocked*."

The chimera sniffs Jan's waist. Sure enough the hair under its eyes is matted against its skull, wet. Though pools could just as easily have gathered there from the sweat running from beneath its hood. Jan sewed the hood, which covers it thumb, to render it less conspicuous—and less self-conscious—among the flock.

"It didn't knock," he says. "It butted."

"No, it was gentler than that. More like—it was tapping, Eddie. It must be starving."

"Tell me the truth," he snaps, "are you feeding them yourself?"

She looks incredulous. "You told me not to!"

"I've been finding things left out," he tells her for the first time. "Things spilled. Like someone forgot to clean up her mess."

"It's not like a sheep to go wandering off by itself. It's like a *human*." She reaches down to rub the chimera's ears, which protrude through perfect-size holes in the hood. She eyes the barn. "They could lift those latches on those doors with their noses. They get out of that sorry-ass pen the same way."

He keeps studying her face. "One time, one of the freezers was left open."

Jan gazes at the field enveloping her house, the subtle hills rippling north. Farther away, a small forest swells west. Her searching eyes are almost hopeful, almost as though they expect something miraculous to emerge any second. "I wasn't looking at what's in those freezers."

Eddie considers the pen he and his mother rigged together. "Maybe we should keep the chimeras in the garage." Though he thinks the garage is too small. He remembers the U-Haul, in which they traveled. The other five that didn't survive the trip.

The one with the thumb nibbles the ends of Jan's hair just above her butt.

The lab is a huge metal building on the outskirts of Lincoln. The lab also contains an office and a room with medical machinery but above all it houses a stretch of simulated pasture. Tender grasses pave the floor, equidistant sprinkler heads popping up and retracting on a schedule. Synthetic trees crafted with the bark of real trees intersperse the setting in a calculatedly haphazard arrangement. There are imported boulders. Potted thickets lining the walls. And overhead hangs a computerized panel that glows with an evolving intensity to replicate the course of daylight. The trees reach precisely fifteen feet below the panel to prevent a fire.

Now, in a sheep's natural habitat, the chimeras act peculiar. When it rains they fall on their knees, tucking their heads between their forelegs, not baa-ing but screaming *Bee-hee! Bee-hee!* Often Eddie catches them staring at the sun. Their eyes begin to trail its path as it burrows through the sky, the blinding disc unlike any light they have ever seen. Eddie must slap them one by one to break their transfixion.

The openness of the outdoors eludes them. The simulated pasture is fenced in a grid to inhibit overgrazing of any area. Now, without an alarm and the release of a gate signaling movement to the next cell, the chimeras sometimes remain in a single section of the field, their confinement imagined. When this happens, as it happens two days later, nothing short of terror can stir them to migrate.

Eddie shouts at them to move. Eddie swings his arms as he shouts. And he bares his teeth and he kicks at the ground and his feet propel clods over the flock, a few crashing on it. The chimeras watch Eddie's performance as they chew and blink heavily. These things have never worked. Still Eddie tries them to avoid the walk to the barn. From here the barn is small enough to fit on a cake. The chimeras turn back to the barren earth, grass gnawed to roots. They scrape the ground with their teeth, taking in more dirt than greenery.

Eddie returns from the barn equipped with an old air horn. Also, he is dressed as a toothbrush, or at least the head of one. He still wears jeans and a denim jacket. The mask is constructed from a box with hay painted white, sprouting from the front as bristles. The mask, which Jan made, is meant to be accompanied by a solid sweat suit, representing a handle. Jan thinks this is the beauty of the costume: one can wear it in different colors. In the ten years since Eddie wore it his senior year of high school, Jan has worn it twice: once as a pink toothbrush and again in aqua.

As Eddie nears the chimeras he begins to run and sounds the horn. The chimeras jerk their heads up. Their chomping jaws freeze. The blast plows over the gaping field far past them. Birds erupt from a tree to the west like seeds blown off a dandelion. The chimeras catch sight of his spiny head and release a shriek not unlike the one they emit for rain. They stampede in zigzags with their eyes trained behind, Eddie barreling toward them, honking. Before Eddie loses his breath, the one with the thumb loses its hood, and Eddie stops to retrieve it. At once the chimeras reform their group, an explosion in reverse. Leery, they watch to see if Eddie will charge again. He jerks off his mask and they relax. Their fat necks elongate to the taller grass below.

In a fit, Eddie chucks the toothbrush head at a small mound covered in a lace of clover. The head lands perfectly on its bristles, without damage, which irritates Eddie further. He storms over to the one with the thumb, who glances up, still skittish. The thumb, unresponsive as ever, hangs limply from its forehead, knuckle bulging, nail in need of trimming. Eddie ties the hood back around its skull, cursing Dr. Wu. Two more days and still no text message. Though the phone Dr. Wu gave Eddie to receive this message only gets reception in certain spots. The recollection of himself wandering aimlessly in his mother's yard, holding the phone out to detect a signal, as if he is searching for gold, nudges Eddie past the bounds of fury. He pinches a tiny piece of his wrist until he can't stand the pain.

The situation reminds him of the other Eddie. Months before, Eddie dated another man named Eddie. When it ended and the other Eddie wouldn't speak to him, Eddie slept on the other Eddie's doorstep. He had woken in the morning to the other Eddie's pinstriped legs stepping over him. Without pause the legs strode forth in a linear flurry.

And still Eddie had lain there.

Eddie feels the doormat's prickly ghost against his tingling cheek. He remembers opening the U-Haul to check the chimeras in Iowa. A U-Haul because Dr. Wu thought it more covert than a cattle trailer. Straw pillowed its bed, buckets of feed hugged its sides. Additional vents were slit in the roof. All the cabinets containing the project's documentation had been secured against the walls with multiple straps. Still, behind an abandoned Exxon off Highway 80, Eddie discovered a chimera collapsed in the middle of the flock, dead, as if it had simply keeled over. The next day he had found another dead chimera, and then another.

Back at the lab, Dr. Wu had instructed Eddie to simply drive: to keep driving. To inspect the chimeras every four hours. There was no destination. There were no provisions for glitches. In the U-Haul there was only enough feed, water, and space to confine the chimeras for days, by which Dr. Wu expected to send the return message. Plans had been made in haste, and Eddie had been eager to accept the duty. He had been trying to remind himself he was dedicated to his work. He had been trying to escape the obsessive aftermath of his break-up. The thought of a dying man offered life in the shape of a homegrown organ once filled Eddie with an intense but reassuring weight, so physical that at times it was the weight itself, not work, that seemed to give him direction—feeling as though the weight were tipping him forward, onward. He needed to remember this feeling. He had sought greater responsibility in the lab. Dr. Wu had actually let him perform the latest injection. Eddie admired this control Dr. Wu wielded over the chimeras, over their organs. The influence he commanded on science, on other people's lives, even Eddie's. Each variation of his actions determined whether infinite patients would die or survive in the future. Dr. Wu had noticed Eddie's dedication to the project, and it was because of this that Dr. Wu had trusted him with the future.

Eddie tells himself he is dedicated to his work. Eddie is dedicated to science.

But with each task Eddie performs in absconding the chimeras, he feels increasingly dedicated to Dr. Wu. And lately, Eddie has begun to wonder if this dedication rooted itself long before Dr. Wu handed him a U-Haul key. When it comes to the men in his life, it seems Eddie is dedicated to dedication, some controlling part of him involuntarily willing.

Each blade of grass the chimeras remove from the field makes a popping sound as it severs. Collectively the noises give the same effect as standing in a giant crackling skillet.

Eddie's wash of anger ebbs and leaves behind a heavy trail of exhaustion. A nap reveals itself as a momentary means of divorcing the chimeras, and thus Dr. Wu. This section of the field will keep the chimeras occupied for hours: ragweed and foxtail and plantain are nestled here and there like hidden prizes. Already the chimeras seem to map out a rough square for makeshift imprisonment. Eddie wads his jacket. He arranges it between his head and the mound draped in clover. The sunlight, slicing his body at an afternoon angle, reminds him of the U-Haul's cab, the sunlight amplified by wide windows. Through the splattered windshield, the light had made dead-bug-shaped shadows across the dash.

Everything, including Eddie, slips away to be replaced by Jan and her three dead husbands. The four of them sit around a green velvet table. Two husbands appear to have played strip poker, while Jan knits a pulsating sweater. The sweater's sleeves, which are still wet, glisten as they dangle from Jan's lap; instead of yarn Jan knits with the men's arteries. Jerkily the arteries unwind from chests and necks as Jan binds them together. This, Jan demonstrates, is what you do with dead husbands. When her first husband empties, Jan disrobes her third husband and digs into his thigh. Eddie understands this husband to be his father, Eddie Senior, though he looks nothing like the man Eddie has only seen in pictures.

Someone shrieks. There are many shrieks. Eddie wakes. The only cloud in the pinkening sky looks like a rib cage.

Like the cloud, Eddie is alone on the grass and upon this understanding experiences a sudden sensation of lightness before panic falls. The chimeras are missing. Searching the field is like skimming a blank page. Eddie's eyes dart west to the forest. He imagines hearts being chewed and slurped by fanged mouths.

But the next set of shrieks come from the house. Far behind him, Eddie spots an amorphous clump of white shifting shape in Jan's yard. The chimeras have only escaped to their pen. Still they are screaming. A tuft breaks off the clump, streaked with electric red. By the time Eddie reaches the pen with mask and horn, that chimera is collapsed, blood decorating its breast like an ascot. Blood trickles down the breasts of others. Three continue to rake their necks across the barbed wire fence in an effort to spring a gush.

For seconds, Eddie can only observe. Eddie stands there observing in shock. Then he drives the chimeras toward the barn, in theory to dress their wounds. Horrified, the one with its throat slit staggers up then falls again, spurting. Up ahead another stumbles and slides on its face. Eddie remains dazed as he honks and runs. In what feels like an instant of clarity, he thinks the one behind will need a tourniquet. He then realizes a tourniquet will choke it if it isn't dead by the time he returns. Either way, Eddie thinks, that chimera will get what it wanted.

But as soon as Eddie enters the barn all thoughts of the chimeras begin to swirl. It is as though a plug has been pulled at the bottom of his mind, the thoughts are draining. At the workbench stands a man with matted hair, tattooed hands, and an air of having been inconvenienced. His arms are stacked with cans of beans. Past the thin, unruly beard, Eddie catches a flicker of his half-brother. Teal, Jan's son from her second husband. The flicker extinguishes. Eddie hasn't seen his only sibling in twelve years. "Hi, Pop," the man says begrudgingly, readjusting his load. "Pop" was what Teal had always called Eddie. After Eddie Senior died, Jan had his semen harvested and frozen, and later, years later, when Eddie was a child, Teal had explained to him that he was the son of a Popsicle.

Teal snorts at Eddie's mask. "She still have you playing dress-up?"

Outside the barn, Jan stitches the chimeras' deepest cuts with dental floss. The floss is waxed—and sturdier than thread, Jan said—and over each slash it forms an angry-looking pattern that resembles the crevice between clenched crocodile teeth. Teal bites the chimeras' ears while Jan laces their throats. Still no words have been exchanged between Teal and his mother. Few have been exchanged between Teal and Eddie. In part this is due to the fact that since Jan appeared, Teal has kept his mouth full. At first this was achieved with fistfuls of peanuts, now it is done with the chimeras. Apparently biting a chimera's ear has the effect of holding its body steady. This so the chimera can be sewn shut.

When Eddie held the chimeras they resisted Jan's needle. In the lab it is Eddie's job to restrain them as Dr. Wu examines their hearts. Eddie also fastens sheep to the same stainless-steel tables before their fetuses are injected. Detaining an animal without a series of harnesses and sedatives, however, has proven a different matter. Eddie pulled their heads and clutched their necks and straddled their shoulders. As soon as each chimera was pricked, it reared up or slithered backwards. Teal, having been discovered, propped himself against the barn and openly peeled an orange. At the first chimera's escape he guffawed, as if to cheer it on, disclosing a mangled wedge inside his mouth, but after Eddie's sixth attempt Teal tossed the last swatch of rind and hunched toward that chimera's ear as though he were about to whisper a secret.

Now Eddie tends the chimeras with minor injuries. He wraps these chimeras with gauze. Against Jan's suggestion, Eddie does not secure the ends of the gauze in bow ties beneath their chins, but small hard knots at the bases of their skulls. Once a chimera is released from treatment at either station, it trots off to rejoin the flock, which Eddie monitors warily. Currently the flock forages daisies planted around the barn and exhibits no suicidal tendencies. Eddie likewise watches his mother. He is watching Jan watch Teal at intervals. She pushes the needle through wounds that look like lips, split, puckered, reddened, and she glances up at Teal when she pulls the floss behind it. Jan's lips are as silent as the wounds, as expectant. She wears the expression of a person within reach of whom an exotic bird suddenly lights. Surprise cloaked by the anticipatory disappointment of the inevitable blink or breath that will scare the bird away.

For Teal has only returned home twice in twelve years. Twelve years ago was when he left them, when he made off in Jan's Town Car. The previous two times Teal returned, he made it clear he had only returned for money. The first time, Jan wrote him a check, taking care to ask the least invasive questions. Teal lingered in the foyer and tendered grunts for answers and fondled a ceramic squash with eyes and an apron that he had admired as a boy. He disappeared as mysteriously as he had arrived the instant the check was torn. It was as though the sound of the check tearing was what drove Teal away.

The second time was identical to the first except Jan wrote slower to prolong Teal's visit. In addition Jan wrote the check for zero dollars, zero cents. Teal failed to notice this before he was gone.

But that was all according to Jan. Eddie was on a different coast and in a different university from one return to the next. Eddie hasn't seen Teal since he dropped off Eddie and Jan at the high school in Paducah where Eddie participated in a quiz bowl tournament. Following the tournament Eddie and Jan waited in the parking lot for hours. They hitchhiked the twenty miles home. Later, the Town Car was found deserted at a tropical fish store in Nashville. In the floorboard were emptied hundreds of pounds of colored gravel. Teal had been angry because Jan finally sold the two thousand acres she had inherited from her first husband. Teal's father, one of the first husband's hands, had continued to manage the first husband's cattle when he married Jan. Eddie's father, who had been Teal's father's hand, sold the cattle and lined the fields with rice and wheat. Then Eddie Senior died, and Jan rented the land to several farmers. Teal had often expressed the intention to reconvert it to a ranch, but his plans never made it past a series of childish sketches. He had last worked with cattle when he was thirteen. He had lived at home until he was twenty-nine, sacking groceries or tinting windows or installing shrubs on and off again.

Seeing Teal, Eddie thinks of the desperate admiration he held for his brother as a child, the authority that, by virtue of this admiration, Teal held over him. It was a crush Eddie had on Teal then and, at the time, felt extremely sexual. Though then Eddie didn't even know what sex was. The feeling that had charged his body was urgent but incomprehensible. Eddie would watch Teal change clothes whenever he could, and when he couldn't, he peered under doors and watched Teal's feet.

The chimera with the thumb now saunters to Jan and Teal to observe their final suture. It is one of two chimeras that remain unscathed, the one still slumped by the pen being the single casualty. Teal releases Jan's last patient. It bolts to the flock where other ears are slick with his saliva. The chimera with the thumb hangs beside Teal and nuzzles his leg. Teal regards the hood with the same sullenly amused look with which he greeted Eddie's mask. On Teal's hands are tattooed the faces of two distinctly different children. Both girls' faces undulate over the bones of his hands as his fingers shift and position.

"I knew it," Jan says abruptly. She drops the needle and floss as if suddenly unburdened of a job she has been forced to perform for days. The spell of hesitation has lifted from her animated face. "I knew it was you," she says to Teal. "Them tools. That food. I knew nobody but my own son would ever steal from me." Her voice climbs and dips with tentative joy. She beams.

Eddie has not heard about the tools. The tools are in the barn, beside the ingredients for the feed, and if any had been taken or rearranged since Eddie has been here he would have noticed.

A long pause unfurls during which it is suspensefully obvious to all that Teal must explain himself or exit. He looks out at the twenty acres that moat Jan's house. The twenty acres are the only scrap of the land that Jan kept. Teal's face says he would like to run, but it also strains, temples corded, declaring him trapped. But nothing apparent holds him there and thus in the way of the chimeras he appears to conjure his own ensnarement.

Jan, reading Teal's dilemma, pushes further. "How long have you been here?"

Then the chimera with the thumb shifts its head and before Eddie can stop it, caresses Teal's thigh with the top of its skull. Teal's leg jolts back as the bony hump beneath the hood drags over his jeans. His eyes narrow and appear to slide down the sides of his scrunching nose, searching the hood for an explanation. "Long enough to see something funny's going on around here."

Eddie hurriedly readjusts the hood. He focuses on the hood long after it has been readjusted, and readjusted, to avoid Teal's gaze. He drags the chimera back to the flock.

"Months," Teal stares at Jan boldfaced and says, seeming to detect a gain of leverage. "That one out there"—he points to the dead chimera by the pen—"should we put that one in a freezer? With the others, I mean?"

The two freezers in the barn were bought to preserve the dead chimeras. This way Dr. Wu can autopsy them upon Eddie's return, though neither this nor even the possibility of death was discussed before Eddie's departure. By the time Eddie made it to Jan's house, another two chimeras were dead in addition to the three he had found on the road. Eddie had taken the chimeras all the way to Jan's house, five hundred miles south, because he had no better, more secluded place to keep them.

Jan gives Eddie a look signaling him to answer. Eddie severs eye contact, defiant, and another lull opens up as questions cease. Freed, Teal strolls into the barn and reappears with the beans. "I don't want to be found," he says. "By anybody." He heads toward the forest. The flock begins to follow his lead, but Eddie shoos them backwards. A chimera spits cud on his boot. The cud is flecked with white petals.

"You don't have to eat out of the barn like an—an animal!" Jan shouts. Teal shrinks and shrinks to the size of a paperweight. A paperclip. Jan says to Eddie, "He used to hide in a pit he dug in those woods, when he was mad at me."

Eddie puts the chimeras on suicide watch. The shoddy pen that took two days to rig is pushed over in less than two minutes. The open field, Eddie thinks, is the next best thing to a padded cell. Or perhaps the

260

open field is better: there not even pillowed walls threaten the chimeras' safety. After witnessing the remaining chimeras' self-destructive behavior, Eddie has begun to imagine the dead chimeras smothering themselves in the U-Haul's corners, or against each other. He feels the burden of lives, the burden of Dr. Wu's lifework, on his shoulders. He feels guilty. Now the chimeras roam the field twenty-four hours a day and are never without supervision.

Jan searches the barn loft for supplies to aid Eddie at night. In the process she discovers a number of other things missing. For instance, a portable stove, collapsible furniture. She first noticed tools gone, she says, weeks before Eddie and the chimeras' arrival. One morning the scarecrow in her garden had been stripped naked. Teal was wearing the scarecrow's pants—Eddie Senior's pants—when he appeared. Eddie keeps thinking of Jan saying, I knew it. But if Jan really knew it, how could she not have told Eddie?

In the loft, only one sleeping bag is present. But Eddie does not sleep in order to monitor the chimeras' every move, though Jan offers to babysit. Upon learning of the chimeras' attempt, she very slowly shakes her head at them as if weighing a lost cause. "Those poor things," she says. "Maybe they're homesick."

And suddenly a cause that was once lost to Jan now seems to her found. She prepares square meals and places them at first in the barn, then on the butane tank, on the picnic table, the back steps, leading Teal to the house, closer and closer. Identical meals are prepared for Eddie and brought to wherever he and the chimeras have wandered. From there Eddie watches a figure divide from the woods and hunt for the location of a paper plate wrapped in foil. As Teal treads back to the woods, the foil twinkles in the sunlight. Then one day Teal explores the yard, stares at the house, returns to the woods without breakfast, lunch, or dinner. The next morning he finally enters the house for five minutes.

Jan makes no mention of this until two days later. By which time Teal has begun taking meals in Jan's laundry room, and Eddie has been awake for eighty-seven hours. Teal eats over the dryer, Jan says, and exits with the last bite still being chewed in his mouth. Eddie stands in the heat being pumped by the sun, listening to Jan, succumbing to the sensation of his body being baked. He would like to close his eyes, to rest, to shrivel and curl inward like a burning leaf. In this state, anything Jan could possibly say would have the same lull as a bedtime story.

"And he's running from someone. He's hiding. But not from me," Jan says proudly.

Eddie's head dips and he staggers to one side. "What did he say?" Eddie blurts, jerking upright.

"He didn't *say* anything, what do you think, he'd just tell me that? I can just—I can tell it. The same way I can tell things about you." Jan studies Eddie as though she has posed a question he should answer. Briefly it occurs to Eddie that perhaps a question *has* been asked which he has missed in an instant of sleep. "I wanted to know if those kids' faces tattooed on his hands were his. That little girl on the right is real cute, but the one on the left—maybe the tattooist messed up. Anyway, he told me all my grandchildren had been wiped off on sheets."

Eddie's head bows until his chin perches on his chest.

"For the *love*—would you just go to bed!"

Slowly fatigue has eroded Eddie's better judgment. Sheer determination to protect the chimeras from themselves fails to keep his body afloat. Eddie gives in to sleep and he tucks himself into the grass directly below. The grass shoots up around his outline like pin art. He clamps his eyes, allowing the chimeras out of his sight only by knowing that they are in Jan's right beside him.

Eddie is in Jan's body. She wears a bolo tie and a milk moustache. Eddie feels the heft of her breasts pulling her shoulders forward. Before her is a field, and the field is a sea of mooing cows in metallic capes. Jan runs toward them without a sound. At first the cows trot, then gain momentum and settle into a gallop, capes whipping and flashing across their backs. Jan chases the cows for miles and miles until a cliff is reached. The front of the herd dives off the cliff then swoops into the sky. The rest of the herd follows their lead, forming a magnificent wave. Jan grabs a hoof at the end and is hauled through the air behind them.

"Eddie?"

He thrusts up through the dream, searching the vicinity. A hundred feet to his left, the chimeras graze serenely.

"Eddie, they're moving," Jan says. "And I've got to start dinner." Jan leaves.

Vaguely refreshed, Eddie sits straight and, remembering, wonders what things, exactly, Jan can tell about him. That Eddie likes men in general, and still loves one in particular? For this has never been discussed with Jan, nor even mentioned. Even when Eddie was sixteen and Jan caught him dipped in her cold cream, masturbating to professional wrestlers. Because the incident was never acknowledged, for a time Eddie was able to convince himself that Jan had not fully realized what she'd seen. He imagines the truth, like so many truths, nestled inside them both, unspoken, small and hard as seeds. Eddie suspects that even without the wrestlers Jan has always seen everything there is to see inside him.

By sunset the chimeras have meandered toward the woods. Teal returns from dinner. He veers from his usual path, the grass flattened, to join Eddie. For some time they stand side-by-side in silence, staring at the chimeras. Eddie grows increasingly uncomfortable until, as if by some spontaneous reaction, the discomfort acquires its own brand of comfort. Eddie notices a fat grain of rice stuck to Teal's lower lip like a maggot. A few chimeras settle onto their stomachs.

"How long do we have to wait before they fuck?" Teal asks.

It is impossible for Eddie to untangle the question, to tell if Teal is serious. "They're neutered."

Teal cocks an eyebrow at the one in the hood. "Figures," he says, resuming the path. From the sky a crow drops dead, wings spread, and crashes directly in front of him. He kicks the crow back into the air like a football.

Eddie cringes.

The end with the other Eddie was just like this. Words had unexpectedly fallen from Eddie's mouth, and the other Eddie had pushed him away for it. One night, the last night, after sex, Eddie had collapsed between the other Eddie's legs and offered to have his babies. The offer had not been the exclamation of an orgasm, though it had erupted from Eddie's mouth with equal force. It seemed to have sprung itself from a place he nurtured in secret, even secret from himself, a place where logic did not and could not exist, where love was logic's opposite and grew rampant. It was as though, working with a scientist who impregnated sheep with human hearts, Eddie had forgotten what was and was not possible between two men.

What proved more impossible for the other Eddie to grasp was the idea of children, a life, with Eddie.

Eddie yanks out the phone Dr. Wu gave him. From here the phone receives full signal and reports no new messages.

One day Teal spends more time inside the house. According to Jan, he had dessert. The next day she says he ate at the table.

Eddie sweats so much that the sweat runs into his watch, causing it to short-circuit. He tries to estimate the length of Teal's meals, but he can no longer differentiate ten minutes and an hour. Instead he measures the increase in time by the change in Jan's demeanor. At first, when she spoke of Teal, hope lurked beneath her face, twisting and sliding like a seductive and arbitrarily vicious creature. Then she allowed that hope, in the form of a resolute smile, to surface. Now Jan revels in playing mother. She makes no attempt to hide her joyfulness. Often her bliss could be mistaken as the effect of an illegal substance. She reminds Eddie of the ewes he has observed with their newborn chimeras. Once, when Dr. Wu tried to remove a chimera from its mother, the ewe bit a small chunk from his thigh, a hole in his khakis. Since then all ewes have been tranquilized prior to separation. Each morning Jan inhales as deeply as she can, swelling her chest. "Both my boys are back," she exhales heartily, grinning at Eddie.

Teal also begins to visit the herd with regularity. Most visits, like the first, hinge on a disconcerting silence that somehow slowly shifts to a blunt and enigmatic solace. Eddie imagines that this is what falling asleep feels like. He tries to remember.

One night Teal materializes from the darkness into the lantern's orb and sleeps among the chimeras. The next night this happens again though to Eddie it still seems like the same night as the night before: Without sleep of his own to delineate the days, one glides into the next, the past into the present. Time is not a progressing line but a fixed point in which everything has happened. Eddie listens to Teal's rolling snore, watches him snuggle in the grass, open and close his mouth, idly paw at his genitals. Eddie looks at Teal and experiences a dull but undoubted warmth that endears his younger self to him as if that self is another, weaker person. He wonders when it was he stopped admiring Teal, how it was Teal lost that power. How, exactly, did Eddie cease to find this man attractive? Things had started to change when Eddie was thirteen, when, by no effort of his own, and almost against his will, Eddie began to shift from Teal's much younger sibling to Teal's equal. Teal was a grown man but still at home, doing nothing with his life except tending to the deaths of palsied dreams. By the time Teal finally left, his sudden, unexpected action had the effect on Eddie of an unsophisticated practical joke. Eddie tries to remember how he outgrew Teal, or if he ever really did. He tries to remember how to outgrow himself, to become another person. He tries to determine the steps to outgrow someone again, he wonders if outgrowing a love is even completely possible.

The following day, Eddie notes it has been exactly four weeks since he and the chimeras arrived at Jan's. He roams into a pocket of reception. He turns the phone off, then on again. Zero messages. Irrationally, he shakes it. Zero messages. When Jan distributes breakfast, he asks her to bring him the *Courier-Journal*. He combs the chalky-feeling pages for renegade sheep, a heart farm in Lincoln. Nothing. He tells Jan to keep her television tuned to CNN. Nothing.

After lunch, Teal emerges from the house with a small cooler. He heads into the barn for an indeterminable amount of time. He comes out with an air mattress on his back, and he carries a tarp, a saw, the cooler, and a can of Diet RC Cola. The air mattress is deflated and has faded, withered straps that look like gigantic sun-dried worms draped over Teal's shoulders.

At the edge of the yard Eddie sits near the chimeras while they eat from his father's boat. Eddie has continued to give them their prescribed feed each day at noon, though by now ingredients for the feed are running low. Soon another run must be made to the bulk food store in Paducah. The chimeras stick their heads in and out of the boat with mechanical motions: bite, chew, swallow, bite, chew, swallow. When Teal draws near, heads momentarily pause then shoot back down like pistons.

"She told me to give you one of these sodies," Teal mumbles, handing Eddie the Diet RC, vaguely cold. He must have washed himself under the spigot inside the barn: his arms are wet to his elbows. He adjusts the straps with his freed thumb and stares at the boat, its heterogeneous contents. He gradually halts, appearing to formulate a question. Eddie struggles to devise an explanation. He nearly blurts, "None of your business!" and, catching himself, he instantly feels like a brat, like a little brother.

"He was the one who showed me about biting ears." Teal taps his foot against the boat to indicate Eddie Senior.

The unexpectedness of this sends what feels like a fissure running through Eddie, as scalding water thrown on frozen glass. "What do you mean?"

"There was this calf that kept getting away from everyone every time Daddy tried to brand it. It had burns all over its butt. Then Ed just bit it. Jackass."

A phone rings. Eddie is too mystified by what Teal has said to reach into his pocket. Eddie has never heard this particular detail about his father. It occurs to him that he has no memories of his father, only memories of other people's memories, and even then only the memories they have chosen to tell him.

Once Eddie realizes he could be receiving a call from Dr. Wu, the phone rings a third time, and the electronic twitter unmistakably emanates from Teal's pants. Teal allows the phone to continue ringing, engrossed by his recollection. Several seconds later a prolonged humming vibration alerts him of a message.

Without another word Teal ambles toward the woods. The morsel of information he leaves in his wake seems to swell and swell until it surrounds Eddie, and then the boat, and then the field, and then the planet. For the rest of the afternoon everything is haunted by Eddie's father.

Teal doesn't return to the house for dinner. Or breakfast or lunch the next day.

Each time Jan brings Eddie a plate she asks Eddie if he has seen Teal, but Eddie hasn't.

Heat radiates from the ground, causing everything it overlays to appear to shiver. Without Teal the field remains disturbingly vacant. Eddie's heightened sense of his father's absence is made acute by Teal's disappearance. Eddie looks at the boat. At the chimeras' ears. There is the barn and the house and all the things the barn and the house hold. The land. Each plant, each object with some tie to his father that Eddie can only imagine.

Eddie imagines himself being viewed through the heat: someone sees Eddie shiver.

Sometime after lunch, Jan brings him an umbrella. For shade, she says. But at this point the sun seems to have done all the damage it can, his skin fully ripened, ginger brown. Jan stares at the woods, mashes her lips together. "Has he showed up yet?" she manages to ask. At Eddie's response, panic seeps into her expression until her face is submerged, distorted. Eddie is too tired to care. Or perhaps it is that Eddie has begun to wonder what else Jan has failed to tell him about his father, of what else he has been deprived by her forgetfulness, her inadvertent neglect. He feels guilty for resenting her. He resents her to varying degrees nonetheless.

Lately the chimeras have displayed exemplary behavior and migrate without incident if Eddie so much as reaches for the mask. Now their suicide attempt might be reassessed as an amateur's misconception. More likely, Eddie thinks, they have adapted to their environment. Regardless, because of their more recent conduct, yesterday Eddie accepted Jan's offer to babysit. After Jan babysat, she called the chimeras little angels. Still Eddie remains vigilant. He doesn't allow himself more than an hour of sleep per day.

Presently he tells Jan to watch the chimeras while he naps. He closes his eyes and thinks this is the part in which he should dream about his father eating a bag of cow ears. Instead he deliberately lies awake and listens to Jan, to what she will say and do if she believes Eddie isn't conscious. There is only silence. The occasional stomp, or the sound of a chimera's mouth gathering spit. Then Eddie senses Jan's frantic gaze at the trees with such intensity he becomes convinced he hears its drone. When Eddie pretends to wake, severing this gaze seems as arduous a task for Jan as sawing off an appendage. Feigning determination, she drives to Paducah to replenish broccoli and oranges.

Finally, sometime after Jan is gone, Teal appears. Eddie spots him coming from the barn, lugging oats. From here Teal is the size of a plastic army man. He is small and hard, retaining this form as he crosses the field, making no move toward Eddie. Teal turns his tiny head. Eddie tries to avert his eyes before he can be observed watching. He imagines himself being observed with the chimeras: at this distance, a Bo Peep play set, minute plastic sheep arranged and rearranged in pleasing formations.

Later, Jan returns. She backs up the old farm truck to the barn. The question she longs to ask is trapped in her dejected eyes, circling: have you seen him have you seen him have you seen him. Eddie knows he should tell her. A part of Eddie wants to tell her, it does. But in the moment he decides to try on the secret of it, like a false identity, and, to some surprise, finds it fits with ease. Jan turns away toward the chimeras as he unloads the goods, his silence all the answer she thinks is needed. The knowledge bubbles up, makes Eddie's head feel buoyant. He could tell her, or not tell her, talk to her, or not talk to her, any second.

It occurs to Eddie that this is the same authority Dr. Wu holds over him. And before that authority there was the other Eddie's. Something inside Eddie breaks for his mother. Yet even as that thing is still breaking, the two pieces of the thing feel as though they are beginning to mend, independent of one another. Becoming things of their own.

"Mom?" He pauses, considers how to phrase it. His head tingles, untethers, drifts away. "What would Dad think of—all this?" he asks, gesturing at the chimeras.

Jan faces him, defeated. "The first thing he did when he married me was sell everything with four legs. What does that tell you?"

He watches her wander across the yard and find her way into the house almost as if by accident. He tells her nothing.

That night, after the sun goes down, the heat intensifies. It is as though the sun did not set but tunneled into the Earth and now swelters it inside out rather than outside in. Sweat collects in the chimeras' eye sockets, where flies promptly assemble. In the sweat, flies drown. Eddie wipes the crisp carcasses away but fresh ones accumulate. He gives up. He turns off the lantern, which he believes attracts the flies and augments the overbearing warmth. But only a clipping of the moon dangles in the sky, providing little light, and still he can hear the insistent hum of flies, orbiting. He reignites the lantern.

Soon Teal materializes bearing lawn chairs. He unfolds the lawn chairs and forces one on Eddie. Teal is shirtless and gleams and has MIAMI tattooed in Gothic letters from shoulder blade to shoulder blade, a small, impotent-looking wing spread at each end. His arms are thick but look soft, smooth with little contour. Eddie remembers Teal's arms, once bulging. The muscles twisted and knotted like balloon animals. Eddie and Teal sit down. A chimera throws its head in Teal's lap and coaxes him into rubbing its ears, its chin.

For once Eddie finds their perfunctory silence intolerable. The urgency to speak forces an anger inside him to germinate at an accelerated rate, and when it blooms, fangs for petals, there is the impulse to leap from his chair and throttle his brother. "Where have you been?" he demands.

Teal sniffs his fingers. In the days since the temperature has spiked the chimeras have acquired an odor reminiscent of nachos. His stomach growls loudly, startling the chimera away. "Who wants to know, Pop—you or her?"

"Don't you know what you've done to her?"

"Yes."

"She's been a wreck! She thought you were gone again!"

"I am. I won't be going back to that house. I've been in syphilitic women I'd rather go back inside."

Eddie huffs. "You'll go as soon as you're hungry enough."

"From now on I'll be taking my meals out here. Like you." Teal smirks and then works his lips as if to prevent laughter from erupting. "Maybe one night you can make me something special? What is it—four parts grain, two parts veggies, two parts lazooms . . . looks like puke?"

Eddie glances away, unsure of what to think, unsure of what Teal knows. Unsure, at this point, of how much he even cares, one way or the other. The chimera with the thumb stares out into the dark, which seems to capture them in a dome of light, at nothing. It blinks laboriously. It drags its head across the ground, scratching its face, and saunters to the lantern's periphery where the dome mingles with darkness.

"Can I see it?" Teal asks. His eyes follow the chimera as it takes tentative steps along the fringes, poking its head into the night. "The thumb?"

Dread courses up Eddie in the form of hot nausea. He wonders how Teal could have recognized what he felt against his leg. He has a flash of guessing games at parties, mysterious objects concealed in velvet bags.

Then he has a flash of Jan's desperate face. Then a flash of his own.

Teal registers the realization in Eddie's expression. "She told me everything she knew to get me to stay. When I finished eating. You know how she is." He makes kissing noises and rubs his fingers together to catch the chimera's attention. On the back of his hand a little girl with intricate hair is illuminated by the lantern. "I couldn't resist knowing what you were doing here. With sheep." He says, with his fingers. "Sheep" again, making hook-like quotation marks. "She told me bit by bit. Every time. Then there wasn't anything left to tell."

Eddie feels like a hostage, at Teal's mercy, but as the chimera's hood comes off, Eddie finds himself willing. He makes no attempt, not even a sound, to prevent its removal. What good would it do to stop Teal from seeing what he already knows is present?

The hood has plastered the hair against the chimera's skull, sopping. The chimera violently shakes its head. Sweat slings across Teal's stomach. When the chimera settles down, Teal braces his palms under its ears and leans in. The thumb is inert, bent impotently at the knuckle, still glistening. "It's just begging to be filed and painted," Teal says, taking care not to touch. Carefully, he blows on it, as if it is a sip of steaming soup balanced in a spoon. "Is it dead?"

"Nonresponsive."

A pinprick of a light bobs toward them like a drunken star. Eddie's sense of betrayal expands and weaves uncertainly with the light as it traverses the yard, the field. Then he sees Jan's face animate once she reaches them, once she glimpses Teal, and he struggles to hold onto the feeling, not to let it escape. But he can't help imagining a call, some word, at last, from the other Eddie. What he would have done, what he would do, to receive it.

"Teal," she says. "Teal, come up, let me make you something, I made Eddie bratwurst, did he tell you?"

Teal is as responsive as the thumb.

She looks from the chimera, exposed, to Eddie. She sets a fan next to Eddie and crosses her arms defensively. Her eyes bear only a momentary glimmer of shame. "Shouldn't it have its hood on?"

"No," Teal says, keeping his gaze tied to the thumb. "There's no need for it to wear some damn *hood*."

Jan's enthusiasm dims to a doggedly optimistic half-grin. "Eddie, I just brought you—you boys—this fan." She lingers, waiting to cling to some thread of conversation, however thin, but neither of her sons speaks for his own reasons. "Battery-operated . . ." she trails off. She turns to leave.

"Maybe you could bring him some chicken strips," Eddie offers. "Nothing fancy."

Jan gives one firm nod and marches off with profound purpose. Teal charms the chimera closer and gently sandwiches its head with his legs and massages the thumb between his fingers. "Some women die right after their husbands—like, they love them so much they can't take it. But look at her, just look at her! She lived through three! Makes you wonder how much she really loved any of them."

"They weren't you," says Eddie. "You didn't see her today, or yesterday. You didn't see her twelve years ago. She did die. She cleaned until she bleached her hands out." He switches the fan on and sets it to oscillate. The fan rattles tremulously as it traces and retraces a path between them.

Teal pulls the thumb straight up and releases it, watching it wilt back into position. "And that hair," he says.

"Last week I swallowed one of her hairs in those mashed potatoes," Eddie says—straining to reach out to his brother—"and the end of it was caught in my teeth and I could feel it all the way down my throat. I nearly choked on her."

A swarm of fireflies crashes into the whirling blades, and the rickety fan appears to spark. When Eddie and Teal catch sight of the jouncing light, marking Jan's return, Teal departs, leaving his chair behind, empty. But before he is gone, before they see the light, his hands rest and he studies the flock and he says, "This was all I ever wanted, I just never knew how to get it. I wish to God it was all I wanted now."

Eddie never confronts Jan for betraying the chimeras to Teal. Nor does Eddie ever tell Jan that, for a day, he kept Teal hidden from her. For a day, he let Jan suffer. Unexplainably, the secret of it, the control he feels at having allowed that suffering, establishes a sense of balance, of evenness, in Eddie's world.

Eddie trusts Teal with the knowledge of the chimeras for reasons Eddie doesn't entirely understand. Perhaps, as Jan said, it is that Teal is running from something as well, and perhaps, as Eddie detects, Teal has something to lose himself. Or maybe Eddie simply *wants* to trust Teal. Still the fact that another person is privy to Dr. Wu's agenda makes Eddie uneasy. He starts to check the phone with greater frequency. When he finds a pocket of reception he is wary to leave it. Often he contemplates calling the lab rather than wait any longer. Then he imagines the lab bugged, men dressed in similar suits ready to pinpoint his location. He sees Dr. Wu interrogated in a dank room with a low-hanging light and a double-sided mirror.

When Eddie thinks of this—and that it has been six weeks since this began—it is hard to trust his trust in anyone. And then there is the other Eddie. Even Jan. He lets Teal interact with the chimeras in an effort to appease him, in hope to keep him silent. Then Eddie begins to encourage it: If Teal helps keep the chimeras concealed, if only for a while, he will be as accountable for harboring them as Jan and Eddie.

The day after Teal uncovers the thumb, Eddie teaches Teal to prepare the chimeras' feed. The next day, Teal goes so far as to sample it. Teal tells Eddie it needs less oil.

By the end of the week Teal thinks the chimeras should exercise more. He waits until Eddie and the chimeras are at the farthest reaches of the field, then dumps the feed in the boat and kicks the boat's sides, goading them into a vigorous run. Sometimes he merely chases them; for this Teal does not need a mask and horn.

Soon Teal tends the chimeras while Eddie sleeps. The weight that once led Eddie forward now seems as though it is pushing him under. Eddie sleeps in the field for hours. He finds himself glad to share the burden. He does not dream, or if he dreams he does not remember. With Teal, Eddie begins to feel free, or at least a little freer. With enough sleep, he begins to have waking dreams of freeing himself altogether.

The two of them sit in the lawn chairs under a beach umbrella Jan has recently purchased. They watch the chimeras graze with varying levels of interest, as if they are spectators of a slow-paced sport. Jan delivers two plates at regular intervals. Often Teal disappears as soon as they see her coming. When he stays to receive his plate from her he does little to acknowledge her presence.

"How can you treat her the way you do?" Eddie asks him one afternoon. "Really, how can you be such a bastard?"

"Who is he? The man who did whatever he did to you?"

Eddie winces.

"What, you thought I didn't know, Pop?"

"Stop calling me that. I've never liked you calling me that." Eddie leans back in his chair and fixes his eyes on one chimera's wound, dark pink and gristly. "What did Mom say to you?"

Teal guffaws. "She didn't have to tell me anything. Listen, this one time? A woman sent me a cat's head in a diaper. It was *her* cat. You've just got to get back at him and get over it."

"The way you've gotten over what Mom did, right? Twelve years ago?"

Repugnance creases Teal's face, nearly causing it to fold. "Pop."

Four meals later he mumbles, "Thanks," to Jan. Then he goes back to avoiding her. As he leaves, her gaze hitches to his back, allowing itself to be dragged across the field. Eddie's hand covers his pocket. He cups the hard plastic lump of the phone. "At least he's here," Jan says. "At least there's that."

Eddie plucks apples, like fat Valentines, with the other Eddie in a Nebraskan orchard . . . He hangs his head in the steam of a cup of Earl Grey in a womb-warm lodge snuggled in the Adirondacks . . . He is deserted on a nameless island with no wish of rescue, only of a book or a song or a movie . . . He injects blind pig eyes with a fizzing serum to make them respond to visual stimuli . . .

Then, between lunch and dinner the next day, Jan traipses into the field and his eyes refocus. His latest dream dissipates as the barn, the field, and eight chimeras are reintroduced to his consciousness. For a second the humid air feels solid, as if he is encased in it.

Teal is halfway to the woods when Jan makes it to the flock. For once she doesn't stare after him. Her face is settled in a worried arrangement. She forks over two short articles, one from the weekly Science & Technology section of the *Courier-Journal* and an identical article, two days old, printed from CNN.com. While Eddie reads, Jan stands too close to him and wrings her index finger.

Research officials at the University of Nebraska–Lincoln discovered the lab of Yingpei Wu abandoned . . . surrogate sheep and heart hosts found euthanized and decomposing . . . dubbed "chimeras" for the Greek mythological creature bearing a lion's head, a goat's body, and a serpent's tail . . . Officials entered the lab by force after Wu failed to attend a routine committee meeting and did not return messages for two weeks . . . Federal Bureau of Investigation has determined all records of the project and Wu himself are missing . . . whereabouts unknown . . . believe Wu to have fled the country with all data and the remainder of the project's most recent grant 500,000 dollars . . . names of persons presently and previously involved with the study are unknown due to lost records . . . The University and the FBI ask all such persons to come forward for questioning . . .

"If *they're* dead," Jan interrupts, pointing at the article, "then what are *they*?" pointing at the animals before them.

The article makes no mention of either the National Academy of Sciences or the Department of Agriculture. It is as if the bioethics investigation never existed.

Then comes a sinking suspicion, hard as truth; heavier than truth—as though truth is not, nor ever has been, sufficient. He suspects he is surrounded by impostors. But then Eddie remembers their bizarre, distinctively unsheeplike behavior. He looks at the chimeras, faces Eddie recognizes from the lab; faces that—even Eddie must admit—seem to convey human emotion. And then there is the human thumb. Eddie's eyes search for and then cling to that thumb desperately. But even as they do so the other chimeras are foggy, seem like apparitions in his peripheral vision. He feels himself, and everything he has ever done, everything he will ever do, begin to fade and brighten with the specters.

Eddie dashes toward the barn. Jan's cries shrivel to a murmur as he runs. He flips the latch with such force that it revolves against the door and scrapes up his leg as he enters. A chopping knife lies in the middle of the workbench. Slices of sunlight slip off and on the blade as Eddie's body blocks and unblocks the light. He shuffles around the U-Haul's bumper and dodges two stray oat bags. He grabs the knife. He only slows as he approaches the freezers.

He wants to reach inside a chimera. He wants to hold its heart in his hands. He needs to know that heart is human. But Eddie realizes he is afraid of knowing.

Still he drives himself toward the freezers.

He lifts one of the freezer's lids. A tender arctic puff is expelled with the release of wet-sounding suction. The draft reaches Eddie's face, greeting him with the odor of cold metal. Opening the pearly new freezer is itself like opening a wound: Inside, the freezer is caked with chunks of blood, frozen. Short, pink icicles hang from the topmost chimera's stiffened hair, its body ravaged, a cavernous gash running the length of its stomach. Where its heart should be packed there is only a deep and empty pocket. Later, but only months later—six, seven months—it will dawn on Eddie that this scene of stolen hearts wasn't nearly as bloody as he might have expected.

But now the chimera's tail snaps off as Eddie lugs it out. Both the chimeras below it are in the same condition. Piles of innards rest on the freezer's bottom, firm and shiny as abstract pottery. He tries to pick them up, to spread them over the workbench, but they are fixed in place. Not a single heart among them.

In the second freezer, Eddie finds the other three dead chimeras hollowed out as well. Suddenly Eddie feels hollowed out. He can't imagine how this has happened. The vacuum of his chest makes it impossible to imagine. He turns in a slow circle, scrutinizing the barn in a daze. He goes back to the second freezer and starts to dig faster and faster. His fingers are painfully cold and feel like they are covered in scratches. He cannot tell if the blood on them belongs to him or a thawing chimera.

Then Eddie notices another frozen substance that is brown and makes his fingers sticky. He sniffs a streak of brown on a chimera's forehead: familiar, and sweet: soda. When he lifts the last chimera out he finds four discarded cans of Diet RC Cola. All but one of the cans has exploded.

When Eddie emerges from the barn he tells Jan nothing.

"But you were in there over an hour," Jan says, apprehensive. "Look at your arms, red as can be!"

He tries to remember the day Teal went to the barn with the cooler. He tries to remember if Teal had taken that long, or longer. But Eddie's eyes remain intent on the closest chimera—or whatever creature it may be. In the barn, he sorted and studied all that was left of the chimeras until finally he understood there were no answers to be found. Not there. Not in the dead. "Isn't it about lunchtime?" he says, as though he is asking this animal. He imagines its heart, still pumping. Pumping. He feels edge of the knife, creasing his thigh, shoved in his pocket.

Jan lingers before she finally becomes exasperated at his silence, huffs, and stomps away.

Eddie waits for his arms to warm. He waits for his hand to grow mobile enough to wield the knife. Eddie's arms feel like slabs of meat as they defrost against his body. They hang limply from the hooks of his shoulders, sunning. The sun creeps approximately a foot across the sky before they lose their hot pink hue and fully regain sensation. Still an occasional, unexpected ache—not unlike heartache, he notes—skates across the bones. The bones' memory of cold.

274

As he is forced to simply stand there, he begins to analyze the flock. They graze. They heave up their cud and gulp it. They defecate. And soon Eddie calms and starts to think: There is the thumb—the human thumb; by that, and that alone, these are chimeras, composed of more than one animal.

But however much the thumb may indicate the presence of other human parts, whether or not those parts exist is irrelevant. Without the project, Eddie sees, these parts are void of meaning regardless, as trivial as a sheep's. The thumb is nothing but a sideshow attraction, and the hearts are powerless to save anything but the bodies they currently save, each time they beat.

But why would Dr. Wu abandon the work to which he had devoted his life when he was on the brink of monumental achievement? Why would he send Eddie on a fictitious mission to save the chimeras when Dr. Wu just as easily could have deserted them in the lab? Or destroyed them as he had the planted sheep?

For such questions, there are no answers, or none that Eddie will ever know. As Eddie wanders the field, waiting for Teal—waiting to ask the only question that can be answered, the one that will have to be enough—he can only picture Dr. Wu continuing his research in a country with more lenient regulations. He can only imagine that, perhaps, Dr. Wu couldn't stand to have the chimeras' deaths on his own hands, not directly—just as now, Eddie sees, neither can he.

From behind, the chimera with the thumb forces its way between Eddie's legs and drags its hood off against his crotch.

There is the thumb.

The thumb, as he, Eddie sees, will have to go.

At feeding time, Eddie watches Teal walk inside the barn. Now, Eddie thinks, Teal is discovering the bloody fingerprints Eddie left covering the freezers purposely. It is longer than usual before Teal exits. He dumps the contents of the wheelbarrow—big as a breath mint—and gongs the boat, propelling the chimeras across the field at full speed.

When Eddie makes it to the boat, Teal has left for the second load of feed. The chimeras are chewing their first bites. The harmonic crunching sounds like loudening static as another and another joins in. Teal returns, dumps, and appears unaffected by the conspicuousness of the fingerprints—impervious, if not accustomed, to accusation.

"Where are they?" Eddie asks. "The hearts?" He thinks that right now he should be struggling to contain his fury. But the truth is, Eddie is empty. He feels he has nothing inside him left to hold, or hold back. Without Dr. Wu, any effort he might make to protect the chimeras would be made in vain. As if the chimeras were mere sheep.

As soon as the thumb is gone, the chimeras *will* be sheep.

"What did you do with the hearts, Teal?" he asks his brother again.

Teal holds up his fists in an awkward, non-threatening stance. "It was for them," he says. At first Eddie thinks Teal is referring to his fists, and when Teal realizes this he shakes them in such a way to indicate the back of his hands, the children's faces, inverted. "Them," he says, "I owe them. And their mother, and she—"

"I don't care about them," Eddie says, intent on the answer to his only question. "Just tell me what you did with the hearts."

The little girls' faces plummet, and Teal's eyes roll. "I was going to sell them. I know this guy—in St. Louis. He deals with kidneys mostly."

Eddie remembers how badly the other organs had decomposed, sunken and gray, some nearly unrecognizable. "But they'd been dead for weeks. Anyone with *any* sort of training—even someone like this *friend* of yours—could see those hearts weren't viable. The host has to be—"

"You think he didn't tell me that?"

Eddie has the urge to run, now. To keep running, just as Dr. Wu instructed. Life is starting to seem like a simple process of acquiring more and more things from which to run. "Does your friend know where we are?"

"Friend?" Teal huffs, exasperated. "He's as much my friend as that doctor is yours. And for your information, I hitched there and back."

The knowledge gives Eddie little comfort. They watch the chimeras finish eating, push past the orange rinds with their noses, lick the boat's bottom for evading morsels.

That night, as she delivers dinner, Jan tells Teal everything while informing Eddie there are no new developments. For the first time in a long time Teal makes eye contact with her. He asks her for pepper. At this progress her body pauses. She smiles cautiously. However small the progress may be, she will take it. She leaves.

"They're yours," Eddie says to Teal as the plates are still cooling on their laps. The chimeras have come across a cache of ragweed. "You stay here, you take them. They're all you wanted."

"All I *did* want," Teal says. "Not all I want now."

They watch a chimera drop and roll.

"Maybe they're all you'll ever have," Eddie says. "And Mom. Ever think of that?"

276

And for weeks, while Jan babysits, Eddie and Teal work in the woods. First they clean out Teal's pit, a cavity larger than Eddie expected, bandaged by a tarp in a clearing. They remove all the things Teal took from the barn, in addition to a bong, cigar wrappers, paper plates, a body massager. They dig his pit wider and wider. Deeper and deeper. Then, finally, they load the U-Haul with the freezers, barricading the filing cabinets, and steer the yellow monstrosity across the field—contents jouncing—down a path just wide enough that the two men have cleared through the trees, Jan screaming and floundering behind it, dissuading the chimeras from following it like a funeral procession.

There is only one thing left for Eddie to do, and Eddie, in the end, cannot bring himself to do it. Instead he bites the chimera's ear—the one with the thumb—as Teal straddles its back and steadies a hacksaw. At the first forward motion of the saw, the chimera lets loose a scream which was once only unleashed for rain. And it keeps screaming until they are done, and even after, long after, but with each successive motion, back and forth, it begins to still, and Eddie feels the chimera surrender between his teeth. Then Teal starts to shout and Eddie opens his eyes and can only see the blurred image of the thumb, moving wildly.

He tells the investigators in Lincoln that he was fired weeks before Dr. Wu's apparent departure. After precisely an hour of questioning—he watches the clock—they are satisfied that, indeed, he knows nothing. And really, he knows hardly anything at all—nothing more than they do. By then, the investigators have identified the bodies found in the lab as sheep and suspect Dr. Wu disposed of the chimeras using a U-Haul rented under an alias.

He gets another assistantship in another lab, this one in Bloomington. He phones home from time to time to check on Jan, on Teal, the sheep. Teal, Jan says, has cleaned out the barn to house the sheep for the winter. Teal, Jan says, lets the sheep graze the yard so it won't have to be mowed all summer. Months pass, nearly a year, in this manner. Then one night Jan reports a sheep has died. In October another. And another. Teal thinks it is a disease. But each time one dies, Jan notices, she is left to care for the sheep for a day, far longer than it should take for Teal to replenish ingredients for the feed. Sometimes when Teal drives to Paducah to replenish the ingredients, the ingredients don't even need replenishing.

When only one sheep is left—the one with a hard pink knot where a thumb used to be—Eddie stops calling.

Woods and Chalices appeared from Harcourt in 2008. **Andrew Hudgins**'s most recent book of poems is *Ecstatic in the Poison* (Overbook Press, 2003). *Shut Up, You're Fine!: Troubling Poems for Troubled Children* is his forthcoming book from Overlook Press. **Peter Johnson**'s recent books are *Eduardo & "I"* (White Pine Press, 2006) and *What Happened* (Front Street Books, 2007). His new novel, *Loserville*, is forthcoming in 2008. **David Kirby** was a finalist for the 2007 National Book Award for *The House on Boulevard Street: New and Selected Poems* (Louisiana State University Press, 2007). He is currently writing a book called *Little Richard: The Birth of Rock 'n' Roll*. **Fred G. Leebron** is the author of three novels and a number of short stories. He directs the MFA program at Queens University of Charlotte and is an English professor at Gettysburg College. **Erica Levy McAlpine** is currently finishing her PhD in English at Yale. Her poetry has most recently appeared in *Slate*. **Doug Macomber** is an award winning videographer and a landscape photographer. He lives in St. Louis, Missouri and Cape Cod, Massachusetts. **Margaret McMullan** is the author of five novels including *My Mother's House* (St. Martin's/Thomas Dunne Books, 2003), the young adult novel *When I Crossed No-Bob* (Houghton Mifflin, 2007), and forthcoming in 2009, *Cashay* (Houghton Mifflin). Her work has appeared in *Glamour*, the *Chicago Tribune*, *Michigan Quarterly Review*, *Other Voices*, *Boulevard*, and *Ploughshares* among others. **D. Nurkse**'s most recent book is *The Border Kingdom* (Knopf, 2008). **Stephen O'Connor** is the author of *Rescue* (Harmony Books, 1989), *Will My Name Be Shouted Out?* (Simon & Schuster, 1994, Touchstone 1996) and *Orphan Trains* (Houghton Mifflin 2001, University of Chicago 2004). He teaches in the MFA programs of Columbia University and Sarah Lawrence. **Elise Paschen** is the author of *Infidelities* (Story Line, 1996), winner of the Nicholas Roerich Poetry Prize, and *Houses: Coasts* (Oxford: Sycamore Press, 1985). Her poems have been published in the *New Republic*, *Ploughshares*, *Shenandoah*, among other magazines, and in numerous anthologies. **Justin Quarry** is a graduate of the MFA Program at the University of Virginia, where he was a Henry Hoyns Fellow and a recipient of other fellowships and scholarships from the Bread Loaf Writers' Conference, the Jack Kerouac Project of Orlando, KHN Center for the Arts, the Ragdale Foundation, and Vermont Studio Center. His stories have appeared in *Sou'wester*, *Fiction*, and the *Southeast Review*. **Donna Seaman** is an associate editor for *Booklist*; editor of the anthology, *In Our Nature: Stories of Wildness* (University of Georgia Press, 2002); and host of *Open Books Radio*. Her authors' interviews are collected in *Writers on the Air: Conversations about Books* (Paul Dry Books, 2005). **Murzban F. Shroff** is a Bombay-born writer. His debut collection of short stories, *Breathless in Bombay*, was published this year by St. Martin's Press, U.S. His fiction has appeared in thirty publications worldwide. He is the recipient of the John Gilgun Fiction Award and has two Pushcart Prize nominations. **Julie Suk** is the author of *The Dark Takes Aim* (Autumn

House Press, 2003); *The Angel of Obsession* (1992), winner of the Arkansas Poetry Award and the Roanoke-Chowan Poetry Award; *Heartwood* (1991); and *The Medicine Woman* (1980). Her poems have appeared in such periodicals as *Georgia Review*; *Poetry*, which awarded her the Bess Hokin Award; and *Shenandoah*. **Kristen Tracy**'s poems have appeared in *Threepenny Review*, *Southern Review*, *Prairie Schooner*, *AGNI*, and elsewhere. She has published two young adult novels with Simon & Schuster, *Lost It* (2007) and *Crimes of the Sarahs* (2008). She also co-edited *A Chorus for Peace: A Global Anthology of Poetry by Women* (University of Iowa Press, 2002). **Lee Upton**'s fifth book of poetry appeared in November 2007 from New Issues Press. Her poetry, fiction, and essays appear widely. **David Wagoner** has published seventeen books of poems, most recently *Good Morning and Good Night* (University of Illinois Press, 2005) and ten novels, one of which, *The Escape Artist*, was made into a movie by Francis Ford Coppola. He won the Lilly Prize in 1991 and has been nominated for the Pulitzer Prize and twice for the National Book Award. He edited Poetry Northwest from 1966 to its end in 2002. He is professor emeritus of English at the University of Washington. **G. C. Waldrep** is the author of *Goldbeater's Skin* (Colorado Prize, 2003) and *Disclaimer* (BOA Editions, 2007). He lives in Lewisburg, Pennsylvania and teaches at Bucknell University. **Lauren Watel** lives in Decatur, Georgia with her son. She has published poetry and fiction in *Five Points* and *Ploughshares*. **Robert von Hallberg** is the author of *Lyric Powers* (University of Chicago Press, 2008) and teaches at the University of Chicago. **Steve Yates** has received two fellowships from the Mississippi Arts Commission for his fiction. His stories are forthcoming in *Harrington Gay Men's Literary Quarterly*, and *North Dakota Quarterly*, and have recently appeared in *Southwest Review*, among other journals. Excerpts from novels in progress have appeared in the *Ontario Review*, in several issues of the *Missouri Review*, and elsewhere. **C. Dale Young** is the author of two books of poetry, most recently *The Second Person* (Four Way Books, 2007). He practices medicine, edits poetry for the *New England Review*, and teaches in the Warren Wilson MFA Program for Writers.

Subscriptions

Three issues per year. **Individuals:** one
year $24; two years $44; life $600. **Insti-
tutions:** one year $36; two years $68.
Overseas: $5 per year additional. Price
of back issues varies. Sample copies $5.
Address correspondence and subscriptions
to *TriQuarterly*, Northwestern University,
629 Noyes St., Evanston, IL 60208-4210.
Phone (847) 491-7614.

Submissions

The editors invite submissions of fiction,
poetry and literary essays, which must
be postmarked between October 1 and
March 31; manuscripts postmarked between April 1 and September 30 will
not be read. No manuscripts will be returned unless accompanied by a stamped,
self-addressed envelope. All manuscripts
accepted for publication become the
property of *TriQuarterly*, unless otherwise indicated.

Reprints

Reprints of issues 1–17 of *TriQuarterly*
are available in full format from Kraus
Reprint Company, Route 100, Millwood,
NY 10546, and all issues in microfilm
from University Microfilms International,
300 North Zeeb Road, Ann Arbor, MI
48106.

Indexing

TriQuarterly is indexed in the Humanities
Index (H. W. Wilson Co.), Humanities
International Complete (Whitson
Publishing Co.), Historical Abstracts,
MLA, EBSCO Publishing (Peabody,
MA) and Informa-tion Access Co.
(Foster City, CA).

Distributors

Our national distributors to retail trade
are Ingram Periodicals (La Vergne, TN);
B. DeBoer (Nutley, NJ); Ubiquity (Brook-
lyn, NY); Armadillo (Los Angeles, CA).

**Publication of *TriQuarterly* is made
possible in part by the donors of gifts
and grants to the magazine. For their
recent and continuing support, we are
very pleased to thank the Illinois Arts
Council, the Lannan Foundation, the
National Endowment for the Arts,
the Sara Lee Foundation, the Wendling
Foundation and individual donors.**

No. 30 Winter 2005

FUGUE

$8.00

Promoting the diverse literary voices of new and established writers since 1990

Win
We award cash prizes and publication for prose and poetry in our annual spring contest. Past judges include Mark Doty, Rick Moody, Ellen Bryant Voigt, Ehud Havazelet, Scott Russell Sanders, Rebecca McClanahan, and Tony Hoagland.

Submit
Fugue invites submissions of fiction, creative nonfiction, and poetry. Send SASE for guidelines or visit us on the web at http://www.uidaho.edu/fugue.

Subscribe

Individual
1 year/2 issues $14
2 years/4 issues $25
3 years/6 issues $35

Institutional
1 year/2 issues $22
2 years/4 issues $40
3 years/6 issues $55

Send orders to:
Fugue
200 Brink Hall
University of Idaho
PO Box 441102
Moscow, ID 83844-1102

Past contributors
Steve Almond
Charles Baxter
Mary Clearman Blew
Stephen Dobyns
Denise Duhamel
Stephen Dunn
Terrance Hayes
Jane McCafferty
W.S. Merwin
Sharon Olds
Paul Perry
Sonia Sanchez
Vivian Shipley
Virgil Suarez
Melanie Rae Thon
Robert Vivian
Robert Wrigley
Dean Young

Writing Published in Fugue has won the Pushcart Prize

Published by the MFA Program at the University of Idaho

THE MASSACHUSETTS REVIEW

LAYLAH ALI

MR_Q

an especially queer issue of

the MASSACHUSETTS REVIEW

A QUARTERLY REVIEW *of* Fiction, Poetry, Essays, and Art, *since 1959*

massrev@external.umass.edu | www.massreview.org

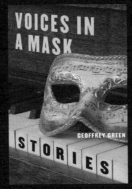

2009 CAVE CANEM NORTHWESTERN UNIVERSITY PRESS POETRY PRIZE

The inaugural Cave Canem Northwestern University Press Poetry Prize is a second book award for African American poets. This annual award celebrates and publishes works of lasting cultural value and literary excellence.

Award Winner receives $1,000, publication by Northwestern University Press, 15 copies of the book and a featured reading.

Judges: Parneshia Jones, John Keene and Reginald Gibbons. Judges reserve the right not to select a winner.

Eligibility: African American writers who have had one full-length book of poetry published by a professional press. Chapbooks and self-published works do not qualify. Simultaneous submission to other contests should be noted. Immediate notification upon winning another award is required.

Deadline: Reading period begins January 1, 2009. Manuscripts must be postmarked no later than March 15, 2009. To be notified that your manuscript has been received, enclose a stamped, self-addressed postcard. Winner announced in June 2009.

Entry Fee: $20. Enclose check with submission, made payable to Northwestern University Press. Entry fees are non-refundable.

Direct packet to:
Northwestern University Press
Cave Canem Northwestern University Press Poetry Prize
629 Noyes Street
Evanston, IL 60208

Media Contacts:

Camille Rankine,
Program/Communications Coordinator,
Cave Canem Foundation: 212.941.5720;
camillerankine@ccpoets.org

Rudy Faust, Publicity Manager,
Northwestern University Press:
847.467.0319; r-faust@northwestern.edu

Guidelines:

Send three copies of a single manuscript. One manuscript per poet allowed.

Enclose a stamped, self-addressed envelope to receive notification of results.

Author's name should not appear on any pages within the manuscript. Copy One must include a title page with the author's brief bio (200 words, maximum) and contact information: author's name, postal address, e-mail address and telephone number.

Copies Two and Three must include a cover sheet with the title only.

Manuscript must be typed single sided with a minimum font size of 11, paginated and 50-75 pages in length. A poem may be multiple pages, but no more than one poem per page is permitted.

Manuscript must include a table of contents and list of acknowledgments of previously published poems.

Manuscript must be unbound. Use a binder clip do not staple or fold. Do not include illustrations or images of any kind. Manuscripts not adhering to submission guidelines will be discarded without notice to sender.

Due to the volume of submissions, manuscripts will not be returned. Post-submission revisions or corrections are not permitted.

CAVE CANEM
A HOME FOR BLACK POETRY

NORTHWESTERN UNIVERSITY PRESS
www.nupress.northwestern.edu